DON'T PANIC!

What to Do and What Not to Do
in All Kinds of Family Emergencies

Don't Panic!

What to Do and What Not to Do
in All Kinds of Family Emergencies

by Ruth Winter

Drawings by Roy Doty

Golden Press · New York
Western Publishing Company, Inc.
Racine, Wisconsin

ACKNOWLEDGMENTS

The author wishes to express appreciation to James Kielty, Hans Grigo, and Dan Consalvo at the National Safety Council for their help in checking several chapters of the manuscript.

She also wishes to extend thanks to the following experts and organizations for their help in the preparation of specific chapters in the book:

APPLIANCES: The National Safety Council

AUTOMOBILE: The National Safety Council; M. R. Darlington, Jr., Director, Auto Dealers Traffic Safety Council; George W. Threlfall, Secretary, Auto Body Association of America

CRIME: The National Safety Council; The Police Department of The City of New York

FAMILY CRISES: Robert Kennedy M.D. former Chairman of the American College of Surgeons Committee on Trauma; Donald Dukelow M.D., American Medical Association; John E. Harmon, Executive Vice President, National Employment Association; Jennifer Schroeder, Administrative Secretary, Continental Association of Funeral and Memorial Societies, Inc.

FIRE: The National Safety Council

ILLNESS AND INJURY: Robert Kennedy M.D., former Chairman of the American College of Surgeons' Committee on Trauma; Donald Dukelow M.D., American Medical Association; Willard Simmons, Executive Secretary, The National Association of Retail Druggists; Meyer Mathis Director, Office of Systems Analysis, Information and Statistics; The American National Red Cross; Mary Bowman, Consumer News Specialist, American Gas Association; Gertrude Lady, Medic Alert Foundation; Dorothea Andrews, Acting Director, Office of Information, Maternal and Child Health Service, Department of Health, Education, and Welfare, Public Health Service

MONEY: Eileen Hyddall, The American Bankers Association; Thomas D. Boyd, Director of Special Projects Information, Services Division, American Stock Exchange; Elaine Spector, Consumer Specialist, Federal Trade Commission; Carl F. Hawver, Executive Vice President, National Consumer Finance Association; Lawrence E. Jaffee, Attorney, Branch of Legal Interpretations, U.S. Securities Exchange Commission; T. M. Alexander, Jr., Assistant Commissioner for Unsubsidized Insured Housing Programs, Department of Housing and Urban Development, Federal Housing Administration; Barbara McNear, Manager, Press Relations, CNA Financial Corp.; Richard Seater, Acting Director, Rural Housing, Loan Division, U.S. Department of Agriculture, Farmers Home Administration; Robert Miskelly, Editor, News Bureau Public Affairs, Allstate Insurance; Thad L. Weber, Security Consultant, The Jewelers' Security Alliance

PETS: Dr. D. E. DeCamp, Veterinarian

STAINS AND CLEANING: William L. Browne, Director of Public Relations, National Institute of Drycleaning; Barbara Meyer, Assistant Office Manager, Melody Glove Suede and Leather Cleaners

TRAVEL: The National Safety Council; Albert S. J. Tarka, Director, Program Services, Travelers' Aid Association of America; Albert E. Kudrle, Director of Information, American Hotel and Motel Association

WEATHER: Marvin M. Frydenlund, Executive Secretary, Lightning Protection Institute; Joseph M. Murphy, News Supervisor, New Jersey Bell Telephone Company; Ann K. Cook, Office of Public Information, U.S. Department of Commerce, Environmental Science Services Administration

CONTENTS

crime, (continued)

family crises, 59 *Professional Help and Referral Services, 59*

fire, 73 *Reporting a Fire, 73; Fire Drills, 74; Precautions, 74; Fire Extinguishers, 75*

illness and injury, 82 *First-Aid Priorities, 82; Emergency Services, 83; Personal Emergency Warning, 83; Checklist of Emergency First-Aid Supplies, 84; Emergency Telephone Numbers, 84; Home Care Services, 86*

illness and injury, (continued)

life's little emergencies, 120

money, 128 *Vital Information, 129; Family Data Bank, 129*

pets, 148

pets, (continued)

plumbing, 160

stains and special cleaning problems, 165

stains and special cleaning problems, (continued)

travel, 193 *Preparation for a Trip, 193*

weather, 202 *Preparation for Weather Disasters, 202*

index, 213

NOTE: *A cross-reference page number within the text followed by f. or ff. indicates that pertinent information can be found not only on that page but on the page or pages following.*

FOREWORD

EVERYONE has experienced that breath-catching, heart-pounding, indecisive feeling known as "panic" when confronted with an emergency. You can't think clearly and you aren't certain what to do first.

One of the reasons this experience is so common is that we rarely expect an emergency—a situation which requires immediate action. We live as if such things happened to other people, not to us. Yet, we are all frequently confronted with emergencies. Most are minor—a sewing machine that quits in the middle of a seam or a stain on the rug. But some are life threatening; such as an automobile accident or a heart attack.

The best way to avoid the mental and physical short-circuiting that occurs during panic is to know what to do—how to cope with an emergency situation. For instance, if you know exactly what to do when someone drips grape juice on your brand new rug (see page 185), you won't panic and you'll avoid a permanent stain. If you know the steps to take when someone complains of chest pains (see page 93), you won't panic and you may save a life.

What do you do when a pipe breaks? Your dog has an encounter with a skunk? Your car's accelerator is stuck? You require a loan in a hurry? The answers to these situations and hundreds more can be found in these pages.

The purpose of this book is to suggest the appropriate actions to take when faced with the emergencies that may be encountered in everyday living. The advice is culled from the experience of experts in a number of fields. It is not meant to replace the physician, lawyer, banker, or other professional. It is meant only to help you handle an emergency situation until expert help is available.

While the information is intended to help you to act quickly, remember it is rarely necessary to react instantaneously. Even when someone has stopped breathing, you have several minutes before permanent damage occurs. Take a deep breath yourself, gather your thoughts, and then begin the proper procedure. It is better to do nothing than to do something that may make matters worse.

The book should be read thoroughly at least once by every member of the family capable of understanding it. It should then be hung or placed in an accessible spot such as a kitchen shelf or near the medicine chest. Everyone in the family and your baby-sitter should know where it is kept.

Remember that if you know what to do in an emergency, you won't panic!

appliances

Because appliance repairs are very expensive and repairmen are often hard to find, no one wants to call for professional help unnecessarily. There is no question of necessity, however, if you receive a shock (no matter how slight) or if you smell something burning when an appliance is turned on. It must be repaired before further use.

The best way to avoid difficulties with your appliances is to have them checked periodically, even if no trouble is apparent. Although they may not be used daily, motor-driven machines need regular servicing. Some public utilities offer a free annual examination of large appliances, so check with them before calling a service company.

ESCAPING GAS

One of the most potentially dangerous problems associated with appliances is escaping gas. If you smell the odor of gas in your home, look for the source immediately. (Because natural gas itself has no odor, the gas companies add an odorant, a garlicky smell, as a warning agent.) Unless you literally want to go through the roof, do not look for a gas leak with a lighted match. If light is needed, use a flashlight.

When the odor of gas is only slight, check for partially open gas valves on the range, heater, or other gas appliance or for extinguished pilot lights. Close any open gas valves and air the room thoroughly. To relight a pilot light, first cut off the supply of gas by turning the adjusting screw clockwise. Open the windows and air the room thoroughly. Then relight the pilot according to instructions in the owner's manual. (Never try to relight a pilot light if you have been away from a stove or other appliance for more than a few hours. Gas that has been escaping for a longer period of time can explode if ignited.) If the source of the gas odor cannot be determined, open the windows to air out the room and call the gas company immediately.

If the odor of gas is strong and its source is not immediately obvious, open all windows and turn off the main gas valve if accessible. (In a house, this may be in the cellar or at a gas tank; in an apartment, it may be behind or to the side of the stove.) Get everyone out of the house, and call the gas company from a neighbor's phone. Do not operate electric switches or doorbells, or light matches, because these could ignite the gas.

For any service problem, call your gas company. If they can't provide service themselves, they will tell you where to get it.

IF THE APPLIANCE DOESN'T WORK OR PERFORMS UNSATISFACTORILY

Before turning an appliance problem over to a professional repair service, here are several things you can do yourself:

Check the owner's manual. Keep the manual that comes with an appliance until you dispose of the machine. Never throw the book away! The information in that little booklet may save you the expense of unnecessary professional service calls.

Check lubrication. Motor-driven machines that are not permanently lubricated need regular oiling. Refer to the manual, and oil the machine in accordance with the manufacturer's instructions.

Check the source of power. Don't wait until you are faced with an emergency to locate the main gas valve and the fuse box or circuit breakers in your home or apartment. Often the source of power must be shut off before you proceed with simple repairs, and you will only add to your troubles if you must search for it before you can start on the repair job at hand. At times, too, turning off the power at its source is an important safety measure. In these cases delay might prove dangerous.

Check the plug or pilot light. If your machine does not run at all, look at the electric cord. Is it plugged in? Believe it or not, a repairman often finds that an unplugged cord is the only problem. Is it a gas appliance? See if the pilot light is out. If it is, refer to your owner's manual and to instructions above before trying to relight it.

Check the controls. Reset the controls. Be sure they are in the correct position by referring to the owner's manual. Give pushbuttons an extra-firm push and turn dials in the proper direction. Sometimes a piece of lint or dust momentarily interferes with the operation of the controls.

Check for dirt. Clogged filters in washers, dryers, refrigerators, humidifiers, vacuum cleaners, and air conditioners may keep these machines from operating efficiently. Check the filters frequently and clean them when necessary. Dust and dirt will also build up on the coils in back and beneath refrigerators and freezers. These coils should be cleaned every two to three months with the brush attachment on your vacuum cleaner.

Check the door. Make sure that appliance doors, latches, or covers are properly closed. Most appliances will not operate unless sealed tightly.

Check the bulb. If the appliance light doesn't work, the bulb probably has to be replaced. (Test the bulb in another outlet to be sure it is the bulb that is at fault.) Your owner's manual will tell you the type of bulb needed. If the light blinks on and off and you know that the blinking is not a normal signal or part of the intended cycling, look for a loose connection.

Check the electricity. When an appliance doesn't run efficiently, it may be because an electrical circuit is overloaded. Temporarily cut down the number of lamps and other appliances on the same circuit. If this corrects the problem, you will know that the circuit is overloaded and you should consult your electric company. A representative will tell you how to prevent a reoccurrence.

If the loss in power is not caused by an overloaded circuit, look at your room lights. Are they dimmer than usual? In this age of electrical everything—from toothbrushes to air conditioners—utility companies are sometimes forced to cut power in peak periods of use. If the house lights are dim and your machine is running inefficiently, it may be because your whole area is suffering a "brown-out" or power cut. Such events usually last only a short time. Do not use the machine until power is fully restored. Running a machine when there is insufficient power can seriously damage it.

Check fuse or circuit breaker. If the appliance doesn't work at all, check to see whether a fuse has blown or the circuit breaker has moved to the "off" position. Before any emergency arises, of course, it is a good idea to know which fuses or circuit breakers control the different circuits in your home. On the fuse box itself, mark the location of the specific circuit for each fuse or breaker. Usually a form is provided on the door of the box on which you can write this information. If there isn't, make out your own and attach it. You'll find that such a list will make checking on lighting problems much easier.

IF YOU CAN FIX IT YOURSELF

Before attempting to make repairs on any electrical appliance or to investigate a problem, be sure to disconnect the appliance cord.

For some repairs you can often save time and money by writing directly to the manufacturer and asking for replacements for frayed cords, worn can opener wheels, and other small parts. Address your request to the Customer Service Department and include the exact model number, if possible. If not, mail back the worn part so the manufacturer knows exactly what is to be replaced.

IF YOU CAN'T FIX IT YOURSELF

If none of the simple things suggested in these pages work, you will need a professional repair service. Make sure the one you choose has a repairman familiar with your particular machine. The Association of Home Appliance Manufacturers defines the following types of services:

Factory service. The appliance manufacturer owns the local company and provides service through the manufacturer's own employees. You can be quite sure, therefore, that the serviceman will be knowledgeable about your machine and will most likely have the necessary replacement parts in stock.

Authorized factory or factory franchised service. These are separately owned and managed, but they have a contract with the manufacturer to provide in-warranty and out-of-warranty service. You can also be quite sure that the repairman will be familiar with your machine and will probably have the parts in stock.

With both of the above services, you have some leverage because the service companies are dependent on the goodwill of the manufacturer and the manufacturer is dependent on your goodwill. If the repair job is not satisfactory, you can take your case directly to the manufacturer.

Independent service. This is provided by a local company not under contract to the manufacturer. You may get excellent repairs done by an independent at a reasonable price, and then again, you may not. Check the store where you bought the appliance or with friends who own the same brand appliance for referral to a reliable service. Chances are that an independent service will have to order replacement parts from the manufacturer.

FOR FURTHER INFORMATION

If you have questions about particular problems in your area that affect the operation of your appliances, such as hard water or "brown-outs," or you want information about new techniques in using particular appliances, contact your State University Extension Center or County Agent, who is listed under your county in the telephone book. Some utilities also have home economists on the staff to help customers and to give courses.

For questions, suggestions, or complaints about major appliances, you may write to: Major Appliance Consumer Action Panel
20 North Wacker Drive
Chicago, Illinois 60606

The sponsors of MACAP, which was organized in 1970, are manufacturers of major appliances and retailers who sell appliances under their own brand names. Products represented are: compactors, dehumidifiers, dishwashers, disposers, gas incinerators, home laundry equipment, humidifiers, ranges, refrigerators and freezers, room air conditioners, and water heaters.

AIR CONDITIONER

Air conditioners usually break down just when they are needed most—on hot, humid days. When this happens, keep cool. Here are a few common air conditioner ailments and some hints on what to do about them:

The motor labors. The problem may be a clogged filter (refer to your manual for the location of the filter). When you do not have a replacement on hand, take the old one out and go over it lightly on both sides with the vacuum cleaner brush. Then put it back into the machine.

The air conditioner turns on and off at short intervals. Move the thermostat up two points; it may be at too low a setting relative to the outside temperature.

The machine is on and no cold air comes through. This may mean that the cooling coils have developed a layer of ice that prevents them from functioning properly. Turn off the unit and wait until the ice melts before turning it on again.

The cooling fluid leaks out. Turn the machine off! Open the windows immediately if there is any odor at all. Heat can vaporize the fluid into a toxic gas. Be sure to have the machine repaired before turning it on again.

With the great drain on electricity during the summer, a drop in voltage may cause your air conditioner to work less efficiently. Listen to the radio and read the newspaper to determine if the electric company did indeed drop the voltage at the time you felt your air conditioner wasn't working well.

BLENDER

When a blender refuses to operate, it is usually because the knife blades are bent. Damaged knife blades are the most frequent cause of blender malfunction, but they can be replaced. If you are able to do it yourself, see page 15 for information about ordering the parts. To avoid bent blades, always use a rubber scraper when emptying the blender. If blades are not the problem, check the cord and switches for defects. These, too, can be replaced. If none of the above solves the problem, the blender needs professional repair.

CAN OPENER (ELECTRIC)

An electric can opener is a joy when you want to prepare a meal in a hurry, but is annoying when it doesn't work. The first thing to do is to disconnect it and scrub the cutting mechanism thoroughly. Use an old toothbrush dipped into detergent solution. Don't wet the electrical parts. If this doesn't help, check to see whether the space between the cutting wheel and the cogwheel is too wide for cans to be held securely. The space can be narrowed by tightening the nut that is found either on the front of the cutting wheel, or on the shaft behind it. If dirt or malfunctioning wheels are not the cause of the breakdown, take the can opener to the service department of the store in which it was purchased, or to a repair shop. If the cutting wheel becomes dull, you can buy replacements for some models (see page 15).

COFFEE MAKER

If your electric percolator fails to perk, try another cord. The original cord may be worn out and need replacement. If that is not the problem, plug another appliance or lamp into the outlet to see if the outlet is working. Have any faulty outlets repaired by an electrician. Check the coffee basket; sometimes grounds plug up the tube. To avoid this, always put your finger over the top of the tube when you spoon coffee into the basket. If the coffee maker is not immersible, it may be that the mechanism got wet. Let it dry thoroughly and try again.

COMPACTOR

Compactors are designed to crush garbage and make it fit into a fairly small bag. The bag lines a drawerlike compartment into which the rubbish is placed. Although compactors can crush glass, it is wise not to feed in bottles, dishes, or jars. The sharp edges of the glass often puncture the bag, the most common compactor problem, and cause mechanical troubles. If you find a ruptured bag is not the source of the malfunction, reset the dial. Sometimes a simple backup and restart will clear the problem. If not, call a repair service.

DEHUMIDIFIER

Used to remove moisture from the air in a damp room, a dehumidifier helps to make the atmosphere more comfortable by preventing mildew, mold, and oppressive humidity. If your machine isn't doing a proper job, it may not have sufficient capacity to dehumidify the area in which it is operating. A dehumidifier with a small reservoir, for instance, cannot be expected to dry an entire damp basement—several small machines or one large one may be needed.

Because dehumidifiers must be emptied when they reach capacity, most of them have an optional hose attachment that allows automatic drainage. If your machine has no such drain, the water reservoir must be emptied by hand. Many machines will automatically stop working when the reservoir is filled.

If you have the appropriate size dehumidifier for the area, and the reservoir is properly emptied, the problem may be icing of the coils. Coils become iced when the room in which the dehumidifier is operating has a temperature below 65 degrees F. This usually occurs in early spring when rooms become damp but are still too cool to permit efficient operation of a dehumidifier. All you can do is to raise the room temperature and disconnect the dehumidifier until the ice melts.

If none of the above explains the problem, check the cord, plug, and outlets for defects, and make sure the circuit is not overloaded. If all these tests check out and the dehumidifier still does not work properly, have it repaired professionally.

DISHWASHER

Dishwashers are marvelous convenience appliances, but sometimes they get balky. Common problems are:

Your dishwasher doesn't start at all, or the water does not enter. Make sure that the cord is plugged in, the switch is turned to the "on" position, the water is turned on, and the fuse has not blown.

The dishes come out dirty. The problem may be that the water entering the machine is not hot enough or not under sufficient pressure. Check the dishwasher during the first wash (you can hear it shut off automatically for a short period). If you see no steam and feel no heat, it is probably a water-temperature problem. If you do not hear the water rushing into the machine during the wash cycle, the water may not be under sufficient pressure. Telephone the water company, and a representative will check the problem and tell you how to remedy it. If temperature and pressure are not the culprits, then it may be the hardness of the water. Use only those detergents recommended for your area. To obtain a list of such products, contact the store where you purchased the machine, the company that services the machine, the extension service of your state agricultural college, or the water company.

The dishes in one section of your dishwasher do not get clean. Be sure the water flow isn't blocked by large platters. Improper loading can cause filming and spotting.

Silver and aluminum come out spotted and discolored. These conditions may be caused by undissolved detergent accidentally sprinkled on the cutlery or utensils. Silver polish will usually remove such stains. Remember, it is not wise to put hollow-handled silver utensils through the dishwasher because the heat of the drying period may cause them to fall apart.

Water does not drain from the dishwasher. Check the drain to see if it is clogged and examine the hose to see if there is a kink somewhere.

When you cannot track down the source of the trouble yourself, then of course, you will have to call in professional help.

DRYER, CLOTHES

Dryer breakdowns are always inopportune, especially when you have a load of wet clothing waiting to be dried. Several problems may arise:

Drying takes longer than usual. If you are absolutely certain you have the correct setting for the size and composition of the load, then check the lint screen. Because a blocked screen can affect efficiency, manufacturers recommend that it be cleaned after each load is dried. If the lint screen is clean, the outside vent may be clogged. If so, clean it with your hand or with the head of a wire hanger.

19

The dryer shorts out. Disconnect it and search for a bobby pin or some other metal object that may have worked through a hole in the basket and rubbed against a part of the machinery behind it.

The pilot light on your gas dryer goes out. Even if there is no odor of gas, do not relight it until you have aired the room and the basket thoroughly. Then relight the pilot according to the instructions in the owner's manual. Wait ten minutes before starting the machine again to allow the automatic switch to reset.

With the ever-changing variety of fabrics, drying clothes has become a skilled art. The law now requires clothing labels to carry cleaning instructions, but if items are unmarked because they were produced before or exempted from the law, or the label has come off, call the store where you purchased the item or your county extension service (see page 16) for advice on cleaning, drying time, and temperature.

For safety reasons, certain items should not be put in a dryer. These include anything made of foam rubber or glass fiber, home dry-cleaned articles, woolen knits, kapok pillows, cleaning cloths or mops saturated with wax, and any item labeled "dry away from heat."

Electric Frying Pan. See **SKILLET,** page 25.
Electrical Fires. See page 80.

FAN

If the blades of your fan are turning too slowly, the cause may be a clogged mechanism or insufficient lubrication. Turn off the fan, disconnect it, and rotate the blades by hand. If you see a lot of grease and dirt around the center of the mechanism, wipe it off with a damp rag and remove as much of the gummy residue as you can with a toothpick. Then wipe again. If the blades feel stiff, the machine may need oiling. Apply 2 or 3 drops of sewing machine oil to the shaft at the point where it enters the motor housing. Turn the blades and wipe off any excess oil. (See also **VENTILATION EQUIPMENT,** page 30.)

FREEZER

When most kitchen appliances break down it is an inconvenience, but when a well-stocked freezer does not work, the financial loss from spoiled food may be considerable. Freezers should be kept at 0 degrees F. or below. If the temperature goes above that, the quality and sometimes the safety of the food may be affected.

Watch for these difficulties:

The cabinet light is off. Check to see whether the bulb has burned out, the freezer is unplugged, or the circuit fuse has blown.

The freezer seems to run continuously. It may be because it has been opened too frequently, or the door has been left open too long. The frequently opened door may also cause heavy frost. If the door is not the problem, check the thermostat to see that it is set properly.

The freezer is noisy. Disconnect it, and clean the dust from the operating mechanism with a vacuum cleaner hose. Check for toys and other loose objects behind the appliance.

Sweating occurs around the door rim. Check the inside of the door to see that the gasket (the strip that lines the inside edge of the door) seals tightly. Wash it with soap and water. If sweating continues, call the serviceman.

Spills inside a freezer. Leave until defrosting time because a damp cloth or sponge will stick to the surface. If the machine is the frost-free type, then you can rub the spill with a hot, damp dishcloth.

The power fails. Keep the door or lid closed to retain the low temperature. Frozen foods in a fully loaded freezer will stay frozen for as long as two days—in a half-filled freezer for about a day. **If the power has been off for more than 24 hours,** try to obtain dry ice, or transfer food to a commercial locker. (See the Yellow Pages of the telephone directory.)

Never refreeze completely thawed meat or other food unless you cook it between freezings. Any food can be safely refrozen if it still contains ice crystals. Otherwise, use defrosted food within 24 to 48 hours. If you cannot use the food or give it away, it is better to throw it out than to take the chance of making someone ill.

GARBAGE DISPOSER

If your garbage disposer has indigestion, you may not have "fed" it right. When it makes loud noises, it is probably because you have forced too much into it, or there may be something caught in it. Turn off the disposer and take out the excess or the indigestible object with a long-handled spoon or pincers.

To prevent tangling, mix fibrous materials such as pea pods or corn husks with other wastes before putting them in the disposer. (Some machines cannot handle such fibrous material so check your instruction manual.) Other problems may be:

The unit stops grinding while operating. Turn it off, wait about three minutes, then turn it on again. If it does not resume normal operation, the rotating mechanism may be stuck. Turn off the current at the fuse box and lift out the top of the disposer. Insert a long-handled object such as a broom or mop handle. Pry against either hammer until the rotating wheel at the bottom of the shredding zone turns freely. Reinsert the top, turn on the switch at the fuse box, and start the disposer.

Disposers are self-cleaning. However, for a periodic flushing, fill the sink with cold water and then open the drain and allow the disposer and the cold water to run until the sink is empty.

Onions or other foods leave an odor. Run the cold water while you grind a lemon or orange rind, or several ice cubes. *Never use a drain-cleaning chemical!*

HUMIDIFIER

Human beings are most comfortable in an environment of 40 percent humidity because then the mucous linings of the nose and throat stay moist and germ resistant. During the winter when homes are heated, or in very dry climates, it may be necessary to install a humidifier to add water vapor to the air. Both room units and central humidifiers have reservoirs with available water supplies. The central unit is attached to the household water system, and the room unit is usually filled by hand.

When a humidifier stops or works inefficiently, chances are that it is clogged with various minerals and other solid deposits held in suspension in the water supply. These solids tend to accumulate in the reservoir, the take-up, and the vaporizing system of humidifiers. Remove the reservoir and scrub off any white film you see. Also scrub as much of the film from other parts of the humidifier as you can reach. Generally, this will remedy the malfunction. If it does not, turn the problem over to a professional repair service.

INCINERATOR

A gas-fired incinerator consists of a heavy metal container with a grate, a gas burner, and an ash drawer built into the bottom. Not all municipalities permit them, so check on the regulations in your area before you buy one. If you decide to purchase an incinerator, be sure it has the American Gas Association's Seal for Smokeless and Odorless Operation. Such appliances have a special afterburner that consumes smoke, fly ash, and odors.

An incinerator will dispose of anything that will burn, including wet food wastes, old shoes, and newspapers. It will not handle metals or glass or ceramic materials, so do not throw them in.

Wherever it is placed, inside the house or out, an incinerator must be connected to the fuel supply and to a chimney with a tiled flue of proper capacity.

The most frequent problem with an incinerator, as with other gas appliances, is a pilot light that has gone out. Learning to relight it is easy because pilot lights are specifically designed to be simple to restart.

If you smell smoke or see it when the incinerator is at work, something is wrong. You may have allowed a buildup in the ash drawer. Ashes should be emptied at least weekly and preferably every two or three days if the incinerator is used frequently. If the ash drawer is not the problem, have someone check the draft. The chimney may be clogged. If the problem still remains, call a serviceman.

MIXER

Most electric mixer problems are caused by a worn-out cord, a battered plug, or a defective speed control device, parts you may be able to replace yourself (see page 15). Sometimes, the answer is much simpler—a sticky residue may be gumming up the works. In this case, wipe the mixer with a damp cloth, and remove the gummy substance from the top of the beater shaft with a toothpick. Unless the manual specifically says you may, do not immerse the machine in water. Wash bowls, beater, wire whip, or metal attachments with a strong detergent solution and rinse well (an accumulation of detergent can affect the taste of the food you put in the mixer). If you can lift off the speed control knob easily, do so, and then wipe the metal contacts with a cloth.

Some machines never need oiling, but if your machine does require regular lubrication, follow the instructions given in your owner's manual. Remember to use oil sparingly.

Bent or damaged beaters can sometimes be straightened out, but usually they must be replaced (see page 15).

If none of the above works, take the mixer to a repair service.

Oven. See **STOVES AND OVENS,** page 26.
Percolator. See **COFFEE MAKER,** page 18.
Range. See **STOVES AND OVENS,** page 26.

REFRIGERATOR

A refrigerator can develop several troublesome symptoms:

The machine labors, rumbles, and shakes. The cure may merely be to vacuum the grid and the coils at the back and at the bottom of the refrigerator. If the machine is a gas appliance, clean the filter. To prevent this common ailment, go over the appliance with the vacuum brush regularly—about every two months.

You feel warmth emanating from the machine. Have it moved so that air can circulate freely around the sides and top. A refrigerator can suffer from suffocation.

High temperature inside the refrigerator. A high temperature may be caused by insufficient sealing of the refrigerator door. You can easily diagnose this problem if you hear the machine running constantly. Wash and dry gasket (the strip that lines the edge of the door on the inside). If this does not solve the problem, have the gasket replaced.

If a plastic part is broken, wash it with soap and water, rinse, and dry it thoroughly. Coat the broken edges with an appropriate plastic adhesive or heavy-duty rubber cement and clamp or tape them together for 24 hours.

Rotisserie. See **STOVES AND OVENS,** page 26.

SEWING MACHINE

A sewing machine is really a complicated piece of engineering. If you know a little about the principal parts and how they work, you may be able to avoid unnecessary repair calls. Always keep the machine in good condition by cleaning and lubricating it frequently according to directions in the manual. Never try to sew with a balky machine. Before you turn it over to a professional serviceman, however, see if you can diagnose the trouble by referring to the owner's manual and this check list:

The machine won't sew.

Is the control switch on?

If you have buttonhole controls, are they in the "off" position?

Stitching is unsatisfactory.

Is the machine threaded properly?

Are thread and bobbin tensions properly adjusted?

In order for the machine to stitch properly, the thread and bobbin tensions must be balanced so that both threads are drawn equally into the fabric. Test the tension and stitch size on a scrap of the fabric you intend to sew.

The upper tension disc controls the thread that goes through the needle. If this tension is too loose, the thread on the *underside* of the stitching will appear to lay flat on the surface of the fabric. If the tension is too tight, the thread on the *upperside* of the fabric will appear to lay flat.

If the bobbin tension is not properly adjusted, the stitches on the *underside* will be uneven, or will bunch up, or break. This may cause seams to split open when the garment is being worn.

To determine whether it is the upper tension control or the bobbin that is giving you trouble, thread the machine with two different colors. You can then tell by the color of the thread where the source of the problem is. No matter which tension is causing the trouble, however, almost all adjustments should be made on the upper thread control. Do not attempt to adjust the bobbin tension unless you are given specific instructions about how to do it in the owner's manual.

The bobbin thread breaks.

Are there loose threads caught in the case?

Is the tension correct?

Is there a knot in the thread?

Is the thread wound too loose or too tight?

The upper thread breaks.

Are you following the threading diagram in your manual?

Is there free movement of thread from the spool?

Is there free movement of thread from the tension disc?

Are there snags in the thread including the thread in the needle eye?

Is the upper tension too tight?

Is the needle bent or loose in the clamp?

The machine jams.

Is there lint or thread caught around the bobbin?

Is the fabric stuck in the needle hole in the throat plate?

The needle breaks.
    Is it the right size for the fabric?
    Is it secure in the clamp?
    Is the pressure foot or attachment in the wrong place?
Ask at a fabric store for free booklets of suggestions for special tricks in sewing various fabrics. Each fabric requires different techniques. There are needles and threads especially recommended for use on leather, knits, and synthetics to make machine sewing easier.

SKILLET

The heating element in an electric skillet is built in and therefore impossible for you to check. However, if the plug and thermostat are worn out or defective, you may be able to replace them yourself (see page 15)

STEAM IRON

Most of the trouble that occurs with an electric iron is caused by dropping it. The impact breaks the element connections, which must then be repaired professionally. But, if you haven't dropped the iron or at least you don't think you have dropped it hard enough to break the elements, check to see if the prongs of the plug are clean. If not, use fine sandpaper or steel wool to remove the dirt. Check the cord and plug to see if they are in good working order. If not, they can be replaced (see page 15). Common difficulties are:

Drops of water instead of steam come through the perforations. Allow the iron to heat up a little longer. Usually, when it reaches the proper temperature, it will emit an even flow of steam.

The iron spits or spurts, or refuses to steam at all. It is probably because the ports are clogged. There is a special steam iron cleaner available in hardware stores, but if you have none on hand, use a toothpick to clean out the holes and then brush away the residue with a cloth or brush. Some irons are advertised as being able to use water from the tap, but if you find the ports become clogged frequently, use only distilled water.

The soleplate is sticky or dirty. Rub it with fine sandpaper, fine steel wool (#00), or an emery cloth. Wipe it clean with a dry cloth and then wax it. Although there are special waxes available, ironing a piece of wax paper with a warm iron will coat the plate nicely.

The iron doesn't glide as smoothly as it should. The soleplate may be coated with starch. Disconnect the plug and allow the iron to cool. Then, rub the bottom with a damp pad of soapy fine steel wool and when it is clean, wipe out the steam vents with a cotton swab. Before using the iron again, heat it and run it over a kitchen towel.

If the soleplate is made of Teflon®, sprinkle baking soda on a damp

25

cloth and wipe. Then rewipe with a clean damp cloth, turn on the iron (low heat) and run it over a piece of wax paper.

STOVES AND OVENS

Because using the wrong utensils or a malfunctioning stove can subtly sabotage your supper, it is a good idea to check the following:

Cooking and baking utensils. Surface cooking utensils with flat bottoms are the most efficient, but they should not extend more than two inches beyond the heating units. If they do, they may cause the temperature to build up and damage the appliance.

Check your recipes carefully, and be sure to use utensils that are the correct size and shape. The choice of cookware depends upon the individual but generally, for double-crust pies, glass or anodized aluminum will give crisper crusts. For cakes, pans with dull, rough bottoms and shiny sides will give the largest volume and tenderest crumb. For cookies, you get the best results with a moderately shiny sheet of a size that allows two inches of free space in the oven on all sides for circulation of heat. The wrong size pan may result in uneven heat and over- or under-doneness, and in some cases, it can cause a cake to fall.

All pots and pans should be in good condition. Warped or rounded surfaces decrease cooking speed. Pans or utensils that have become darkened with use absorb more heat than bright, shiny ones, and can, therefore, be responsible for unevenly browned or burned foods. A product used to clean ovens is effective in cleaning heavily encrusted pots and pans. Be sure to follow the directions on the container carefully.

Burners. One cause of unreliable cooking may be crusty surface units on the burners. Pot boil-overs and spills should be wiped up as soon as the burner has cooled. Then take out and wash the surface units with a solution of detergent and hot water to which ½ cup of ammonia has been added. Rinse well and dry immediately.

Gas burners. A yellow flame often indicates a need for general cleaning. Lift burners out and soak them in household ammonia for several hours. If they are still dirty, boil them in a weak solution of washing soda and rinse in clear water. Dry thoroughly. See page 14 for instructions on relighting a pilot light.

Electric burners. Electric units, on the whole, are self-cleaning, but they may be impaired if the reflectors are encrusted with spilled food. Soak dirty reflectors for several hours in a strong solution of household ammonia. Then polish with steel wool and rinse clean.

If the cause of the trouble in an electric burner is neither dirt nor incorrect utensils, then the problem may be at the fuse box. If all four burners do not work, check the fuse. If only one burner is malfunctioning, check the wires. Make sure the switch is off, then raise the unit, and remove the reflector. Look to see whether the wires are connected to their terminals or whether any of the wires are broken. If there is a disconnected wire, reconnect it. If the unit still does not heat, call a repairman.

OVENS

Just as a thermometer can signal when something is wrong with a person, it can also help you to determine if cooking appliances are malfunctioning. Meat, candy, and deep-fat thermometers differ slightly, so be sure to select the proper one. The numbers should be easy to read. If the instrument shows that your oven consistently cooks too fast or too slow, you can compensate by adjusting cooking time or temperature until you have the appliance serviced.

If the oven does not work at all, check the automatic timer (if you have one). Manufacturers claim that having the oven set to go on at the wrong time of day is one of the most common causes of unnecessary repair calls.

Just as surface units must be kept clean for maximum cooking efficiency, ovens should be dirt- and grime-free. Some newer gas and electric ranges have ovens that clean themselves. One type locks while the temperature rises to 850–1000 degrees F., cleans the oven, and then leaves just a little powdery ash. The other type is made of a material that causes food soils to oxidize gradually whenever the oven is used for cooking. If something goes wrong with the self-cleaning system, do not try to repair it yourself.

If you do not have a self-cleaning oven, and for some reason you do not want to use a commercial oven cleaner, turn the oven on at 450 degrees for a few minutes and then turn it off. Pour straight household ammonia into a pan and place it in the oven overnight. In the morning, you will be able to wash the walls and bottom of the oven clean with plain water and without much effort. Dry thoroughly.

Gas ovens. If your gas oven does not work at all, call a repairman. (See also **ESCAPING GAS,** page 13.)

Electric ovens. If the electric oven does not work, check to see whether the element is connected firmly to the receptacle (outlet). If the oven doesn't heat, remove the element, clean the terminals, and reinsert it in the receptacle. If it still doesn't work, it has probably burned out. Call the repairman.

Portable ovens and rotisseries. Designed to supplement or substitute for a stove oven, portable ovens provide fast, controlled heat at high wattages. To use them efficiently, the home wiring system must be adequate to carry the wattages indicated on the name plate of the appliance.

Portable ovens and broilers come in a variety of sizes. Many are equipped with thermostats and timers. Check the timer and the switch to see if they are on. Then check the cord. If it is defective and replaceable, buy a new one (see page 15). If the appliance still does not operate, it needs professional repair.

On a rotisserie, foods are cooked as they turn on a motor-driven spit. Some rotisseries may also be used for broiling. If the rotisserie doesn't work at all, and the appliance has a timer and a switch that turns off the motor, check both of these first. Determine whether the spit is inserted properly. Check the wires and cord for breaks. If the rotisserie still doesn't work, have it repaired professionally. (See also **TOASTER AND TOASTER-BROILER OR BAKER COMBINATION,** below, and **SKILLET,** page 25.)

Microwave ovens. Microwave ovens operate heatlessly by means of high-frequency microwaves that penetrate the food to a depth of about two and a half inches on all sides. Cooking time is, therefore, substantially decreased. Because food does not brown in these electronic ovens, conventional high-speed broilers are sometimes incorporated in the top for browning.

Metal reflects microwaves, thus glass, china, or paper cooking containers that transmit the waves must be used in these ovens.

Microwave appliances operate on standard voltage outlets, so if an oven is not operating efficiently, check to see that the wiring is not overloaded (see page 15). If the wiring is sufficient, do not use the oven until it is checked by a *qualified* repairman.

Microwave ovens may leak and release harmful radiation. Because this radiation gives no warning such as pain, heat, or light, it is very important to be sure that the oven door seals tightly, and that the appliance is in top working order at all times.

TOASTER AND TOASTER-BROILER OR BAKER COMBINATION

Although table-top toasters and toaster-broiler or baker combinations use a lot of electrical current, they are convenient, time-saving appliances. If yours doesn't work satisfactorily:

Is it plugged in and does it feel warm? If it does, the appliance is not at fault. It may be that it is just putting too much of a burden on the electric supply. This happens most frequently during the summer months when air conditioners are in use. Therefore, it is wise not to use any other appliances on the same circuit when you are toasting, broiling, or baking with a table-top model. Don't even use the electric coffee pot that is usually plugged in at the same time as the toaster, unless you can use an outlet that is on another circuit.

Is the heating element intact? Take a flashlight and look into the toaster or broiler to see whether the heating element is broken. In the table-top toaster combinations, the heating element is quite simple and you may be able to replace it yourself (see page 15). To avoid trouble with toaster heating elements, do not allow melted butter or other liquids to drip on them.

The toaster heats but the toast doesn't eject. If a piece of toast or large crumbs are clogging the mechanism, do not use a metal instrument, such as a knife or a fork, to take them out unless the toaster is disconnected. Remove the crumb tray and clean it. Disconnect the appliance and blow the crumbs out of the inside with a vacuum cleaner hose.

If all these measures fail, take it to a repair shop.

VACUUM

Vacuum cleaners are very versatile and can perform many unusual chores from grooming the dog to cleaning the venetian blinds. Check your manual for ideas and for proper operation and care of your machine. Vacuum cleaners can suffer from punctured "intestines" or may choke on pieces of debris too large to swallow, so to avoid trouble don't use the vacuum to pick up sharp or bulky objects unless the owner's manual specifically says it is possible for your model to do so. Shag carpets need a special attachment or they will clog up most machines. If your vacuum cleaner:

Doesn't work at all. Disconnect and examine the cord for a break. If the plug is broken, replace it (see page 15).

Makes a rattling noise and then stops. Something is caught in the fan. Disconnect and disassemble enough to get at the fan and shake the cleaner. The object should fall out. A broken fan belt can cause a rattle. In some older-type machines, you can fix it yourself. (Consult the instruction manual.) In others, you have to have it repaired professionally.

Won't pick up dirt. The bag may be too full, or the brush may be worn or packed with dirt. Disconnect, disassemble, and inspect the parts. A flashlight can help you to see dark recesses better. Are there threads wound around the brush? Cut them with a pair of scissors and remove. Is the outlet from the machine to the bag clogged? Poke out lint and dirt with a stiff wire. Is the hose clogged? If so, clean with a long wire. (Loop the end so it doesn't puncture the hose.) Remember: the efficiency of any vacuum cleaner drops when the dirt container is more than half full.

If an upright vacuum cleaner is still not picking up dirt and nothing is jammed, check the position of the nozzle. It may be too close or too far from the surface being cleaned. If so, turn the screw until a quarter will slide easily between the nozzle and the floor. For cleaners with revolving brushes, double the space between the nozzle and the floor surface.

Has a hole. To patch a hole in a vacuum bag made of plastic or paper, use plastic mending tape. If the bag is cloth, cover the hole on the inside with adhesive-backed or press-on mending tape.

To fix a hole in a plastic hose, wind plastic tape over the hole and around the hose. For a fabric-covered hose, use a strip of strong fabric. Coat one side with rubber cement and wind it around the hose. The edges of the strip should overlap as it goes around. Let it dry before using the vacuum.

Has hose troubles. The hose may fall loose from the machine, a common problem with cannister-type cleaners that have hoses made of plastic over a flexible metal coil. If the plastic sleeve on the end of the hose separates from the hose, coat the end of the hose with plastic mending adhesive and screw it into the sleeve. Let the glue dry overnight. If the plastic sleeve slips off the metal tube, wrap adhesive or plastic mending tape around the end of the tube to form a slight ridge. Then force the sleeve over this.

If the hose won't hold the cleaning tools, one of the metal fittings may be bent. If so, attempt to straighten the part with a pair of pliers. Check to see whether the metal clips that are sometimes used to secure the joints are catching properly. If this doesn't work, tape the tools to the hose with plastic mending tape as a temporary measure. Then have the troublesome parts professionally repaired.

VENTILATION EQUIPMENT

If you see or smell cooking smoke and your appliances are clean and free of debris, chances are the oven vent or the kitchen fan is not working properly. The vent may be cleaned with a toothbrush or dull knife. Just place a piece of paper toweling or a pan on the oven floor to catch the debris.

The kitchen fan may be cleaned by unscrewing the face plate and disconnecting the plug. With a toothbrush or dish brush dipped into a detergent solution, scrub the blades and the casing and then dry them thoroughly with paper towels.

WASHING MACHINE

The many varieties of fabrics and colors used today sometimes make operating modern washing machines a fairly complicated procedure. The size of a load and the kind of fabric in a load can seriously affect cleaning efficiency. Water temperature is also an important consideration when cleaning certain types of materials. Therefore, it is important to check the labels on all the garments being washed. Such labeling is now required by law to provide washing instructions for every kind of fabric. If there is no label, or if you have a question that cannot be answered by the label or your washing machine manual, call the county agent (listed under your "County" in your telephone book), your utility company's home economist, or the store in which you purchased your machine. Some common problems are:

The washing machine doesn't work. First check to see whether it is plugged in. If it is, check the fuse. Then look to see if any clothing has been tangled in the agitator. Such tangles not only prevent the machine from working, but they can also clog the machine so that the water cannot drain out. If there is no tangle of clothes, but the agitator does not move, remove the cap that holds it in place and clean it. (The agitator cap should be removed and cleaned regularly—about every two weeks—to prevent this problem.) If you cannot remove the cap, you will have to call a serviceman.

The water comes in cold. You probably have used up your hot water supply. But check to see whether the hot water valve near the machine is turned on and in operating order.

The water does not enter or the machine fills too slowly. Check to see if there is a kink in the hose. The trouble may be caused by sand or sediment that has collected in the filter washers at the faucet connections. This can block the water supply completely. Remove and clean the filter washers and replace them.

The machine starts disgorging bubbles. You have probably used too much detergent or the wrong kind of product for your machine. Turn off the machine. Let the suds settle down, then empty the machine and start over.

The laundry comes out of the machine still dirty. You may not be using enough soap or detergent, or you may be using the wrong kind of washing product for the water in your area. Check your instruction manual or ask for professional advice (see page 16).

WATER HEATER

Bathtubs, dishwashers, washing machines, and showers all use plenty of hot water. Although modern water heaters stand ready to supply the needs of the household, they are always subject to corrosion and should be checked.

Always shut off the source of power before touching the water heater. Water and electricity do not ever mix safely. Turn off the water supply to the appliance before attending to it. The valves are usually right at the junction where the pipes supplying water lead into the unit.

Corrosion and sediment buildup. To prevent buildup on the inside of the tank, drain it every month if your water is hard and every two or three months if it is soft. Most water heaters have spigots to which a garden hose may be attached. Screw the hose onto the spigot and then run the hose into a sink or outside the house. If you do not wish to use a hose, substitute a gallon bucket. Allow the water to drain until it is clear.

Insufficient and inconsistent supply of hot water. You probably need a tank with a larger capacity. In the meantime, try to schedule uses of large amounts of water (for bath or laundry) at least one hour apart.

The water doesn't heat. If you have a gas heater, check the pilot light. If the pilot is out, call a service representative to relight it. If the heater is run by electricity, check the fuse. If the trouble is not caused by the fuse or the pilot, call a repairman. (The newer models are both gas and electric, so you will have to check both sources of power.)

Water on the floor. To determine the source of the problem, you have to observe the amount of water and its location. Water heaters automatically turn off when temperature or pressure build too high. There is also a relief valve or outlet that is a safety feature. You should be familiar with its location. Check your owner's manual or ask a plumber or repairman to point it out. If you see water dripping from the valve, do not touch the heater. Immediately summon a representative of the utility or a repair service. When you explain the situation, they should respond promptly because this is a potentially dangerous situation.

If you see a small amount of water on the floor around the heater after you return from a trip, chances are nothing is wrong. Before leaving the house, you probably turned down the temperature of the water heater and the house. When you returned, you may have turned the house and water heater temperature up, causing condensation to form and drip on the floor.

The heater has sprung a leak. In this instance, water will be running from the tank. If it is a slow leak, just let the water heater alone and call the repairman. You cannot patch the leak yourself, but you will still be able to keep the appliance in service until it is repaired.

A fast leak, however, requires draining the tank. Turn off the source of energy and the water, as mentioned before. Hook up the garden hose to the tank's outlet (or use a large bucket) and drain the water heater completely.

automobile

When you are driving a car, a breakdown is not only frustrating and time-consuming, but it can also be frightening and dangerous.

Since there is rarely time to consult the manual that comes with your car at the time of an emergency, it is important to study it carefully and be prepared. Familiarize yourself with the location of the various parts of the car (see illustrations on pages 34 and 41) and what to do if any part needs attention. For example, learn how to open the hood so you can do it easily when you have to look for trouble inside. Read the instructions for changing a tire—and better still, try doing it before you need to, so you can do it yourself if no help is available. Become familiar with the tools that are part of standard equipment so you know what each one is for and can handle it easily. You will find many helpful instructions in the manual that will tell you how to diagnose trouble, what you can do, and when you should turn to a professional repairman for help.

An accident may be as minor as a slight bump or as major as a serious injury or death. In a dangerous situation, there is often only a split second to make a decision. Knowing the right thing to do can save your life, the lives of your passengers, and the lives of people in other cars.

SAFETY CHECKUPS

To avoid breakdowns and accidents, a car must be in safe condition. The following should be checked periodically and always before taking a long trip or at the start of the winter season in the north:

Battery. Test the battery; fill and recharge it if necessary. If you suspect that the battery may fail, even if recharged, get a new one.

Tires. If the thread is not clearly visible in regular tires, have them checked at a service station. A bald tire is always unsafe. When winter approaches, and as soon as local law permits, put on snow tires. Carry chains in the trunk of the car if you think there is a chance they will be needed.

Brakes. Equal pull on all four wheels is necessary. If the pull is uneven, have brakes adjusted to assure straight-line stopping. (See page 40.)

Parts of the automobile found under the hood.
Although the position of these parts may vary in different cars,
you can generally recognize each of them by shape.

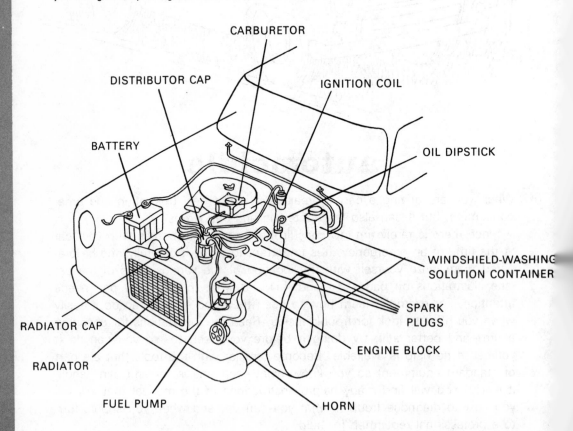

Exhaust system. Have the muffler and exhaust checked for leaks. A carbon monoxide leak can be lethal (see page 41).

Windshield. The defroster and wiper blades should be in good condition. Replace worn wiper blades, and adjust tension. Use antifreeze windshield washing solution for winter driving (see illustration on page 34).

SAFETY TIPS FOR DRIVERS

If you hear any unusual sounds or sense a problem while operating a car, have the vehicle attended to as soon as possible. These symptoms may be warnings of a serious breakdown. At the first sign of any mechanical trouble, slow down, pull over to the curb or the shoulder of the road, and stop.

Even if the car is in excellent operating condition, always drive defensively. Know the motor vehicle laws in your area, the various traffic signs and signals, and drive as if the other fellow might not obey them. Adjust your speed to the weather. Posted speed limits are usually for ideal conditions only. If you feel at all sleepy or begin to get a kink in your neck, stop the car and rest.

Keep in mind, too, that you are vulnerable to crimes in your car as well as on the street. This chapter contains advice from police experts on how to protect yourself.

EMERGENCY EQUIPMENT

To be prepared for most emergencies, it is wise to carry the following equipment:

Emergency lights or flares. There are many types on the market. If you do not have a set, keep several empty milk cartons in the car trunk. They will burn for about 15 minutes.. In windy or stormy weather, stones placed inside keep them from blowing away.

Reflector tape. This is used for the same purpose as emergency lights. In the event a taillight or headlight goes out, reflector tape can be attached to the car to warn others.

Small first-aid kit

Standard equipment for changing a tire

Fire extinguisher (see page 75)

Rag

Window scraper (for winter travel)

Can or spray deicer (for winter travel)

Sand and a shovel (for winter and mud conditions)

Flashlight (useful for signaling and for reading street and house signs)

Send Help sign (obtained from a service station or home-made)

Jumper cables (and learn how to use them to start your car)

ACCELERATOR STICKS

If the car fails to slow down when you take your foot off the gas pedal, don't hit your brakes even with a pumping action, because it will jerk the car and burn up the brakes. Given the time, try to raise the accelerator pedal with your foot. This may free the accelerator linkage, or at least improve your chances of pulling off the road safely. Do not bend down and try to free the accelerator with your hand; this will only increase the chance of an accident.

Should you be in heavy traffic or in a danger spot, and you cannot lift the pedal with your foot, shift the car immediately into neutral, and apply your brakes gently but firmly. If possible, signal your intention to turn toward a safe place at the curb, or on to the shoulder of the road. The car's engine will race when it is put in neutral and this may cause damage, but it is far better to save your life than to worry about the car.

If you are not in heavy traffic and there is little danger of being hit from another direction, turn off the ignition. Then brake to a stop as you try to maneuver your car to the side of the road.

In any event, do not drive the car again until it has been repaired.

ACCIDENT

If you are involved in an accident, stop immediately at the scene or as close to the spot as possible. Turn off the ignition and do not smoke. Gas fumes from a damaged car could literally send you up in flames.

Check to see if anyone has been hurt. If there are injuries, ask a passerby to call the police and inform them of the injuries. The police, in turn, will speed to the scene and send an ambulance. If you are qualified, give first aid (see page 82 ff.).

Even if there are no injuries, it is wise to notify the police. Some states require that any accident involving damages of more than $50 be reported to the police.

Be considerate of other drivers by moving the car out of the way, if possible. If not, put on flasher lights or set out flares, if available. Do not let honking horns or angry yells force you to get into your car or move it if you do not believe it is wise to do so.

It is helpful to keep in your glove compartment a list of information you will be asked to give, and the information you should ask for, if another car is involved in the accident. You might want to copy the form suggested on pages 37ff. for this purpose. In any case, be sure to obtain the other driver's name, address, license number, and registration number. Write down a description of his vehicle as well. In states where insurance is compulsory, the laws require that drivers involved in an accident provide this information. This also holds true in states where there are "No-Fault Insurance Laws." In general these laws make it unnecessary to prove guilt in accident cases in order to obtain reimbursement for damages or personal injuries, but since the laws vary from state to state, it would be wise to find out the exact provisions of the laws in your area. If the car is not owned by the driver, get the owner's name and address. To speed up claims, also ask for the name of the owner's insurance company.

Make a list of the names and addresses of the occupants of the vehicles involved in the accident. As soon as possible, ask for the names and addresses of all witnesses, including those who saw the accident or might have information about the circumstances surrounding it. Get the same information, as well as badge numbers, from all police officers involved.

Except in very minor accidents, attempt, if possible, to have photographs made of the scene (including tire marks) and of the vehicles. If there is no police photographer, have a commercial one called. If the vehicles have been removed to a garage, they should be photographed there.

Never apologize to or make accusations against the other persons involved. Give only the information required. Cooperate with the police investigating the accident, but do not volunteer your opinion of how the incident occurred. Try to avoid making any statements, and do not sign a written statement before you have consulted a lawyer.

Do not speak to an insurance representative for the other party, and do not deal with any adjusters without legal advice. Also consult your lawyer and/or your insurance company if you are required by law to file a motor vehicle accident report with the city or state.

GLOVE COMPARTMENT ACCIDENT FORM

YOUR NAME: _____

Address: _____

Home phone: _____

Person to be notified in case of serious injury: _____

_____

INSURANCE COMPANY: _____

Address: _____

Phone: _____

DRIVER'S LICENSE NO.: _____

REGISTRATION NO.: _____

LICENSE PLATE NO.: _____

PERSONAL PHYSICIAN: _____

    Phone: _____

AUTO CLUB OR TOW SERVICE: _____

    Phone: _____

HEALTH INSURANCE COMPANY and NO.: _____

_____

OTHER CAR

OWNER'S NAME: _____

    Address: _____

    Phone: _____

INSURANCE COMPANY: _____

DRIVER'S LICENSE NO.: _____

OWNER'S REGISTRATION NO.: _____

MAKE AND YEAR OF CAR: _____

    Color: _____

DESCRIPTION OF DAMAGE: _____

_____

DATE OF ACCIDENT: _____

TIME OF ACCIDENT: _____

SCENE OF ACCIDENT (exact location: street and house or pole number):

_____

Draw Diagram

WEATHER: _____

ROAD CONDITIONS: _____

PERSONS INJURED (in all cars involved):

Name: _____

Address: _____

Description: _____

Name: _____

Address: _____

Description: _____

WITNESSES:

Name: _____

Address: _____

Phone: _____

Name: _____

Address: _____

Phone: _____

Police Officer: _____

Badge No.. _____

Police Precinct No.. _____

ATTEMPTED ENTRY AT A TRAFFIC LIGHT

Always keep your doors locked and your car in gear at a traffic light. If anyone should try to enter, drive off, even if it means you have to go through a red light. Sounding your horn at the same time will serve to frighten the intruder, to attract attention, and to warn other drivers at an intersection.

If someone succeeds in getting into your car at a traffic light, scream and run. Grab the car keys if possible, but get out fast.

BLOWOUT

When a tire blows out, the car usually starts to wobble violently. Don't step on the brakes or you will lose control of the car. Grab the steering wheel firmly and hold on. Lift your foot slowly from the gas pedal and gently put it down on the brake. Ease the car to the side of

39

the road. Do not try to drive on a flat tire unless there is a dire emergency, because it can be costly. In general, slowing down gradually with a blowout will not severely damage a tire.

Put up a distress signal—a white handkerchief tied to the door, the raised hood, a commercial flare or a flasher, a sign, or all of them together.

If you want to tackle changing the tire yourself, look in the car's manual for instructions. It can be done, and it does not require the strength of Hercules.

BRAKES FAIL

One of the most panic-inducing situations occurs when you press on the brake pedal and nothing happens. If you step on the pedal and it goes down to the floor, don't stiffen and hold your foot there. Lift your foot and then slam it down quickly several times. This action may pump up sufficient pressure in your failing brakes to stop the car. If this doesn't work and you have the leeway, immediately shift into low, which uses the engine as a brake, until your speed is reduced to approximately 20 miles an hour.

If you must stop instantly, shift gears and begin applying the parking brake. Do it rather slowly because the emergency or parking brake locks the two rear wheels, and under slippery conditions, this can send you into a tailspin.

You can encourage your car to stop by turning off the ignition. If you have power steering, however, don't do so unless the road is clear; you may need to steer the car out of the path of trouble.

You can also slow your car down by rubbing the tires against a curb, a wall, or a fence, but you must have strength and skill as well as time to execute this maneuver.

As with any malfunction, brake failure is best avoided by taking preventive measures. Have brake linings checked at least one a year and be aware of the following danger signs:

Car swerves to one side when you apply the brakes.
The pedal seems soft and spongy.
The brakes make a squealing, metal-to-metal sound.
The brake pedal must be depressed almost to the floor to work.

Any of these conditions indicate that brake trouble is imminent, and the car should be checked by a serviceman as soon as possible.

BUMPERS LOCKED

Locked bumpers can occur as a result of a minor bumping accident or in a tight parking situation. But whatever the cause, never stick your hands between the cars in an effort to free the bumpers or you will risk very serious injury.

Try the simplest solution first. Rock the car whose bumper is on the bottom by pressing both hands on a fender. If this does not work, put a board behind the front wheels of the car whose bumper is on top. By backing the car over the board you may be able to raise it enough to clear the other car's bumper. If no board is available, or you still cannot get the cars apart by this method, try lifting the top car bumper with a jack. Still locked? Call a serviceman.

CARBON MONOXIDE

Carbon monoxide is a colorless, odorless, and highly toxic gas found in the exhaust fumes from an internal combustion engine. Because this gas can be lethal, it is important to be aware of certain safety precautions, many of which are usually taken care of in a regular maintenance check.

Underside view of automobile showing exhaust system.

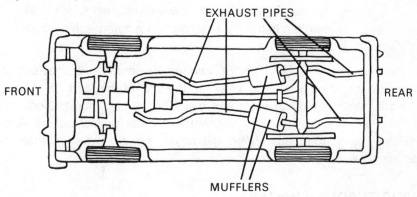

EXHAUST PIPES

FRONT

REAR

MUFFLERS

Make sure that your car's exhaust system (see illustration above) is free of defects. The tail pipe should be long enough to clear the back end of the car. Rust frequently corrodes exhaust pipes causing holes and sometimes breakage, so be sure that the pipe is in good condition.

See that the connection between the exhaust pipe and the engine compartment is properly sealed. Fumes escaping at this juncture sometimes leak into the passenger area or the heating system. Have heater connections checked as well.

Examine the floor of the car to see that there are no holes in it.

When driving, always keep the window at least slightly open. In heavy traffic, open it wide (unless, of course, your car is air conditioned).

Never leave the engine running if you are parked in a garage or an enclosed area. (See also **POISONS INHALED**, page 107.)

Car Following Your Car, see page 55.
Car Following You While You Walk, see page 55.
Car Sickness. See **MOTION SICKNESS,** page 105.

COLLISION COURSE

Head-on collisions are generally the most deadly. If another vehicle is heading straight toward you, slow down immediately. Flash your lights, and blow your horn. Pull over to the shoulder of the road, if necessary, but never try to swerve to the left. The other driver might cut back into his own lane when he realizes the predicament, and a crash could result (see page 36).

DANGEROUS DRIVER

Defensive driving includes being on the alert for dangerous drivers who may be behaving in any of the following ways:

Driving noticeably slower than other drivers
Weaving in and out
Crossing or "riding" the dividing line
Failing to stop at stop signals or otherwise demonstrating
    a slow reaction
Being aggressive and taking unwarranted risks, such as
    jumping lights, tailgating, sounding the horn
    repeatedly.

Such drivers may be drunk or emotionally unstable, so get out of the way at once. If necessary, pull over to the side of the road. Then note the license number and the color and make of the car. Flag the next police officer you see, or stop and phone the nearest police station. A patrol car will be sent to apprehend the driver, hopefully before there is an accident.

DRIVING THROUGH WATER

You can drive through water up to the frame of your car without damage, if you proceed with caution. Depress the brake pedal nearly enough to stop the car, and move slowly. Heat from the friction will help to keep the brake linings dry. After you have driven through the water, test the brakes lightly to see if they are wet. If they grab on one wheel or don't hold, keep the brake pedal slightly depressed for a few minutes; again, frictional heat will help to dry them. If your car stops in the middle of water, it is probably because the water has caused a short circuit (see **Wet ignition,** page 49).

DRIVING THROUGH WINTER STORMS

In areas of heavy snowfall, be prepared for winter automobile travel by equipping your car for emergencies. A storm kit should contain blankets or sleeping bags; matches and candles; an empty three-pound can with plastic cover to receive wastes; facial tissues; paper towels; extra clothing; high-calorie, nonperishable food; compass and road maps;

knife; first aid kit; shovel; sack of sand; flashlight or signal light; windshield scraper; booster cables; two tow chains; fire extinguisher; an axe.

Every car should be winterized well before the storm season begins, and the gas tank kept full.

If you must travel when there is danger of a winter storm, select primary and alternate routes and check the latest weather information on the radio or with the appropriate weather bureau before you leave and during your trip. Try not to travel alone; it is better to have two or three people in the car or to travel in a convoy with another car if possible. Always fill your gas tank before entering open country, even for a short distance. Drive with extreme caution.

If your visibility is at all restricted because windshield wipers aren't working properly, the best thing to do is to stop immediately. Do not drive with nonfunctioning windshield wipers. Wait until the snow lets up, and then proceed to a nearby service station for repairs.

If a blizzard traps you while you are driving, avoid overexertion. Don't attempt to push your car, shovel heavy drifts, or perform other such difficult chores during the storm. Stay in the car, and do not attempt to walk out of a blizzard. You can become disoriented quickly in blowing and drifting snow, and being lost in open country during a blizzard results in almost certain disaster. You are more likely to be found if you stay in your car, and your chances of survival are better in the shelter of the auto.

When sitting in a car, always allow fresh air to circulate. Be sure that freezing wet snow and wind-driven snow do not completely seal the passenger compartment. Beware of carbon monoxide poisoning and oxygen starvation. Run the motor and heater sparingly, and only with the downwind window open for ventilation.

Exercise by clapping your hands and moving your arms and legs vigorously from time to time. Do not stay in one position for long.

Turn on the car's inside light at night to make the vehicle visible to work crews or possible rescuers.

Do not permit all occupants of the car to sleep at the same time!

EXPRESSWAY OR FREEWAY DRIVING

Driving on superhighways demands quick reflexes and caution. Don't try it unless you are an experienced driver and have been taught how to enter an expressway safely.

If you are on an expressway and find you are going in a direction opposite from the one you intended, or you go past your exit, you must proceed with traffic until the next interchange. Only then can you leave the expressway and re-enter by the proper approach. Never attempt to cross the center strip or back up to the place where you entered. Both are not only illegal, but potentially suicidal.

Drive within a 25 percent range of the speed of traffic. If most cars are going 55 miles per hour, you shouldn't drop below 40. Stay in the right-hand lane if you want to drive at minimum speed. Be sure to signal if you decide to change lanes.

If you are driving at a speed of 55 miles an hour, you will require 275 feet to stop. Therefore, in good weather you should allow at least one car length between your car and the car in front of you for every 10 miles an hour of traveling speed. In bad weather, the distance should be increased. If you keep a two-second interval from the car ahead, you will be following safely. You can do this by noticing the car ahead as it reaches some fixed object such as a sign or tree on the roadside. At that moment, count at a medium pace—one thousand-and-one, one-thousand and two—until your vehicle reaches the object. Each count approximates a second. If your vehicle passes the object before the count of one-thousand-and-two, you are following too closely.

Should it be necessary to stop, signal for a right-hand turn as you decelerate. Drive completely off the right side of the road—all four wheels and fenders.

When you have to get off the expressway, look for the signs that tell you your turnoff is coming up. Signal and move to the correct turnoff lane. Decrease your speed and begin signaling your intention to exit well in advance.

If a car is coming at you in the wrong lane, honk and blink your lights and try to pull off the road if you can (see page 42).

When watching road and traffic, you can't always read all words on signs. Road signs have therefore been standardized throughout most of the country for quick recognition. Learn the basic shapes of the principal regulatory and warning signs and use them as an instant "alert" (see illustrations below).

ROAD SIGNS

FIRE

The way in which you deal with an automobile fire depends on its location.

Engine. Turn off the ignition immediately and use a fire extinguisher. If you do not have one, there may be snow, dirt, or sand nearby to throw on the flames. Or, you may use a woolen—not a synthetic—blanket to smother the flame. If you have nothing with which to extinguish the flames, stay clear of the car. Signal oncoming traffic to alert them to the danger, and ask someone to send for help.

If you are able to put out the fire, check the spark plugs and other wires for burns. If there is any evidence of charring, do not drive the car and be sure to have a mechanic check the engine before you do drive again. If there is no such evidence, you may be able to drive a short distance to the nearest service station for a thorough check.

Upholstery. If the car's upholstery is smoldering, get out and soak the seat with water or snow. If possible, remove the seat and check for burning embers. Be sure the spark is out—car seats can smolder for a long time and then catch fire again.

Should you be in an accident in which gasoline has spilled, get away fast. Do not smoke. There is great danger of fire.

FOG

Whether you continue to drive in fog or not depends on your judgment. Consider how far you have to go to get out of the fog, how dangerous the road is, and your chances of pulling off the road to safety. If you must drive through fog, slow down gradually, flash your brake lights frequently, and put on your low headlight beams to avoid blinding oncoming drivers. Turn on your windshield wipers and defroster. Should you have to pull off the road, turn on your right signal light well in advance, and then drive as far off the road as possible. If you can do so safely, pull off the shoulder of the road onto the grass. Put on your emergency lights or your parking lights. If it is necessary to get off a highway or road, try to find a service station where you can park. In any event, you should avoid traveling on an expressway during fog. If you have to continue driving, take a secondary road on which the traffic is slower.

HELP NEEDED

When your car breaks down on the road, or on an expressway, put on the safety flasher lights immediately. If your car is an older model and does not have them, turn on a directional signal and the parking lights.

If your car is well off the road, sit in it until help arrives. If it is in a hazardous spot, get out and wait for help on the side of the road.

Tie a white handkerchief to the handle of the driver's door and put up the car's hood, if you can do it safely. These are international distress signals.

Should another car stop and offer help, ask the driver to notify the police at the nearest toll booth or phone station.

If you are a travel club member, you should have a directory which gives you the names of towing services in the area. If you do not have a directory, ask the police, or look up the nearest affiliated station in the telephone company's Yellow Pages.

Before you give the go-ahead for any on-the-spot repairs or towing, ask how much the job will cost and have the price put in writing.

HOOD FLIES UP

If the hood of your car isn't shut securely, it could fly up suddenly while you are driving. Although this is a very frightening situation, you can resolve it safely if you stay calm. First take your foot off the accelerator. Look in the rearview mirror and observe the traffic behind you as you slowly begin applying the brakes. Lean out the left window just far enough to be able to guide your car safely to the side of the road. Then get out of the car, and slam down the hood.

HORN STUCK

If turning off the engine does not stop the honking, lift the hood and locate the horn, which is usually in front, or to one side of the radiator (see illustration on page 34). Most of them look like miniature French horns. The wire clips on each of the two wires leading to the horn are made to be easily unplugged. To stop the noise, pull out the plugs, and then have the horn repaired as soon as possible.

INTRUDER

A number of people have been unfortunate enough to get into their cars and find a stranger hiding in it. The intruder usually says something like: "Get moving or I'll kill you." Unless there's a gun or knife aimed at you, do get moving—but out of the car! Let out a shriek as you open the door; get out and run. Police emphasize that you should not stay in the car and follow orders. If you always lock the doors and close all the windows when you leave the car, you can avoid such an incident.

LIGHTS OUT

Should you find you must drive when your headlights have gone dead, hold a flashlight or have someone else hold it out the window to light the road and to warn other cars of your approach. If possible, arrange to have another car lead you to the nearest service station.

If it is a taillight that has gone out, the flashlight can be held so it shines out the back window. An alternative solution is to attach reflector tape to the back of the car until you can get the taillight fixed.

LOCK FROZEN

Do not force the key into the lock. Heat the key with your hand or with matches or a cigarette lighter. Put the key in the lock, and attempt to turn it very gently.

LOCKED OUT OF CAR

Whether you have locked your keys in the car or simply lost them, you'll need to get help to open the door. Call the nearest dealer who sells your type of car. They often have master keys and may be able to send a serviceman to open a door. If this isn't feasible, call the police. They have techniques for opening cars and may be able to help you or refer you to a garage or locksmith with master keys.

The National Safety Council does not recommend placing an extra key in a magnetized box hidden somewhere on the car—a thief can find a second key no matter where you hide it.

OUTDOOR PARKING IN SLEET OR SNOW

If you have to park your car outdoors in the kind of weather that freezes the windshield, place the rubber floor mat over the windshield. Adjust the windshield wipers to keep it in place. Even if you come out several hours later, when you remove the mat you'll be able to drive off with vision unimpaired. Don't try this in a neighborhood where you think there is danger of having the mat stolen. (See also **DRIVING THROUGH WINTER STORMS,** page 42)

OUT OF GAS

Even when the indicator reads "empty," there is usually a reserve supply of gas to get you to a service station several miles away. However, to conserve your remaining supply, drive in high gear at about 20 miles per hour keeping your acceleration as steady as possible. Take advantage of momentum from hills, and coast without using the gas pedal.

If you feel that you can't make it to the service station or, if the tank is really empty and your car won't move at all, signal another car and ask the driver to send an attendant from the nearest service station with a five-gallon tank. Don't ever get into a car that stops along the road to help, even if someone else can stay with the disabled car.

OVERHEATED ENGINE

In most modern cars the temperature gauge on the instrument panel flashes a signal when the engine is overheating. In older cars, or for unobservant drivers, the first indication may be water squirting from the front of the car.

When overheating becomes evident, pull over to the side of the road and turn off the ignition. Wait several minutes for the engine to cool off. Then protect your hands with a thick glove or a heavy wadding of rags. With your face as far away as possible from the radiator area, slowly loosen the radiator cap (see illustration on page 34). (If the cap is equipped with a lever, button, or other pressure-release device, use it to allow steam to escape.) Turn the cap a little counterclockwise and listen for the escape of steam, then turn and remove the cap.

If the water level is low, let the engine cool for several minutes and then add water. Hot water is preferable. In any case, it should not be very cold. Adding cold water too quickly to an engine that has not cooled properly could crack the engine block (see illustration on page 34).

If there is no water available, wait until the engine cools off of its own accord, and then drive very slowly until you reach a source of water, stopping again as necessary for a cooling-off period.

PLUNGE INTO DEEP WATER

When it plunges into deep water, a car will usually float from four to eight minutes if the windows are closed and the body is not structurally damaged. Before the car sinks, the best chance of escape is through the windows. Try to roll down the window nearest you and climb out. If you cannot use this means of escape, try to climb into the back seat if the engine is in front, or into the front seat if the engine is in the rear. The end of the car containing the engine tends to go down first, leaving the opposite end out of the water.

If the car goes nose down, try to knock out the back window with a sharp object such as a pen or nail clipper. A hard blow with a pointed object will cause the tempered glass to crumble. Something sharp and pointed is more effective in breaking this type of glass than a blunt instrument.

Even if the car sinks, you may still have sufficient time to get out. As the passenger compartment fills with water, a bubble of air is usually trapped inside, which allows you to breathe. At first, as the car descends, the air may be forced to the rear of the car, but if the vehicle settles wheels down, the bubble of air shifts to the top.

Do not try to escape while the car is submerging. It is almost impossible to swim out of a car window while the water is rushing in. Wait until the pressure equalizes inside and outside the car. When this happens, you can open a door or roll down a window and escape.

RIGHT WHEELS OFF THE ROAD

If your right wheels go off the road pavement, do not apply the brakes, or you may lose control of the car. Stay in gear and reduce your speed to about 10 miles an hour. Look in your rearview mirror to determine when the road is clear of traffic. Turn left sharply and you will be back on the road again. Then turn right to straighten the car in the lane.

SKIDDING

Although the natural reaction is to jam on the brakes and turn the car away from the skid, that will only add to the danger. Take your foot off the gas, and steer in the direction of the skid until the wheels regain rolling traction. Then pump the brake pedal to slow down.

STALLING

The most common causes of stalling are an empty gas tank, overheated or flooded engine, a wet ignition, or a vapor lock. Keeping the engine going until you can get to a service station for help requires skill.

Empty gas tank. When your car begins to sputter and behave as if it is about to stall, check the gas and temperature gauges first. If your gas gauge reads "empty," you may still be able to make it to a service station by keeping your foot gently and consistently on the accelerator, running the car at 20 miles an hour, and taking advantage of hills to gain momentum. However, if you sense the car is about to stop altogether, pull over to the side of the road. Don't take the chance of getting caught in a dangerous situation in the middle of traffic.

Overheated engine. If either the temperature or oil gauge flashes red (indicating that the engine needs water or oil), pull over to the side immediately. Check the oil supply by pulling out the oil dipstick (see illustration on page 34), wiping it clean, and then reinserting it. When you pull it out again, the oil level will be indicated on the stick. Driving without oil or water will severely damage the engine. (See page 47).

Flooded engine. Stalls are frequently caused by too much gas in the engine. This may happen when you keep trying to start a reluctant engine in cold weather, or when you have to make repeated stops and starts in heavy traffic. If you notice a strong smell of gasoline after you have tried to start the car several times, the engine has probably choked.

Wait a few minutes and then, with the ignition off, press the accelerator to the floor. Hold it there without pumping and then turn on the ignition. If the car does not start in 10 to 15 seconds, switch off the ignition and wait. Then repeat the procedure.

Wet ignition. If your car stalls after you have driven through a rain storm or through an area covered with water, the ignition may have been short-circuited. Turn off the ignition. Lift the hood, and wipe any excess water from around the distributor cap, wires, spark plugs, and ignition coil (see illustration on page 34). If the engine was hot before you stalled, its heat may dry the wet parts, so wait a few minutes and turn on the ignition. You may be able to start your car without difficulty. If not, arrange to have your car towed to a service station.

Vapor lock. In hot weather, stalling may be caused by "vapor lock." The gasoline vaporizes in the fuel line and the fuel pump (see illustration on page 34), cutting off the supply of fuel to the engine. You will

49

have to pull to the side, lift the hood of the car, and allow the fuel lines and pump enough time to recondense the vaporized gas. If available, cool, wet rags placed around the fuel lines and pump will speed the cooling.

STARTING

If your car won't start, first make sure the ignition key is fully on and the transmission is in proper gear for starting. Then check the gas gauge. Other causes of trouble may be:

Battery. If the ignition key does not turn the motor at all, the battery (see illustration on page 34) may be dead, or there may be a poor connection or broken line. Try the horn and the lights. If they fail to work properly, the diagnosis is a weak or dead battery.

Carburetor. If the motor turns but does not catch and you smell gas, the carburetor (see illustration on page 34) may be flooded. Turn off the ignition; press the accelerator to the floor and hold it there without pumping. Then turn on the ignition. If the car does not start in 10 to 15 seconds, switch off the ignition, take your foot off the gas, and wait a few minutes. Then repeat.

Wires. If the car still doesn't start, turn the ignition switch off. Lift the hood and gently test all the wires. If any seem to have shaken loose, try to push them back where they belong.

STEERING WHEEL FAILURE

Although it is very frightening and dangerous when the steering mechanism fails, don't slam on the brakes. Instead, put your hand brake on slowly. For the sake of others, turn on a signal light or safety flasher light if you have one. Stop the car gradually and get out as carefully and as quickly as possible.

TAILGATER

When you are aware that someone is following you too closely, put on your turn signal well in advance. Then pull over to the side and allow the tailgater to pass.

WHEELS STUCK

On ice or in snow. If you live in a cold climate, your car should be equipped with a container of sand, a shovel, and perhaps a special mat sold in auto supply stores that can be placed under the back wheels of a car to provide traction. Or, carry a burlap sack, which serves the same purpose.

Start your car slowly by gently applying pressure on the gas pedal. In a manual shift car, use second or even high gear. If you have an automatic shift, put it in "super" or "low." Try to keep the front wheels straight. If this technique doesn't work, rotate the steering wheel back and forth to open a path for the front tires. If the back wheels are blocked by deep snow, try rocking the car loose by alternately shifting from forward to reverse gear, but with a light touch on the accelerator so the wheels will not spin and dig deeper into the snow. If you still cannot move the car, take the shovel and dig a path in back of the tires. Place the mat or sand behind the tires and try again.

In mud. If you are stuck in mud, start your car slowly by gently applying pressure on the gas, but don't go forward. Back up. Don't move the front wheels right or left because this will only make them dig in further. Try to keep the front wheels in the tracks they made when they went into the mud.

crime

Your best protection against becoming a victim of a crime is prevention. Never open your door automatically to a caller. When you go out at night, walk on lighted, well-traveled thoroughfares. If you are driving, keep the doors of your car locked. When you leave home for a vacation or for an event which has been announced in the newspaper, create a "lived-in" look for your house. Keep a light or, better still, two lights lit at all times, or install an automatic timing device which turns on your lights at dusk. Leave shades or blinds in a normal position—not completely drawn or closed. Keep a radio playing while your home is empty. It is an inexpensive method of keeping burglars out. If you are to be away more than twenty-four hours, cancel milk deliveries and have newspapers and mail held. Do not mention your planned absence to strangers. Make arrangements to have your lawn mowed and watered, and snow shoveled or plowed in winter. Leave your keys with a neighbor and ask him, or her, to check your house periodically. Place valuables and important papers in the bank vault if possible. Notify the police of dates of departure and return.

According to police, you can protect yourself, your family, and your neighbors by being observant. If you see a person acting suspiciously, or you notice a dangerous situation, report the incident to the police. Never assume that somebody else has already reported it. Time is of the essence. The police can help most when they are called promptly.

In some states, crime victim compensation is available to persons who have suffered an injury as a result of crime. Check with the local police, the sheriff, or the State Attorney General's office.

ATTACKER STRIKES

If you are confronted by a thief who merely wants your money or your possessions, do not protest. Hand them over. However, if the person confronting you is intent on bodily harm and is not armed, there are a few defense techniques that may help you defend yourself (especially if you are a woman):

> Your voice—Scream as loudly as you can and keep screaming.
>
> Fingernails—Use to gouge, scratch, poke.
>
> Teeth—Bite anything you can reach.
>
> Legs—Aim a kick in the groin (if the attacker is a man) or in the stomach (if the attacker is a woman). A forcible blow with your knee is effective, too.
>
> Feet—Come down hard with your heel on the instep of the attacker's foot.
>
> Hands—Aim a blow at the face—especially the eyes or the bridge of the nose.
>
> Devices to carry—A shrill whistle or an inexpensive siren kept in an easy-to-reach pocket. (Hard to find in a purse.) Sometimes the sound of this will scare an attacker away.
>
> A long nail file or hat pin. A painful jab with either of these may throw an attacker off guard.
>
> Your purse can sometimes serve as a weapon to hit the attacker in the face.

ATTEMPTED RAPE

According to police and physicians, many women have been killed or severely injured by responding in a contemptuous way when approached by a man seeking sexual contact. Refusing in a calm manner may turn him away without trouble. If you panic, it may cause him to panic and your life will be in great danger. If he is armed, do not attempt to resist.

If an unarmed man should attack, you are advised to scream and fight. As the theory goes, it is difficult to thread a moving needle. Aim a kick or a knee at his groin and make sure it is forceful enough to incapacitate him long enough for you to flee. (See other defense techniques on page 53.) Report the incident to the police as promptly as possible.

If you are injured, or the attacker was successful in his rape attempt, seek medical attention from your own physician or at a hospital emergency room. There are medications to prevent infection and conception.

BURGLARY

The best way to protect your home against burglary is to take preventive measures.

Install a peephole in both front and back doors. Inexpensive, tube-shaped devices for this purpose can be purchased at hardware or variety stores, and they are not difficult to put in.

Install chain bolts as well, and use them when you open your doors to any strangers. The chain should be short enough to make it impossible for a person to reach through the opening and unchain it. Always ask strangers for identification. If the person has none or gives you one you even suspect may be phony, close and lock the door immediately.

There are many types of locks on the market, but it is important to realize that no lock is absolutely foolproof. Before buying one for your house or apartment, check with the local police or the Better Business Bureau and get their advice.

Burglar alarms can act as a deterrent by scaring a burglar into flight. Such devices range from $2.95 in a variety store to thousands of dollars for those that are professionally installed. Before you buy, check with your local police, Better Business Bureau, or consumer group for a recommendation.

If you do install an alarm, it is not advisable to have a sign or plate outside your home announcing that the house is protected by a burglar alarm system. Burglars may activate it and watch from a distance to see how long it takes for the police to arrive. When they really break in, the burglars will know approximately how much time they have to do the job and get out safely. Also, the fact that you have an alarm system informs burglars that you must have something valuable to protect.

It is also a good idea not to put your name on the door, mail box, or light post. All the burglars have to do is look up your name in the telephone directory and place a call. If you are not at home, they will know the coast is clear. In apartment houses where it is necessary to have the name on the mail box, use only an initial and your last name. This is added protection for women living alone, and it makes it a little more difficult to look you up in the phone book.

Everyone should have a list of valuables. Keep the list in a safe place, preferably a bank vault. Include the serial numbers of television sets and other small appliances. Police departments are now suggesting that you etch your social security number onto all portable appliances so that if the items turn up after being stolen, they can be easily identified.

See page 52 for information on how to protect your home when you are away for extended periods of time.

If your house is burglarized. Should you come home and find obvious signs of burglary, do not enter your house—the buglar may still be there. Go directly to a neighbor's home and call the police.

After the police have made their investigation, start taking inventory by checking against the list of valuables. If you carry burglary insurance, report any missing items to your insurance agent.

CAR FOLLOWING YOUR CAR

When a car is deliberately following yours, don't attempt to reach your home. Police say many a man or woman trying to dash from the garage to the safety of the house has failed to make it in time. They advise blowing your horn and heading for the police station. If there is not one nearby, they suggest driving to a well-lit store or service station.

If another car attempts to force you off the road, sound the horn continuously, and keep going until you reach safety. Try to get the license number of the car if you can. Should you be forced off the road, make sure all doors are locked. Roll up the windows, and keep blowing the horn until help arrives.

CAR FOLLOWING YOU WHILE YOU WALK

Sometimes a slow-moving car will follow a man, woman, or child. Police say no one should assume that such a driver is harmless. The driver may try to induce the person to get into the car or make a robbery attempt. They advise screaming and running in the opposite direction. The driver will then have to turn the car around to follow. If there is no harm intended, the driver won't bother, but if the pursuit continues, keep screaming and run for the nearest lighted house or store.

GOING OUT AT NIGHT

When you go out on the streets at night, walk on lighted, well-traveled thoroughfares and avoid taking shortcuts through lonely places. Police recommend carrying a loud whistle or a battery-operated pocket siren to summon help (you can buy these at a hardware or variety store).

If you are being followed, head for the nearest lighted store or home. Do not attempt to go into a multistoried building even if it is your own apartment house, unless there are other people in the lobby or hallway.

If you ring a stranger's bell and the householder refuses to let you in, remain standing by the door as if waiting for the police to arrive. It will probably scare the culprit away.

If you are driving at night, keep your doors locked. (See also **CAR FOLLOWING WHILE YOU WALK,** and **CAR FOLLOWING YOUR CAR,** page 55.)

INTRUDER IN YOUR HOUSE

If you sense that someone has forced an entry into your house, do not turn on the lights. With a light behind you, you will make a perfect target. As a safety precaution, if possible, have a telephone by your bed. If you do not, go quietly through the dark to your phone, dial "O" and tell the operator your address and that you need help immediately.

Police advise that if you are awakened at night by an intruder, you should not try to apprehend him. He might be armed. Instead, lie still, observe carefully, and at the first chance, call the police.

Having a safety room in the house is a good idea although most people will never have to use it. The room—it can be any room in the house—should have a telephone and a strong inside lock. Everyone in the family should be instructed that in case an intruder enters the house, they should run for that room.

If you have a basement with windows or doors, have a lock on the door at the top of the basement stairs. Burglars often break into the basement, and a lock at the top of the stairs may prevent them from entering the living quarters, or give you time to summon the police.

KIDNAPPING

Fortunately, this is a rare occurrence today, but if you have reason to suspect someone has abducted your child, telephone the local police or the nearest Federal Bureau of Investigation office listed in your phone book. (Kidnapping is always considered a federal offense.) If you cannot find the number, phone the FBI Emergency Headquarters in Washington, D.C., Area Code 202: Executive-3-7100, and give all the details about the disappearance.

MOLESTERS AND SUSPICIOUS CHARACTERS

Child molester. To protect your child, you should provide him or her with the proper information about sex without frightening him. You should also instruct the child never to accept a ride from a stranger or to accompany a stranger anywhere on foot. Explain to him that the stranger may say, "Your mother sent me," or that he may say he has a kitten or puppy or candy somewhere.

Know how long it takes your child to come home from school, and teach him to let you know if he goes to another child's home to play. Instruct him to walk along heavily traveled streets, and to avoid isolated play areas.

Tell him that if anyone tries to bother him or annoy him, on the street, in a theater or on public transportation he should report it to the nearest person in authority—a policeman, usher, bus driver. If anyone tries to force him into a car or a building, tell him to cry out as loudly as he can.

If your children are to arrive home after dark, arrange to meet them at the station or bus stop.

Should your child be molested, your reaction can either increase or ease the harm. You should question the child calmly, but not force an answer. The child should be examined by a physician and the police should be informed of the incident even if the molester is a relative or friend. The police and judges are very considerate of children in such situations, and the questioning will usually be done very gently in private.

Many parents fail to report such incidents because they want to spare their children the discomfort of a court proceeding. However, the child molester is a dangerous person, and may continue to harm other children if not stopped.

Molester in the movies or on a public conveyance. If someone physically molests you in a theater, or while you are riding a bus or train, don't just get up and move to another seat. If there are other people around, say loudly, "This man is bothering me." Just the words are usually enough to get rid of the pest. If there are no other people nearby, get up and notify the usher, bus driver, or conductor.

Suspicious character in a self-service elevator. If you have the slightest suspicion about someone in the elevator, do not board it. If you are already on it get off immediately. Make it a habit to stand near the alarm button on the elevator whenever you get on. If attacked press the button and scream.

Before you board an elevator on the ground floor to go up, make sure that it is ready to go up instead of down to the basement (where a mugger may await you). Let an elevator headed down go down and come back up before you board.

MUGGER

Muggers forcibly take your money and your belongings from you on the street or in a building. They often work in pairs or threes and may be of either sex. There are a few precautions you can take:

If you must walk in a dangerous neighborhood, do so with at least two companions, if possible. Muggers seek single victims or at the most two at once. Do not flash large sums of money in public. When you cash a large check, look around casually to see if anyone is unusually interested in the fact. If you find you are being followed out of the bank or store, or if someone suspicious is following you on the street, go into another store or to a house with a light and ring the bell. Ask the owner to call the police. If the owner refuses, bluff the mugger and stand on the steps as if you were awaiting the police.

Never enter a hallway or darkened building to try to elude a pursuer.

Police advise you not to resist a mugger. They suggest you try to remain calm, and if you can, observe your assailant carefully so you will be able to describe your attacker to the police.

Should the mugger attempt to abuse you physically, scream as loudly as you can and try to run away. If you can't flee, bite his or her hand as hard as possible and kick or punch as hard as you can at the most vulnerable spots—the groin for a man, the breast for a woman.

Usually, the mugger will take your money and valuables and run. Even if what was taken has little value, you should report the incident to the police and provide them with a description of the mugger or muggers.

PURSE SNATCHER

Purse snatchers are often desperate addicts or unpredictable teenagers. Do not carry large sums of money in your purse. If someone attempts to grab your purse, give it up. It is not worth life or limb to resist. Scream, and a policeman or a passerby may be able to catch the thief.

If you must carry a large sum of money, pin it inside your clothes or put it in your shoe where you can feel it. Open pocketbooks or purses with loose handles attract purse snatchers. Choose a zippered or latched bag. In a crowded place, hold it under your arm.

You may be able to prevent a pickpocket from quietly lifting your wallet out of your purse by tying two little bells to a key chain and attaching this to your wallet. It will act like a miniature burglar alarm.

RIOTS AND DISTURBANCES

If you are in a car or on foot in an area in which a riot or disturbance (such as a protest march or a police chase) occurs, get out fast. Do not stop to watch as you may become an innocent victim. If you cannot get out of the area, get into a doorway or up against a building. If there is shooting, either sit or lie down. Do not run.

family crises

At one time or another every family has to deal with an unexpected emotional crisis or an emergency situation that can turn into a harrowing experience for any household. Such crises can be as major as a death in the family or as relatively minor as being locked out of the house.

As with physical emergencies, knowing what to do before, during, and afterward can help to prevent panic. This chapter deals with some common solutions to a varied range of crisis situations.

PROFESSIONAL HELP

Although most families try to deal with a majority of their problems privately, it is important to realize that professional "first aid" is available.

Because there are so many different organizations, it is often wise to find a referral service that will help you locate the proper agency for your particular problem. In practically every community—large cities as well as smaller towns—Community Councils are the coordinating and planning agencies for organizations in the area. Usually listed under United Way, United Fund, United Givers Fund, or Community Chest, these groups have staff members who can refer you to the proper agency for help. In more populous areas, the councils may be listed under Information and Referral Bureau or Service.

If you or someone in your family is a member of a union, trained counselors are usually on hand to guide you to the right social agency. Most A.F.L.-C.I.O. unions have at least one such counselor. Your doctor, clergyman, or local public welfare department may also offer advice and assistance.

When asking for a referral, provide enough information about your situation so that the service you've contacted can select the agency best suited to help you.

To obtain information about legal services call the local Bar Association listed in your phone book. The staff will give you the names of local lawyers or refer you to the proper agency for help. For information not provided by the local Bar Association, write to American Bar Association, 1155 East 60th Street, Chicago, Illinois 60637.

If you cannot afford private legal services, contact the local Legal Aid Society listed in the phone book. If you do not have a Legal Aid Society or cannot obtain local referral for legal services, write to National Legal Aid and Defender Association, 1155 East 60th Street, Chicago, Illinois 60637.

ABORTION

An abortion to save the life of the mother is available in every state in the Union. An abortion for emotional, social, or economic reasons may be obtained in several states. If you desire an abortion for yourself or for someone in your family, discuss it frankly with your obstetrician or family doctor. Act quickly; an abortion is less complicated when performed very early in pregnancy. If he will not help you because of legal, ethical or religious objections, discuss it with your clergyman. If he cannot help you, look in the classified section of your telephone book under Social Service Agencies. There are now non-denominational groups of clergymen around the country who have set up abortion referral services. They may be listed under "Abortion" or "Family Planning" in the phone book. Planned Parenthood Federation of America has local chapters throughout the country which provide information, abortion counseling, and referral services. Some will help to arrange low cost or free abortions for those in need of financial assistance. If you cannot find a branch of Planned Parenthood near you, write or call the national headquarters at 810 Seventh Avenue, New York, New York 10019.

ARREST

Anyone, no matter how respectable, may at some time be arrested unexpectedly. This has happened to people who inadvertently allowed their driver's licenses to expire or to teenagers participating in peaceful demonstrations that suddenly got out of hand. Any number of situations may result in a forced visit to the police station, an emotionally upsetting experience not only for the person involved, but for the family as well.

It is mandatory that a person who is arrested not resist arrest, regardless of how unfair he thinks the charges are. It is also generally not a good idea to talk to the police concerning the facts of the alleged offense until an attorney has been consulted. This is a constitutional right.

A person who is arrested is often allowed one phone call. It should be used to contact a family member or close friend to say where one is, why one is there, and to ask that a lawyer be contacted as soon as possible. If no lawyer is known, then the friend or family member should call the local Bar Association, the Legal Aid Society, or the public defender's office and ask for suggestions. If the services of a private lawyer are not within the means of the person arrested or the family, the free services of a public defender or the Legal Aid Society are available to eligible applicants (see page 60). (See also **ARREST, AC-CIDENT, OR DEATH OVERSEAS,** page 195.)

DEATH IN THE FAMILY

In spite of the fact that everyone dies eventually, few people are prepared to handle the death of someone close. For this reason, it is always wise to enlist the aid of a relative or good friend who is not as emotionally involved, who can help to handle the arrangements objectively. Some of the immediate steps which should be taken are these:

Death certificate. Obtain at least five copies of the death certificate right away; you will need copies for various insurance forms and legal and financial proceedings.

Funeral arrangements. Before making funeral arrangements, check to see if there are any special burial requests or instructions. Such information is frequently contained in a personal letter or a copy of the will that might be found among the personal effects of the deceased. If these papers are not immediately available, contact the family lawyer or estate executor who will have a copy of the will if there is one and who will advise you of any special instructions. These could include any of a number of alternatives to conventional funerals.

If the body has been bequeathed for medical research and teaching, the medical school to whom it has been bequeathed will usually pay for transportation of the body. Arrangements should be considered in case the medical school should refuse the body because of death caused by contagious disease or damage by accident.

If organs are to be donated, this will have been arranged by the deceased through a doctor or through a private organization. The Medic Alert Foundation, Turlock, California, provides a nationwide service in which, for a small fee, a member is provided with a card on which he can fill in his wishes.

If the deceased has made no previous arrangements, choose a funeral director. He will tell you what he will take care of, and what you need to do. If a clergyman is to officiate, contact him. You will have to decide where and when the funeral services will be held, and where friends may call. Also select and notify pallbearers.

If previous arrangements for a cemetery plot have been made, the deed or necessary papers should be turned over to the funeral director when needed. If no previous arrangements have been made, the funeral director can assist in providing a place for burial or arranging for cremation, if desired.

Notification details. Make a list of the immediate family, close friends, and employer or business colleagues, and have someone notify them by phone. Notify lawyers and executor.

Write the obituary including age (optional), place of birth, current residence, cause of death (optional), occupation, college degrees, memberships held, military service, outstanding work, list of survivors in the immediate family. Give the time and place of services, and deliver or phone the facts to the newspapers. If flowers are to be omitted, designate the preferred memorial or charity to which gifts may be made in the deceased's honor. If flowers are sent, arrange for their distribution after the funeral—to a rest home or hospital. If just an announcement in the obituary column is to be printed, the newspaper usually charges a line rate. The announcement should appear the day before or on the same day as the funeral. Some funeral directors will handle the obituary notice for you.

Other arrangements. Provide for child care, meals, and cleaning during the time of mourning.

Prepare a list of persons to be notified by letter.

Keep a list of persons who send memorials, flowers, gifts, and expressions of sympathy so these may be acknowledged later.

Monetary and insurance arrangements. Check carefully all life and casualty insurance and burial benefits, including social security, credit union, trade union, and fraternal and military insurance, and notify these organizations. (Contact the Veterans Administration for GI insurance). Policies should be kept in a safe place available to members of the immediate family. Check also on income for survivors from these sources.

Determine promptly all debts and outstanding installment payments. Some may carry insurance clauses that will cancel them. If there is to be a delay in meeting payments, consult with creditors and ask for more time before the payments are due.

If money is needed immediately to cover expenses incurred by the death, or to pay current household expenses, check the deceased's bankbooks and savings bonds, if any.

If the deceased had joint bank accounts, all or a portion of the money can be withdrawn, depending on state laws, by the survivor.

Savings bonds issued in the name of the deceased jointly with a survivor can be cashed immediately by the joint owner of the bonds. If they are marked P.O.D. (Payable on Death), a copy of the death certificate must be submitted to the bank where the bonds are to be cashed.

Bank accounts that are in the deceased's name alone may be tied up for quite a while, so they cannot be counted on as an immediate source of funds. However, a bank will often make a small personal loan on a signature to the known kin of the deceased account holder as an accommodation. (See also **FAMILY DATA BANK,** pages 129 ff.)

DRUG ABUSE

It is important to be able to recognize the symptoms of drug abuse because such signs may mean both a physical and emotional emergency. Here are the drugs most commonly abused:

Amphetamines: Usually called speed but also called whites, dexies, pep pills, crosses, uppers, A's, bennies, drivers, etc. Includes such drugs as benzedrine, methedrine, dexamyl, etc.

Look for: Tablets or capsules, often colored green. The user may suffer excitability, unclear and rapid speech, restlessness, tremor of the hands, enlarged pupils, sleeplessness, and profuse perspiration. The user may be talkative and have delusions and hallucinations, or unexplained "black-outs," abundant energy, and may stay awake for 24 hours or more.

Barbiturates: Sometimes called downs, barbs, reds, yellow jackets, goofballs, or blue heavens.

Look for: Pills, capsules or, rarely, powders. Common symptoms of drunkenness occur in the users, but without the telltale odor of alcohol unless both have been ingested. A small amount of the drug may make the person appear relaxed, sociable, and good humored. The drug may also make the user sluggish, depressed, and sometimes quarrelsome. There is a loss of physical coordination, and the speech may be slurred. The abuser may slip into a deep sleep or a coma, depending on how much of the drug has been taken.

Cocaine: Sometimes called coke, dust, the leaf, and snow (also slang for heroin).

Look for: A white, odorless powder. Although cocaine does not cause a physical addiction, ingesting large amounts of the drug results in prostration. Formerly used as "snuff," it is now more commonly injected into the vein causing a short period of elation or numbness. The user may twitch, have convulsive movements, sleeplessness, extreme nervousness, confusion, hallucinations, delusions, and mania. Sometimes there is an impulse toward violence.

Hallucinogens such as LSD, STP, DMT, Mescaline, Psilocybin: Sometimes called Acid or Taking a Trip.

Look for: Powders, liquids, pills, or sugar cubes. The pupils of the eyes are often dilated. Dark glasses are often worn, even at night. The user may be restless, with an inability to sleep until the drug wears off or may exhibit no noticeable physical signs of drug intoxication at all. The mental effects are quite unpredictable, but may include euphoria, depression, hallucinations, panic, psychotic or antisocial behavior, and sometimes an impulse toward violence and/or self-destruction.

Heroin: Sometimes called dope, H, Horse, junk, snow, smack, and Miss Emma.

Look for: White powder or burnt spoons, hypodermic needles, or eyedroppers. The user may have pinpoint pupils, chills, needle marks on the arms and legs. Addicts often wear long-sleeved sweaters, even in summer, both to keep warm and to hide their scars. Withdrawal symptoms include nervousness, anxiety, sleeplessness, yawning, running eyes and nose, sweating, enlargement of the pupils, gooseflesh and muscle twitching, severe aches of the back and legs, hot and cold flashes, vomiting, diarrhea, increased breathing rate, blood pressure and temperature, a feeling of desperation, and obsessional desire to secure a "fix."

Marijuana: Sometimes called pot, grass, reefers, sticks, rope, joints hay, tea, weed, bhang, or Mary Jane. (A much more potent form is hashish.)

Look for: Cigarettes, usually appearing home made, or loose "tobacco." The most telling sign of use is the odor of "burnt rope." The marijuana user may appear to be drunk, talkative, silly, or confused. Chronic abusers may become listless, neglect their personal appearance, and feel that they are failures.

Solvents: Fumes from glue, gasoline, paint thinner, lighter fluid, and various aerosol-packed products.

Look for: Excitation, exhilaration, and other symptoms resembling the initial effects of drunkenness. Blurring of vision, ringing in the ears, slurred speech, and staggering are common, as are hallucinations. This phase of intoxication lasts from 30 to 45 minutes after inhalation and is followed by drowsiness, stupor, and even unconsciousness. Upon recovery, the individual usually does not recall what happened during the period of intoxication. Solvent abusers are often very young, and although physical dependence does not appear to be a consequence of solvent sniffing, permanent and often fatal damage may result to the brain, kidneys, liver, and bone marrow.

What to do if someone in your family is abusing drugs. If someone shows any of the above symptoms or suddenly seems to have undergone a great change in personality and habits and is always out of money, or items around the house mysteriously disappear, it is important to investigate. It could indicate a drug problem, and a drug problem will not go away by itself.

When a youngster is involved, psychologists with extensive experience in the field of drug abuse suggest that parents sit down *calmly* and talk to their child. Threats and punishment are not the answers; a mature approach must be used. Point out the consequences and adverse effects of drug abuse. Everyone concerned must understand what is to be lost by the use of drugs. Even smoking marijuana or sniffing glue cannot be ignored. Drug abuse is a multifaceted problem. Parents should not be permissive. They should take action.

If you are unable to obtain the services of a private psychiatrist, psychologist, or social worker trained in drug abuse therapy, contact the local chapter of the National Association for Mental Health, the State

Bureau of Narcotics Addiction and Drug Abuse, or your clergyman for referral to an agency that will help.

EMOTIONAL DISTURBANCES

You may be faced with the problem of handling a person who behaves in a disturbed or unusual way. Below are some of the most common behavior problems and suggestions for emergency action that should be taken, especially if the person appears to be on the verge of doing himself bodily harm or endangering the lives of others.

Dangerous behavior. A person subject to this type of behavior, although often portrayed in books, TV programs, and movies, is relatively rare. You must handle such a patient calmly and firmly without confusion or threats. If danger is imminent, do not hesitate. Call the police. Sometimes the sight of a blue uniform is enough to send a patient off into wild behavior, but many policemen today have special training and experience in handling a person in this condition.

In general, it is always better to treat a patient with respect, no matter how bizarre or abusive he becomes. Try to divert his attention away from what is bothering him. Do not argue with him and do not physically restrain him unless he is about to harm himself or others.

Drunkenness. If the intoxicated person is endangering or hurting himself or others, call the local chapter of Alcoholics Anonymous, which is usually listed in the phone book, for advice or, if the person's behavior is dangerous, call the police. When delirium tremens (the "DT's") accompany drunkenness—the patient trembles and has hallucinations. He should be taken to a hospital at once. En route he should be watched carefully because a person in this condition may try to escape from the horrible things he is "seeing" and as a result may be killed or injured.

Severe anxiety. A person suffering from anxiety may become panic stricken or disoriented and may act bizarrely. Try to calm him by speaking quietly and reassuringly to him to help him over the attack. If he seems unable to understand or respond to you, call a physician, mental health center, or hospital emergency room and ask for advice.

Severe depression. Depression is a profound feeling of sadness and dejection often without just cause. Depressed patients may suffer from insomnia, loss of weight, decreased interest in work and living in general, and sometimes they may be agitated. There is always danger of suicide when a person is severely depressed. (See **SUICIDE, THREAT,** page 70.) A severely depressed person needs prompt medical attention. Call your physician, the local mental health center, mental health association or hospital to ask for advice.

LOCKED IN BATHROOM

The bathroom is one of the most frequent scenes of home accidents, involving children as well as adults. It is therefore vital that a potential rescuer be able to enter the room quickly. No bathroom door should have a lock that cannot be opened from the outside with a key. If your bathrooms have such locks, it would be wise to change them. A spare key should be kept above the bathroom door frame or in some other equally convenient place.

If a child is locked in the bathroom, talk to him very calmly and try to coax him into opening the door. If the child is incapable of opening the door, keep him interested and near the door. You can do this by sliding drawings or a piece of paper and pencil under the door. Adults who have fallen or are ill and cannot open the door also need reassurance. When there is a sound of water running and you can't open the door within a reasonable time, turn the water off at its main source.

If possible, detach the door hinges and remove the door. If you can't do this, telephone the fire department—firemen are skilled in such rescues.

LOCKED OUT OF HOUSE

Never leave a key under the front mat, on a window sill, or anyplace else adjacent to the house. The police claim that a burglar can find a key wherever you hide it. A sound alternative is to leave an extra key with a neighbor or with a relative.

If you are locked out of your home and there is no extra key available, try all windows and doors; you may have left one open. If not, call the police or fire department. They are usually most helpful in such circumstances. As a last resort, break a window panel near the handle of your back door (the most frequent way thieves enter homes). If you do not have a glass-paneled door you will have to break an accessible window. Then, carefully avoiding jagged glass, reach in and open the door or window. (See also **LOCKED OUT OF CAR,** page 47.)

LOSING A JOB

Suddenly losing a job, especially when you are supporting or helping to support a family, can be a shattering experience. If this happens to you or to someone close to you, the following procedure is suggested for the person involved. Instead of giving way to panic or depression, get busy and begin looking for work.

If a résumé of your job experience is required, prepare one. Place your name, address, and telephone number at the top left-hand corner of the page. Start with the most recent employment and work backward to your educational background. Do not include your salary preference, your reason for leaving your current job, your personal description, or your references. (You may be asked to supply this information when you apply for a job.)

Look for job possibilities in the classified advertisements of your local newspaper. Contact your state employment agency, which will try to find employment for you free of charge. If you belong to a professional association or union, contact its headquarters for possible job offers.

You may want to place a classified ad in daily and weekly newspapers or in a trade paper in your field stating your qualifications and the type of position you are seeking.

To help you find a job locally or in another area of the country, you may contact one of the 8,600 employment agencies that function throughout the country. Not all employment agencies are honorable. Some overcharge, promise jobs they don't have, and waste your time and money. Approximately 2,600 reputable agencies belong to the National Employment Association, which requires all members to adhere to a stringent code of ethics. The organization puts out a directory that includes a listing of agency specialties. For further information, write to the National Employment Association, 2000 K St. N.W., Washington, D.C. 20006.

Service charges for employment agencies vary, so read any contract carefully before signing. Some employers will pay the entire fee, but if you have to pay part of it, you can probably arrange with the agency to pay it in installments.

If you do not accept a position, you do not have to pay the fee. If you accept the job and then lose it, that situation may be covered by state or local laws and is usually spelled out in the contract.

While you are job hunting, you may want to contact your State Unemployment Division. Waiting periods vary before unemployment benefits begin.

MARRIAGE PROBLEMS

There is first aid available for ailing marriages. And just as with physical injuries, if this aid is applied early enough, more serious problems may be averted.

Your clergyman or family physician may be able to counsel you or refer you to a counselor. The national organizations listed below will assist you in finding help in your area:

Department of Family Life
National Council of Churches of Christ in the U.S.A.
475 Riverside Drive
New York, N.Y. 10027

Family Life Bureau
National Conference of Catholic Charities
1346 Connecticut Ave., N.W.
Washington, D.C. 20015

Family Service Association of America
44 East 23rd St.
New York, N.Y. 10010

National Association for Mental Health
1800 N. Kent St.
Arlington, Va. 22209

National Council on Family Relations
1219 University Ave., S.E.
Minneapolis, Minn. 55413

Bernstein Center, The Jewish Theological Seminary
3080 Broadway
New York, N.Y. 10027

National Council on Alcoholism
2 Park Ave.
New York, N.Y. 10016

To help you get on your feet again should a divorce take place, there is:

Parents Without Partners
P.O. Box 1002
New York, N.Y. 10001

However, there are certain problems that need immediate action:

Assault. A husband or wife who physically assaults a mate is liable to criminal prosecution. The injured spouse must file a criminal complaint, which in turn, may lead to a jail sentence and its consequences, such as loss of support and embarassment to the family. However, if there is physical danger, it is always wise to call the police, not only to obtain immediate protection but to aid in more permanent protection through court proceedings. The police can give testimony to back up the complaint.

If the injured party does not wish to involve the police and yet wants to obtain a separation or divorce on the basis of this dangerous behavior, a visit to a physician who can examine the injuries and to relatives or friends who may act as witnesses, may enable the case to be proven in court. Furthermore, photographs of the injury may also be added proof.

Of course, expert legal advice is warranted and perhaps counseling. (See pages 60, 67 f. See also **EMOTIONAL DISTURBANCES,** page 65.)

Desertion. A man or woman who deserts a spouse and family is not fulfilling recognized legal obligations. A complaint may be filed in criminal court and the law will force the deserter to live up to these obligations. But since no action can be taken until the absent spouse is located, assistance may be required from the local police, the District Attorney's Office, or the Welfare Department. If private legal services cannot be obtained, seek legal advice immediately from the Legal Aid Society (see page 60).

Divorce. Sometimes divorce seems to be the only answer to an unhappy marriage. But it is wise to consider all the decisions that have to be made during divorce proceedings before the step is taken. When the difficult problems listed below are pointed out, some couples, especially those with children, discover that it is better to try to make adjustments and stay together. A professional marriage counselor may be able to help make this possible. Even if it is decided that divorce is the only solution, it saves time and heartache if the spouses can agree before going into court on the terms of the divorce decree. Judges today welcome pre-trial settlement. These are some of the questions that will be decided in court but it is advisable to consider them before actual proceedings are started:

Who gets the house, apartment, or any other real estate belonging to the couple?

How shall the household possessions be divided?

Who gets the car or cars?

Should there be alimony and if so how much? Should it be in one large settlement or paid weekly, monthly or yearly? What security will there be to make sure payments are met?

Who will get custody of the children if they are minors? How will visitation rights be arranged?

How much will be paid for child support?

Who shall decide where the children will go to school? On vacations?

What should be done about the beneficiaries named in the husband's and wife's insurance? What provisions will be made if the children or wife become seriously ill?

Who will pay the taxes on the property transfers and on the alimony payments?

Who will get the pet or pets?

What division should be made of stocks and bonds and bank accounts owned by both parties?

Should the wife turn over the property in her name which actually belongs to her husband?

The legal agreement should be drawn up by an attorney representing the wife and an attorney representing the husband. The local Legal Aid Society will provide assistance if the parties cannot afford private attorneys. (See page 60.)

Removal of children from the home. Should your spouse remove your children from your home against your will and prevent you from seeing them, you should contact a lawyer or the Legal Aid Society at once. Except under unusual circumstances, both parents have the right to see the children. Custody of children when parents separate or divorce is decided by the court. Mothers are generally given custody, particularly of young children, but there are exceptions. Courts are always reluctant to permit children of divorced or separated parents to be taken out of the state. However, again there are exceptions. If a parent should attempt to remove children from the state before, during, or after court proceedings the other parent should immediately contact a lawyer. (See page 60.)

MISSING PERSON

Report a missing person to the police in the precinct in which the missing person resided. In general, the police consider a "missing person" to be:

> A youngster under 18 years old whose parents or guardians report the child missing
>
> Anyone 18 years or over who is mentally or physically affected to the extent that hospitalization may be required, or who is a possible victim of drowning, or who has indicated an intention of committing suicide
>
> Anyone who is missing without any apparent reason under circumstances indicating a possible kidnapping

All the above, of course, generally eliminates runaway husbands and wives and persons over 18 who just take off without telling their families where they are going.

RUNAWAY CHILD

Whether a small child or a teenager runs away, you must always take action (see **MISSING PERSON,** above) and not assume he will come back by himself. The child may be in danger. Once your youngster has returned, or been found, do not punish him. Try to find out the reason for running away and if you feel you cannot deal with it yourself, seek professional counseling.

SUICIDE THREAT

Suicide is ranked as the tenth leading cause of death over all in the United States, but in the 15 to 19-year age group it is ranked third, and it is the second most common cause of death on college campuses.

A suicide threat should always be taken seriously! There is a common misconception that a person who threatens to commit suicide, never does. Doctors say quite the contrary is true. People who do commit suicide usually signal their intentions before they take their lives.

A person who is considering suicide always has mixed feelings, according to medical experts. He wishes to live at the same time he wishes to die. A successful suicide does not occur suddenly or impulsively, unpredictably, or inevitably, but is always the last step in a desperate descent. Doctors list as high-risk potential suicides:

> Severely depressed patients
>
> Chronically ill and isolated persons
>
> Bereaved people
>
> Disoriented or delirious patients
>
> People who have threatened suicide
>
> People who have attempted suicide before
>
> People who have had other suicides in the family

Doctors agree that the most dangerous period may be when a depressed patient or a person who has threatened suicide suddenly becomes cheerful even though nothing has apparently changed to warrant it. It may mean that he has finally made up his mind to take his life.

If you suspect a potential suicide, contact your personal physician or a suicide prevention center. If no such center is listed under "suicide" in your phone book, call the local mental health center, your local chapter of the National Mental Health Association, the nearest state mental hospital or the local police to ask where you may obtain help. Trying to handle a suicidal patient yourself is folly. Experienced, professional help is needed immediately.

TELEPHONE PESTS

There are three general types of annoying calls:
Unsolicited sales or survey calls
Nuisance calls designed just to irritate
Abusive, harassing, or obscene phone calls

If you are bothered with unwanted sales or survey calls, the telephone company advises that you find out who is calling, including the name of the person as well as the company he or she represents. If you don't recognize the name of the company, offer to call back, or ask the caller to contact you again after you have had time to check with the Better Business Bureau.

A good way to handle this kind of call is to ask the caller to send you all the information by mail so you can consider it carefully. If the caller refuses to do this and won't take "no" for an answer, just hang up.

Nuisance calls can come from almost anyone, but they usually come from a relatively small group of people: unsupervised youngsters, misguided or frustrated people, or sometimes the mentally ill. Often these calls are placed at random. Ask the caller for identification. If the caller asks, "Who is this?", don't reply directly, but ask instead, "What number did you call?" or "Who do you want?" This usually ends it. If a caller remains silent after you answer, hang up! The phone company says this type of caller gets a kick out of listening for your reaction. If the line goes dead there is not much satisfaction.

Instruct your children and your baby-sitter never to give information to strangers on the phone. A comment such as "Daddy's out of town" may invite a burglar. Teach them always to ask for the number of the person calling so the call can be returned later.

The worst types of calls are the abusive, harassing, or obscene calls. They are usually designed to infuriate and to terrify. The telephone company says that you should not give the caller a chance to get started. As soon as you hear anything that sounds suspicious, hang up! Such callers like nothing better than recipients who excitedly demand to know their identity, or ask repeatedly what they want.

A woman living alone can often avoid this kind of call by listing only her initials, not her given name, in the telephone book.

If you receive several abusive or obscene calls or repeated threats to life or property, call the police and the telephone company. They have trained people with special equipment who can usually trace these calls.

One trick that people on their own have employed successfully is to say to an annoying and persistent caller, ''Here he (or she) is again, officer!'' The implied threat may frighten the pest off permanently.

Another technique is to keep a police whistle by the phone and blow it vigorously next time the caller phones. The result is that the harasser may be too busy with a pain in the ear to be a pain in the neck.

fire

No one expects a fire, but everyone must be prepared to fight one.

What would you do if you walked into your living room and found the couch in flames? If your clothing caught fire, would you run to the nearest source of water? Knowing the answers to such questions could save your life and the lives of your loved ones. At the very least, it might prevent the loss of your possessions.

Your first line of defense in fighting any kind of fire is having the appropriate fire extinguisher in working order and within easy reach (see page 75).

REPORTING A FIRE

All but the most minor fires should be reported to the fire department. A fire is considered minor when it is small and contained—for example, grease suddenly catching fire in a pan or a flame from a spark dropped on an upholstered chair. But, small fires can grow within a matter of minutes, so if you cannot put the fire out with your first try, call the fire department. If the fire starts getting out of control, get everyone out of the house and then summon help from an outside phone.

It is a good idea to tape the telephone number of the fire department to each phone in the house, but if you need to call for help, and you do not

have the number, dial "O" for the operator. Say slowly: "My name is
_____. I want to report a fire at _____" and then wait for
any questions. Teach your children the procedure as soon as they are old
enough to learn and always give careful instructions to the baby-sitter.

Find out the location of the fire alarm box nearest your home. If you turn
in the alarm at a fire box, have someone stay at the box until the fire
fighters arrive.

FIRE DRILLS

Everyone in your home must be made to realize that a fire can break out
at any time. Planning ahead may prevent a disaster, so conduct regular
fire drills until you are sure that every member of the family knows just what
to do in case of fire.

First of all, figure out and discuss two possible routes to safety from all
rooms in the house, especially from the bedrooms. Be sure exit windows
work easily so that even a child or an elderly person can open them.

Pick an outside meeting place well away from danger where the whole
family will meet. Many lives have been lost unnecessarily by people returning
to a burning building to look for someone who had already escaped.

Be sure everyone understands that, once outside, no one is to return to
the house for any reason. No furs, jewelry, money, valuable papers, or even
pets are as important as a human life.

PRECAUTIONS

To reduce the chances of having a fire in your home, here are some proven
preventatives:

> Don't overload electrical circuits. Have adequate wiring for
> heavy-duty appliances. Protect exposed electrical cords, but
> avoid having them pass under rugs or through doorways. Ex-
> amine all cords periodically. Replace any that are worn.

> Television sets give off heat, so allow space at the top and
> between the back of the set and the wall.

> Have a qualified serviceman check heating equipment when you
> move into a house and once a year after that. Don't forget
> to check the chimney flue. Every eighth fire is the result of a
> defective heating unit or overheated chimney and flue.

> See that the damper is open and the flue is clear before you
> light a fire in the fireplace. To test, light a match and see if
> the flame is pulled upward by the draft. If the damper is not
> open or the flue is blocked, flames and smoke from the fire
> may back into the room. A slightly open window in the room
> will help the flue draft.

Be sure to use protective screens for fireplace openings.

Check cooking units in the kitchen, and make a point to clean accumulated grease from the broiler, oven, and range hood regularly.

Do not keep plastic or cellophane covers on lampshades.

Do not replace a plastic cover on a toaster or broiler while the appliance is still hot.

Use large metal or glass ashtrays. Make sure all fire in the ashtray is out before dumping contents into the garbage. (Metal garbage cans are the safest.)

Clean out your attic and cellar regularly. Be realistic and throw away the things that you will probably never use. A good rule which, like all good rules, has exceptions, is that if you haven't used it in a year, dispose of it.

Throw out cleaning cloths or papers soaked with oil, wax, or paint. A pile of such materials can catch fire spontaneously.

Remove oil puddles from the garage floor.

An approved fire and smoke alarm system is a wise investment, but see that the system you buy is labeled by the Underwriters Laboratory. Consult your insurance company and the Better Business Bureau to be sure that the system you select is reliable before it is installed. When it is installed, be sure to comply with local fire department recommendations or national fire codes.

FIRE EXTINGUISHERS

Water and sand are probably the oldest and simplest fire-fighting tools. A mop and pail of water, or a wet rug or wet rag, can effectively douse any small fire except those involving electricity or flammable liquids. Long-handled shovels, lawn rakes, and brooms are also useful when snuffing out small fires. Nevertheless, it is always advisable to have several commercial fire extinguishers available in both the home and the office.

How many do you need? You should have fire extinguishers to protect the bedrooms, the kitchen, the living room, the basement, and the garage.

What type to buy. There are four categories of fire extinguishers suitable for the home: Water, Foam, Carbon Dioxide, and Dry Chemical. The type of fire for which an extinguisher is most effective is indicated on the canister of approved fire extinguishers by the letter "A," "B," or "C," which indicates one of the three basic types of fires:

Type A. The most common fires around the house involving combustible solids such as paper, wood, textiles, and rubbish

Type B. Flammable liquid fires that involve grease, oil, paint, gasoline, or similar chemicals

Type C. Fires that start in or involve electrical appliances or wiring

The following chart will tell you which fire extinguishers are most effective for the three basic types of fires described above, and in which part of the house each is most useful.

TYPE OF EXTINGUISHER	TYPE OF FIRE FOR WHICH IT IS TO BE USED	FOR USE IN	REMARKS
Water	Type A	Bedroom Living room Recreation area	Canister weighs over 20 pounds and is heavier than other extinguishers. Contents freezes in low temperatures unless treated with antifreeze solution.
Foam	Type A Type B	Kitchen Workshop Garage Furnace area Laundry area (Wherever flammable liquids are used)	Foam smothers burning surface. (If used on Type C fires involving electrical equipment, may cause electrical shock.)
Carbon dioxide (CO_2)	Type B Type C	Same as for foam extinguishers	Knocks down flames of type A fires but can't put them out.
Dry chemical (1) Dry chemical (2)	1. Type B Type C 2. Types A, B, and C	1. Same as for foam extinguishers 2. Same as for water and foam extinguishers	There are two kinds: 1) Smothers Type B or Type C fires but does little good in Type A; 2) Is multipurpose—effective against all kinds of fires. If choosing one type of extinguisher, choose one labeled ABC.

Fire extinguisher labels also indicate by the numbers in front of the letters (2-A or 10-B:C) the approximate size of the fire they can extinguish. The numbers start with 1 and increase by whole numbers. The higher the number, the greater the ability of the extinguisher to put out a fire. For example, an extinguisher marked 10-B:C would be able to extinguish a flammable liquid or electrical fire twice as large as one that could be fought by an extinguisher marked 5-B:C.

Depending on the kind of extinguishing agent, the cost of a good extinguisher will vary. It pays to shop because prices for similar models with identical ratings vary among manufacturers. But don't buy on price alone. Match the type of extinguisher to the class and potential size of the fire hazard.

Be sure that the extinguisher you buy has the Underwriters Laboratories (UL) or Factory Mutual (FM) label because some fire extinguishers are unreliable. Extinguishers labeled by the UL and FM must meet certain standards and must be explicitly labeled as to the type of extinguisher, the type of fire it fights, and directions for refilling.

Caution! The National Fire Protection Association cautions against the use of aerosol or plastic extinguishers that are limited in the amount of chemical or powder they contain and are unreliable. The Association also disapproves of vapor extinguishers that contain carbon tetrachloride (now illegal) or chlorobromomethane, both of which are toxic to humans when inhaled, especially during a fire. Check your extinguisher, if you have one, and if it contains either of these two chemicals, throw it away.

How to operate a fire extinguisher. When you are faced with fighting a fire, you will have no time to learn how to use an extinguisher. Familiarize yourself with the operation of your unit or units, and see that other members of the household know how to use them as well. Basically there are three different types of canisters:

Pump. You supply the pressure on this type by grabbing the handle and pumping vigorously. It then shoots a stream of water.

Turn-over. Although it is found in some public buildings, this type is becoming increasingly rare. It must be carried to the fire in an upright position. At a fire, it is turned upside down to release pressure in the tank. Some must also be bumped on the floor after they are turned upside down.

Lever. This type has a pull-out locking pin or some other safety device to keep it from operating accidentally. After you pull out or release the device, press or squeeze the operating lever located at the tank.

To use any of these three types of extinguishers, aim at the base of the fire not at the smoke or flame. On floors, use a sweeping motion, from the edge inward. On walls, use a sweeping motion from the bottom up. Remember, when fighting a fire, stay near the door so you can escape if necessary.

Where to keep a fire extinguisher. Keep an extinguisher within easy reach and in full view (never use it as a coat rack). Suspend it on one bracket (which should be supplied when you buy it) near a potential fire source, but be sure it is installed near an escape route such as a doorway or first floor window. Should you determine that your efforts to fight a fire with an extinguisher are not succeeding, you can still escape easily.

Care and maintenance. Fire extinguishers should be inspected periodically for any signs of leakage or damage and should be refilled immediately after use. Refilling instructions are on the canister. If the pressure cannot be maintained in a pressurized unit, do not attempt to fix it yourself. Take it to a fire-equipment servicing company. Disposable extinguishers must be discarded and replaced.

Automobile Fires. See page 45.

BUILDINGS

APARTMENT OR OFFICE BUILDING

Because multistory buildings create special hazards when fires occur, all members of your family or office staff should know where the fire exits are and how to reach them in the dark. Periodically, everyone should walk to exits in a fire drill. They should also be able to recognize instantly the alarm signal in the building.

The moment the alarm is sounded, get your family or fellow workers out of the building. Never stop to take clothing or valuables.

Feel doors before opening them. If the door feels cool, open it cautiously, bracing your hip or foot against it and tilting your head to the side in order to take a quick look. Be ready to slam the door shut if smoke or heat rush in.

If the hallway is clear, proceed. Shout the alarm on your way out so that any other occupants who have not been alerted will know there is a fire. To slow the spread of the fire, close all doors behind you as you go.

Never take an elevator! During a fire the power may fail, and you could be trapped. Take the stairs, or use the fire escapes. In some high-rise buildings, it may be advisable to go to a refuge area on the same floor, rather than try to get down the stairs.

If you feel a door panel and it is hot or smoke is seeping in, and you are trapped in an area, cover the cracks around the door with rugs or clothing and do not open it. Open the window a few inches at both top and bottom. Stay near the floor; cover your face with a damp cloth, if possible, while awaiting rescue. Do not panic and jump unless instructed to do so by firemen holding a net.

Once you are out of the building, do not reenter. Go to a predetermined outside meeting place to be sure everybody is safe.

HOUSE

The first objective in a house fire must be to get everyone out. Do not stop to phone or to pick up possessions! Many a tragedy could have been averted if time were not taken to phone the fire department or gather valuables.

Test the door to any room before you open it. If the panels do not feel warm and you see no smoke seeping around the edges, brace your hip or foot against it. Tilt your head to the side in order to take a quick look, but be ready to slam the door shut if smoke or heat rush in.

If you find that you can safely leave the room, help to get everyone out of the house in whatever they are wearing. Even if it's snowing and the children are dressed only in night clothes, it is better to risk a cold and live than to die in a fire.

Once everyone is out of the house, phone the fire department from a neighbor's home or pull the nearest fire alarm.

If you are in a room in the house and the door panel feels hot, or smoke is leaking around the edges, do not open the door. Take towels, blankets, rugs, or clothes and stuff them around the door's cracks to seal out smoke and heat. If circumstances permit, get into a room with an outside window.

If you are on the second floor and the window leads to a porch or garage roof, you can get out. If there are children with you, you may be able to lower them by firmly gripping their arms, leaning over the window sill, and gently dropping them to the ground—preferably into someone's arms or into bushes that will break the fall.

Don't risk serious injury or death by jumping in a panic from a window that is high above the ground. If smoke and heat seep into the room, open the window a few inches at top and the bottom for ventilation. Staying near the floor is recommended because hot air rises. Take short breaths and cover your face with a cloth—a damp one if possible. Then await rescue.

PUBLIC BUILDINGS

Make it a habit to look for the fire exits or other ways out whenever you go into a theater, restaurant, hotel, or other public building. If a fire does occur and people start running, do not rush blindly for the door through which you entered. Everyone instinctively rushes out the way he came in. Try to leave by the closest exit and, most important, stay calm.

CLOTHING

A question at the beginning of this chapter asked whether you would run to the nearest source of water if your clothing were on fire. The answer is "no." By running, you would fan the fire and risk breathing in the flames. Instead, fall to the ground and roll yourself up in a coat, rug, or blanket or roll on the grass or floor to smother flames. If you are with someone whose clothing catches fire, assist him in following the same procedure.

Although all fabrics burn, some are more flame-resistant than others. Most synthetic fabrics such as nylon, acetate, acrylic, and polyester burn less easily, but when they do, they may melt and cause deep burns. Heavy smooth-surfaced fabrics resist burning better than lightweight, long-napped ones. A number of fabrics containing blends of natural and synthetic fibers can burn readily and will also melt. Cotton, rayon, and silk catch fire and burn quickly.

When you shop for fabrics, especially for children or for elderly or ill persons, keep flammability in mind. If possible, buy garments such as robes and sweaters that are made of wool, the one material that is difficult to ignite and slow to burn. When selecting children's Halloween costumes, choose only those marked "flameproof." Children's sleepwear is required by federal law to be flameproof, but remember that the flame-proofing may wear off after repeated washings.

Also keep in mind that a person wearing a very full skirt, billowing folds, or long, loose sleeves runs a greater risk of fire, because she can unknowingly brush against a flame. This type of clothing admits lots of air to feed a fire, thus it is especially dangerous.

ELECTRICAL

When an electric appliance catches fire or smells as though it is burning, try to unplug it. Unless you see the insulation of the appliance's wiring burning, it is usually safe to pull out the plug with your hand. If the wire is smoldering or you do not want to touch it, you may be able to pull out the plug by twisting the wire around a broom or mop handle. If you cannot unplug it, shut off the electricity at the fuse box by throwing the switch or removing the fuse.

Use a carbon dioxide (CO_2) or dry chemical extinguisher (see pages 75 ff.). If neither is available, and you are sure the appliance is unplugged, or the electricity is shut off, you can use water to extinguish the fire. Always call the fire department when a fire involves an electrical appliance or electric wiring—if the wires in the wall have overheated, they may be smoldering.

When an outside wire is down, do not attempt to fight any fires near it. Keep everyone away and call the fire department.

GASOLINE, OIL, KEROSENE, OR PAINT

Unless such a fire is very small, do not try to handle it yourself. Get away immediately!

When combating a small flammable liquid fire, *do not use water*. It will cause the liquid to splatter and spread the fire. Instead, use a dry chemical or carbon dioxide (CO_2) extinguisher. If the fire is in a container, try smothering it by putting on the lid or cover.

A small outdoor flammable liquid fire can be put out by covering it with a couple of shovelfuls of sand or dirt.

KITCHEN

Kitchen fires can occur either in a cooking utensil or in the oven or broiler. When a pot or pan is on fire, never attempt to pick it up. Turn off the burner, and try to smother the fire with the cover of the pot. If the fire is still burning, use a fire extinguisher, or throw baking soda on the utensil. If the fire is in the oven or broiler, turn off the stove and keep its door closed. If necessary, use a fire extinguisher or baking soda. Remember to close the doors leading to the kitchen in order to limit air circulation and contain the smoke.

Oil. See **GASOLINE, OIL, KEROSENE, OR PAINT,** page 80.

OUTDOOR

To prevent outdoor fires, keep the grounds around your house free of dead grass, weeds, trash, and dried brush. Should a grass or similar fire start, protect your house by closing all the windows and by removing anything nearby that might feed the fire. Then with a garden hose wet the house down from the roof to the ground.

Whenever a barbecue is held outdoors, there should be a bucket of water handy. If the flames grow higher than necessary, douse them with water. If a barbecue fire gets out of hand and involves burning fat, smother the flames with sand or dirt.

Paint. See **GASOLINE, OIL, KEROSENE, OR PAINT,** page 80.

illness and injury

Fortunately, life and death emergencies are rare, but when they do occur, it is always wise to take a few deep breaths and gather your thoughts before you try to help. Familiarize yourself with first-aid techniques and stock adequate first-aid supplies in advance of an emergency to help avoid panic and to save lives. This chapter is designed to tell you what you can do to prevent complications when an illness or injury occurs.

FIRST-AID PRIORITIES

The object of first aid is to keep the patient alive and to prevent further injury until medical help arrives. Those rendering such aid must know proper procedures so no harm is done. They should also inspire confidence to keep both the patient and emotional onlookers from panicking.

The first priority in handling a physical injury is to control very heavy bleeding, because a victim may bleed to death in three to five minutes (see page 88). If there is no severe hemorrhaging, the next priority is respiration. Because irreversible brain damage or death can occur in three to five minutes after breathing has been arrested, mouth-to-mouth resuscitation, the most effective form of artificial respiration, should be started immediately (see page 106).

Always keep the patient comfortably warm to avoid shock.

EMERGENCY SERVICES

For your own and your family's protection, you should find out what emergency or rescue services are available in your area. When you move into a new home, this should be done immediately.

In almost all locations, you must contact the police, who in turn summon the rescue squad. In some municipalities, the fire department handles the situation, and in others a hospital. Poison control centers, located in most urban areas, provide emergency services in cases of poisoning. You can find the number in your phone book or by asking your physician or local hospital for it.

If none of these emergency services exists, you must investigate to find an alternate method of summoning aid. Precious time may be lost if you have to waste phone calls or thumb through a telephone book when an emergency arises.

PERSONAL EMERGENCY WARNING

If a condition such as diabetes or hemophilia exists, which could be aggravated by a first aider who is unaware of it, a warning should be carried on the person. Some nonprofit charitable organizations provide a metal emblem that bears the American Medical Association's Emergency Medical Identification symbol. Write to the American Medical Association, 535 N. Dearborn Street, Chicago, Illinois 60610, for a list of emblem manufacturers and retailers. On the reverse side of the emblem is engraved the immediate medical problem or problems of the wearer, such as "Diabetes" or "Allergic to penicillin." Some emblems have a registered serial number that can be transmitted by a physician to a 24-hour answering service. The patient's medical history is then given to the caller to enable quick and proper treatment.

You can also make your own emergency card to carry with you. It should look something like this:

Name: _____

Address: _____

Phone: _____

Name of person to call in emergency: _____

Phone: _____

Present medical problem (e.g. epilepsy, neck breather, wearing contact lenses, dangerous

allergies, etc.): _____

CHECK LIST OF EMERGENCY FIRST-AID SUPPLIES

Below is a basic list of supplies that should be kept available at all times in one cabinet or on a readily accessible shelf. Be sure everyone in the family knows where these supplies are stored and mark all bottles and packages that do not have an easily identifiable label. Medicines or lotions that might be harmful if swallowed by small children should be kept out of reach.

Take stock periodically, and make necessary replacements so that you don't find yourself without something you may need quickly.

Box of sterile gauze dressings, 4 × 4 inches, individually wrapped, for cleaning and covering wounds

Two rolls of gauze bandage, 2 inches wide, for bandaging fingers and tying sterile dressings over wounds

Adhesive tape to hold dressings and splints in place

Box of assorted Band-Aids.

Roll of absorbent, sterile cotton.

Triangular bandage (37 inches × 37 inches square, cut, or folded diagonally with two safety pins for a sling, a covering, or a dressing

Mild soap

Baking soda (bicarbonate of soda) in a small package to be mixed with water and salt for shock (1 teaspoon salt, ½ teaspoon baking soda in 1 quart of water)

Paper drinking cups

Flashlight, tested periodically to ensure that it is in working order

Package of 1½-inch safety pins

Scissors (do not depend on finding a household pair in an emergency)

Tweezers to remove splinters and insect stingers

Packet of needles for removing splinters

Eyecup for rinsing eyes

Tongue depressors for splinting broken fingers or for stirring solutions

Measuring spoon set

Measuring cup

Small bottle of aromatic spirits of ammonia or commercially packaged smelling salts

Hot-water bottle.

Ice bag

Box of wooden safety matches

Bottle of syrup of ipecac, used to induce vomiting *only if recommended by a physician*

Small bottle of oil of cloves for emergency toothaches

Bottle of lotion for sunburn, insect bites, etc.

Petroleum jelly for small burns and lubrication

Fever thermometer

Rubbing alcohol for sterilizing

EMERGENCY TELEPHONE NUMBERS

To avoid having to search frantically for telephone numbers at a time when every minute counts, make up a list like the one below, and keep a copy available next to each telephone in the house.

IN AN EMERGENCY CALL:

DOCTOR _____

    Address _____

    Office phone _____ Home phone _____

COUNTY MEDICAL SOCIETY EMERGENCY SERVICE*

_____ Phone _____

HOSPITAL _____

    Address _____ Phone _____

POLICE DEPARTMENT _____ Phone _____
                                                      or dial "O" for operator

FIRE DEPARTMENT _____ Phone _____
                                                      or dial "O" for operator

POISON CONTROL CENTER _____ Phone _____

UTILITY COMPANIES

    Gas company _____ Phone _____
                                                      or dial "O" for operator

    Electric company phone_____ Phone _____
                                                      or dial "O" for operator

HUSBAND'S OFFICE_____ Phone _____

WIFE'S OFFICE_____ Phone _____

NEAREST NEIGHBOR_____ Phone _____

NEAREST RELATIVE_____ Phone _____

DENTIST_____ Phone _____

PHARMACIST_____ Phone _____

TAXICAB_____ Phone _____

BABY-SITTER_____ Phone _____

* Most county medical societies now have emergency services staffed on a rotating
basis by physician-members. The answering service will obtain the doctor on call
for you. Even if you have your own physician, you should have this number in case
your own doctor cannot be reached.

HOME CARE SERVICES

Given the choice, most people, even those with extremely serious illnesses, would rather be cared for at home.

If the homemaker in the family is ill or needs assistance to care for someone else, try to obtain professional help. Specially trained personnel will act as substitute ''housewives.'' They do not do professional nursing, but shop, cook, do light housekeeping, care for children, and tend to the patient's everyday needs. To find a homemaker, check your local telephone book, (sometimes listed under ''Nurse'' in the Yellow Pages, or contact the social service department of your local hospital. If you still cannot find a local service, writer or call the National Council for Homemaker-Home Health Aid Services, 67 Irving Place, New York, N.Y. 10003, for the address of the nearest organization that can offer help.

Should the patient require professional nursing, contact the local visiting nurse service. Most communities have access to one. A registered nurse will visit the home just as a hospital nurse visits a patient's room to administer medication and to check his condition. Look under ''Visiting Nurse Service'' in the telephone book or contact the municipal health department or local hospital to obtain the name of the closest visiting nurse service. If the patient is eligible, Medicare and a number of insurance plans will pay for a visiting nurse. Some municipalities pay the bill if the patient's family cannot.

Another source of aid may be one of the voluntary health organizations. There is such a group for almost every major ailment. They offer information and may provide needed services such as the loan of a hospital bed, kidney machine, or transportation to and from therapeutic treatments.

If you cannot find a local organization listed in your phone book, contact the United Way or the social service department of the local hospital. You may be able to find the names of nearby organization chapters by writing to national headquarters. Look up the national headquarters in reference texts in your public library.

ALLERGIC ATTACK

An allergic attack can range from a mild itch to almost instant death. The greatest allergy emergency is the anaphylactic attack that is so severe the patient cannot breathe. Although it is often mistaken for a heart attack, it is different in that the patient usually suffers itching and flushing of the face, wheezing, or hives before the onset of actual symptoms. In a heart attack, these initial symptoms do not occur.

There are emergency kits that persons subject to anaphylactic attacks should carry at all times. These kits usually contain an injection or a tablet (prescribed by a physician) to be placed under the tongue. If no emergency medicine is available, however, the patient should be driven to the hospital without delay, or an emergency squad summoned immediately. Minutes count! (See also **ASTHMA ATTACK,** page 87; **INSECT STINGS OR BITES—ALLERGIC OR POISONOUS,** page 104.)

ANIMAL BITES

Any bite that breaks the skin (including bites by human beings) should be flushed immediately with running water and then washed with soap and water and flushed again. Even if the offending animal is a family pet, the victim should see a doctor as soon as possible. Often a shot for tetanus or a treatment to prevent rabies is indicated.

If the bite is from an unknown dog or cat, it is important to locate the animal and have it turned over to the police or health department for observation. (See **RABIES,** page 113). Advertise or broadcast an appeal for help, if necessary.

As a precaution, teach your children not to pick up any bird or animal they see lying on the ground. They should also learn to approach a strange dog or cat with care.

Artificial Respiration. See **MOUTH-TO-MOUTH RESUSCITATION,** page 106.

ASTHMA ATTACK

When a person has an asthma attack—difficulty in breathing, usually with a whistling sound—the best thing you can do is to offer reassurance. People rarely die of an asthma attack, but the more frightened a person becomes, the more severe the attack. Turning on the hot water in the sink and allowing the asthma victim to breathe in the moist steam may alleviate the symptoms. If a severe attack continues and the patient is obviously in distress, take him to a hospital emergency room. The patient's own physician can either meet him there, or give instructions to emergency room personnel by phone. Most emergency rooms are better equipped than doctors' offices to handle severe asthma attacks.

Bee Stings. See **INSECT STINGS OR BITES—ALLERGIC OR POISONOUS,** page 104.

BIRTH

There is ordinarily plenty of time after the beginning of labor to obtain medical assistance. Signs of labor are low backache, bloody-tinged mucus, or a gush of water from the birth canal. If no medical help is available at the moment of birth, however, this is what you can do:

Have the mother lie down and prepare for birth by bending her knees. As the baby begins to appear, support the baby with your hands and arms to keep him above the fluid or waste material on the bed. No attempt should be made to pull the baby out in any way.

If the baby should appear with the membrane or water sac over his head or face, the sac should be taken between the fingers and torn, so that the water will run out and the baby can breathe. If the umbilical cord is around the baby's neck, try to slip it gently over his head or down over his body to prevent strangulation. Do not cut or pull on the cord.

When the baby is free from the mother, he will still be attached by the umbilical cord. The cord does not have to be cut immediately. The first thing to do is to make sure the baby is breathing. Any fluid in the baby's nose and throat must be drained. Wrap a towel around the baby's feet and hold him firmly by the ankles upside down. Let the cord be slack; do not pull on it. Most babies cry and breathe when the fluid runs out, but it may be necessary to stroke the throat toward the mouth with your free hand to clear the fluid.

If the baby does not cry or begin to breathe quickly, begin mouth-to-mouth resuscitation. Cover baby's nose and mouth with your mouth. Breathe very gently in short puffs into the baby's mouth every five seconds. Stop as soon as breathing begins. Then wrap the baby in a towel or blanket or newspaper, and place him on his right side across the mother's abdomen with head lowered and facing away from the mother's face.

The placenta, or afterbirth, is a round, flat structure about six to eight inches in diameter. This breaks from the womb and must be expelled along the birth channel. The mother undergoes slight contractions while the placenta is expelled. This usually takes 20 to 30 minutes. During this time, do not pull on the cord. When the placenta is expelled, it is still attached to the baby by the cord. Wrap the afterbirth separately, allowing the cord to hang loosely from the baby. Place the wrapped placenta beside the baby, and then wrap them together securely in a blanket so the placenta will not drop and pull the cord. Then lay the baby next to its mother or in another safe place. Place a sanitary pad or cloth between the mother's legs to soak up the blood. If bleeding increases, gently massage her stomach until the womb feels firm. You should not have to cut the baby's cord unless no help is available for several hours. If you do have to cut the cord, tie a piece of string or strong cord or clean cloth strip about four inches from the baby's navel. Cut on the placental side with a knife or a pair of scissors that has been sterilized by boiling in water or by holding it in a flame for several minutes. Then wait for the doctor.

BLEEDING

Because superficial bleeding will stop spontaneously, just cleanse the break in the skin with soap and water and cover it with an adhesive bandage.

Heavy bleeding, however, may kill within three to five minutes if not controlled. Application of pressure is therefore imperative. Place a sterile gauze pad, a clean handkerchief, or a clean cloth directly over the wound, and press firmly with one or both hands. If no bandage or cloth is available, use your hand or fingers. Hold a pressure bandage firmly in place with a length of bandage, necktie, belt, or any strip of material, but do not tie it so tightly that the pulse throbs near the wound.

Raise the bleeding part higher than the rest of the body unless there are broken bones. Keep the victim lying down and warm to avoid shock.

Older first aid manuals always recommended the use of tourniquets to control heavy bleeding, but experience has shown that such binding often did more harm than good. Use a tourniquet to control bleeding only if an arm or leg has been crushed, amputated, or mangled. To apply a tourniquet, wrap a piece of cloth—never wire or rope—around the upper part of the limb above the wound. Tie a half-knot, place a stick, pen, or pencil in it, and then complete the knot. Twist the stick just tight enough to stop bleeding. Loosen the tourniquet every 15 minutes for a few seconds. Be sure to tell those who take over the care of the patient that a tourniquet has been applied.

BLISTERS

Both friction and fever blisters heal best if left alone. A friction blister should merely be soaked in clean, soapy water, gently dried, and then covered with an adhesive bandage. Fever blisters that persist and friction blisters that become infected should be examined by a physician. (See also **BURNS,** page 92.)

Breathing Trouble. See **MOUTH-TO-MOUTH RESUSCITATION,** page 106.

BREATH HOLDING

Breath holding by an angry child—even if he faints, turns blue, or goes into convulsions—is more harrowing to the parent than harmful to the child. Most pediatricians consider it a harmless habit of otherwise healthy children who outgrow it by the age of five.

The only treatment necessary is to display an attitude of ''purposeful neglect'' in order to prevent the child from acquiring satisfaction from the spells and using them as a means of dominating the family.

BROKEN BONES

When a person falls or is struck, be on the alert for broken bones. Often the snap of the bone may actually be felt and heard. Fractures frequently cause the affected part to move into an abnormal position or to stop functioning. As always, the first thing to check is bleeding and breathing. Hemorrhaging must be stopped. If respiration has ceased, proceed with mouth-to-mouth resuscitation. (See Page 106.) Don't move a person with broken bones unnecessarily—especially if the fracture is in the neck or back. Movement may cause further damage, or even death.

The best first aid in cases of broken bones is to do nothing but prevent further injury until help arrives. To ward off shock, make sure the person is warm. Do not allow the victim to move or be moved until the affected part is properly splinted and supported, unless of course further danger is imminent.

There are two types of fractures:

A closed or simple fracture in which the bone is broken
but the skin has not been punctured.
An open or compound fracture in which the skin as well
as the bone is broken.

Do not try to straighten the limb or return it to its natural position. *Do not* try to clean the injured part. If the fracture is open, place a sterile dressing over the wound and press to control bleeding. If you have a pad available, hold it firmly in place with a bandage, necktie, or cloth strips. When no sterile dressing is available, use your fingers to close the edges and press with your other hand. Once the bleeding is controlled, or if there is no bleeding, apply a splint.

There are inexpensive inflatable splints which are growing in popularity. Purchased in sets of various sizes, they can be slipped on or zipped on the injured part and then inflated just as you blow up a balloon. They are becoming part of the emergency supplies stocked by first-aid facilities and carried by scouts and campers. For your own home or camping emergency supply kit, you can obtain inflatable splints through your druggist or directly from a medical supply house. The splints come with individual directions but none should ever be over-inflated because too much air pressure can cut off circulation in the splinted limb.

If you do not have an inflatable splint on hand, any material that will prevent movement of a fractured or dislocated extremity may be used. This includes a sturdy stick, a board, broomstick pole, golf club, metal rod, cane, umbrella, thick magazine, folded newspaper or even a pillow. A soft fabric such as a woman's slip or a man's shirt should be used to pad a rigid splint to avoid skin injury.

The main purpose of a splint is to prevent motion of fragments of bones or of dislocated joints until medical help is obtained. Fasten splints on the affected limb with bandages or ropes or any other suitable ties. The ties should hold the limb to the splint but should not be so tight that they cut off circulation.

If the fracture is closed, place the limb in as natural a position as possible without causing discomfort and apply the splint. Do not try to set the fracture.

An arm may be placed in a sling after splinting to keep it immobile. A sling can be made of any piece of cloth. It should be large enough to support the arm, when bent comfortably at waist level. Tie the ends of the cloth around the back of the neck.

A hand or a foot with broken bones can be tied on a magazine, a pillow, or a folded blanket for support.

Once bleeding, breathing, and splinting have been taken care of, the person may be moved—if absolutely necessary—on a firm stretcher. A door, ladder, large table top, large wide board or surfboard may be used. A stretcher can also be made by buttoning two men's shirts or a coat over two sturdy branches or poles. Or fold a blanket over two branches or poles as shown below. Just make sure that the improvised stretcher will adequately support the weight of the person to be transported.

A stretcher may be fashioned of two men's shirts and two poles or branches.   *A stretcher can also be made by folding a blanket in thirds over two sturdy poles.*

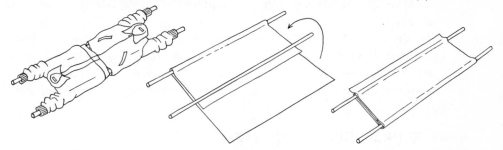

The stretcher should be placed alongside the victim. It is better to have several people lift him at once so his body is kept in a straight line and not bent. As the victim is gently lifted, another person should quickly slide the stretcher under him.

BROKEN NECK OR BACK

One of the most extreme emergencies and one in which well-meaning first-aiders may do the most harm involves a broken back or neck. This often happens in a diving accident when the rescuer feels impelled to get the victim out of the water quickly or in an automobile accident when the first impulse is to get the victim off the road. If the patient is conscious, a few simple tests will help to evaluate the situation and avoid further injury.

If an accident victim cannot move his fingers or toes easily, or if there is tingling or numbness around his shoulders, his neck may be broken. If he can move his fingers but not his feet or toes, or if he has tingling or numbness in his legs or pain when he tries to move his back or neck, his back may be broken.

Loosen clothing around the injured person's neck and waist. Cover him to prevent shock, Watch closely for breathing difficulty. Do not move the victim for any reason—not even to give him a sip of water. The spinal cord extends through the neck and back bones and controls breathing and movement of the arms and legs. Any movement or pressure may cause further injury, permanent paralysis, or death. If there is imminent danger of further injury and the person must be moved without professional assistance, it should be done with the utmost care. A hard, flat surface must be employed such as a board, surfboard, or door. Do not take a chance with anything that might sag or collapse. Place the board next to the person. Every part of the body must be supported. It is vital that the body be kept in a straight line without bending. The board should be slipped under the victim, and he should be tied or held to the board so there is a minimum of movement.

Diving Accident. When a person is hurt in a diving accident, it should be assumed that his neck is broken and he should be treated accordingly. It is better to be safe than sorry. Do not move the victim out of the water until a hard surface (as described above) has been placed under him. The support should be rigid and must not bend or break. Therefore, do not use styrofoam paddleboards, sailing boards, or inflated mattresses.

Tie the person to the support before coming out of the water. A large beach towel, several towels tied together, bathrobe ties, or rope may be used. If only one tie is available, encircle the chest area. The idea is to "splint the victim where he floats" before attempting to remove him from the water.

BRUISES (INCLUDING BLACK EYES)

A bruise is usually the result of a blow that causes bleeding under the unbroken skin. Place a cold compress or an ice bag over the bruise as soon as possible to reduce pain and swelling. After a black and blue mark has developed and the pain has subsided, warm compresses will help to dissolve the discoloration.

BURNS

Emergency treatment of burns depends upon what caused the burn, and how deep and extensive it is. In first-degree burns, the skin is merely reddened as in a mild sunburn. Second-degree burns blister. Third-degree burns are the most serious because there is deeper destruction. The burned area may appear either white or charred. A burn frequently appears more minor than it really is—even a first-degree burn may be serious if it extends over a wide area of the body. All burns except those you are certain are minor should be examined by a physician.

Minor burns. Immediate application of ice or cold-water compresses (which should be kept on for 30 minutes) is the recommended first-aid treatment for minor burns. After the ice has been applied, a solution of tea on a sterile bandage is a soothing remedy. Then, if the skin is not blistered, petroleum jelly, mineral oil, or any other similar product may be applied. If the skin is blistered, just cover the burn with sterile dressings to exclude air and prevent contamination.

Extensive or severe burns. Shock is the first thing to consider in any burn except the very mildest. Signs of shock are cold, clammy skin, beads of perspiration, a pale face, shivering, complaints of cold and often nausea, vomiting, and shallow breathing. In "burn shock" the liquid part of the blood rushes to the burned areas and not enough blood volume may be left to keep the other body organs functioning properly. Treat the victim for shock even if all the above symptoms do not appear. Although the burn itself may not be fatal, shock can kill. Have the person lie down and elevate feet and legs 12 inches or more to help the flow of blood to the heart and head. (The only exception is if he is having difficulty breathing or has other serious injuries that make it unwise to move him.) Keep him warm but not hot.

If the victim is conscious and able and willing to swallow, dissolve ½ teaspoon of baking soda and 1 teaspoon of salt in 1 quart of water. Give the victim half a glass of this solution every 15 minutes to replace lost body fluids. Stop if he vomits, and do not force the solution on him. Any fluid, except an alcoholic one, is beneficial.

Do not apply grease, ointment, baking soda, or anything else to extensive burns. If the burned area is too large for sterile gauze pads, place a clean sheet over the victim. Avoid breathing on any burn, and do not attempt to clean debris from burns.

Chemical burns (lye, acid). Wash copiously with water. The faster you wash away the chemical, the less extensive the burn will be. Apply as much water as possible while removing clothing, and put the cleanest material available over the burned area. Sunlight may make this type of burn worse if the chemical is not entirely removed from the skin, so protect the victim from the sun.

Thermal burns (fire, electricity, scalding liquid). If the skin is not blistered or broken, immerse the burned part in clean, cold water for five minutes. Then, if the area is small, soak a sterile gauze pad or clean cloth in a solution of 2 teaspoons of baking soda to 1 quart of luke-warm water. Place a pad over the burn and bandage loosely. If the burned area is extensive, place the cleanest cloth available over the burned area. Do not break blisters.

CHEST PAIN

When there has been no recent injury, chest pain may arise for a number of reasons. If the pain becomes more severe with deep breathing or coughing, it is often due to inflammation in the lung or chest cavity. The symptoms of a heart attack may include pain in the chest (see page 103).

A person complaining of chest pain should be placed in the most comfortable position, whether it be lying down or half lying, half sitting, or sitting in a chair. Loosen belt, tie, collar, and other restricting clothing. A woman's bra and girdle should be opened if possible. Encourage deep breathing. Cover sufficiently to keep warm, but not hot. Do not allow the person to walk or exert himself or herself in any way.

Call a physician for further instructions. Keep outwardly calm, because a patient with chest pain is usually very frightened. Give reassurance and try to keep the victim from becoming excited, because anxiety can worsen the condition.

Do not give any medication without a doctor's advice.

Do not offer food or drink without a doctor's instructions.

CHIGGERS , TICKS

Pick off a mite with tweezers if it is not embedded. If it is, cover with heavy mineral or machine oil or turpentine. Wait until the mite disengages itself, and then pick it off with tweezers. Scrub the affected area with a brush and soapy water. Then bathe bites with baking soda or alcohol.

CHOKING

When someone chokes on something and gasps for air, do not slap him on the back, reach into his mouth, turn him upside down, as formerly recommended in first-aid manuals! These actions may actually increase the hazard. The natural cough spasm will usually expel the object. If the person is choking, but able to move air in and out of his lungs, do nothing, but rush him to the nearest hospital emergency room. *Only as a last resort, if breathing has stopped, and help is not immediately available,* slap the victim sharply between the shoulder blades. If this does not work, open his mouth, pull his tongue forward, and keeping your fingers to the side of his throat, try to get under the offending object and flip it out with your fingers. Be extremely careful not to push it farther down the throat. If that still does not work, try pressing hard— not with your full weight—on his diaphragm, in the hopes of expelling the obstructive material by the bellows action of the lungs.

If you have not succeeded in removing the object and breathing has stopped completely, use mouth-to-mouth resuscitation (see page 106) until help arrives. This can keep a person alive even when the obstruction is still in the throat, because some air almost always gets through.

CONVULSIONS

Convulsions may occur in a mild form, called petit mal, during which the person stares for a minute or two, does not respond when spoken to, and does not remember the incident. Dramatic and potentially more serious convulsions, or grand mal, cause the patient to fall, lose bladder and bowel control, foam at the mouth, shake, and become unconscious.

Convulsions or seizures are frightening to the onlooker, but they usually last only a short time, and require no action other than making sure the person does not injure himself. If possible, let him lie on the floor so he cannot fall and hurt himself. Do not restrain the victim, slap him, douse him with water, or place anything in his mouth.

If a small child is having a convulsion, place him on his back on the floor to make breathing easier. Do not put the child into a bathtub!

After the convulsion is over, remove the victim to a comfortable place and let him sleep if he wishes to. Often a convulsion marks the onset of an infection or disease. If the seizure lasts longer than five minutes, even if the victim has been a long-time epileptic, summon medical aid immediately. If the patient's own physician cannot be reached, call the emergency squad for help.

CRAMPS

A cramp is caused when a muscle goes into a spasm, usually during or after vigorous exercise, or when the limb is fatigued or subjected to sudden cold or heat.

Exercise cramps can be relieved by working the limb, or by rubbing the muscle.

Heat cramps in abdominal or skeletal muscles occur during physical exertion in high temperatures. Prior to onset, the victim sweats profusely. (See also **HEAT EXHAUSTION,** page 103, and **HEAT STROKE,** page 104.)

Leg cramps that occur at night, or that start after a patient has been ill in bed or suffers heart or vascular disorder, should be diagnosed by a physician. Do not massage the leg or apply heat unless a physician prescribes these treatments.

Swimming cramps occur in the calf of the leg or the sole of the foot. When you feel the ''warning tingle'' before a cramp occurs, immediately stretch the affected muscle to try to prevent the spasm. Once the cramp strikes you, take a deep breath and float face down using both hands to massage the affected muscle. Usually the pressure will ease the pain, but sometimes vigorous kneading is needed to keep the cramp from recurring. As soon as the cramp is relieved, head for shore.

If the cramp occurs in the abdomen, do not try to swim. Turn on your back and float, keeping your hands under the water and moving your hands and feet slowly. Drift until the cramp passes or help arrives. Relaxation and deep breathing may speed relief of the muscle spasm. (See also **STOMACH PAIN,** page 116.)

CROUP

Croup resulting from an infection most often occurs in children between the ages of two and four years. It comes on suddenly, usually at night. A child who may have seemed perfectly well during the day or may have been suffering from a seemingly slight upper respiratory infection suddenly has difficulty in breathing and a high-pitched, barking cough. Croup always requires prompt medical attention. While awaiting a doctor or on the doctor's instruction, take the child into the bathroom. Run the hot water in the shower or the bathtub to quickly steam up the room. Don't place the child in the hot water.

In the event the water in your home is not hot enough to steam quickly, use an electric steamer.

Although croup improves rapidly in warm, moist air, an adult should stay awake and be with the child until it is certain that croup symptoms have gone. Even then, the adult should sleep in the same room with the child, waking periodically to check the child's breathing. It is important to reassure the child. Anxiety can aggravate the condition.

Diving Accident. See **BROKEN NECK OR BACK,** page 91.

illness and injury

DROWNING

When you are the rescuer. When someone is drowning, even experienced life guards heed the advice to "Row (when necessary), throw, tow, and then go." In other words, at lakes and shore areas the first attempt at rescue should be made by rowing out to the victim. If there is no boat available or if the victim is in a pool, throw a buoyant object: a beach ball, thermos jug, slab of wood, or a plastic picnic cooler all make good temporary floats. One of the best life preservers is a spare tire. (Demonstrations have shown that a fully inflated tire mounted on a wheel can support six people in the water with their arms hooked over the rim.)

If the victim is near shore or in a pool, extend a belt, shirt, oar, branch, or fishing pole. Assuming he is still conscious, even a submerged person will instinctively grab a pole if you press it against his chest. All backyard swimming pools should have a long pole or a life preserver attached to a rope to enable a swimmer in trouble to be pulled out of the water.

If you swim up to a drowning person, hold a shirt between your teeth or float a paddle, plank, or log in front of you. Give the free end to the victim and then tow him in. Do not get close enough for him to grab you.

Only as a last resort should you dive in and attempt to drag a person out bodily.

As soon as a drowning victim is pulled into a boat, onto shore, or to pool side, elevate his legs above his head to drain water from his lungs. If breathing has stopped, begin mouth-to-mouth resuscitation at once (see page 106).

To keep from drowning until help comes. Even if you're not a good swimmer, it is possible to save yourself from drowning by using a simple "drown-proofing" technique (see illustration below). You merely rest under water, totally relaxed. Then you make a slight movement to rise above the surface, take a breath, and sink back down again. Once you master the inhaling, exhaling, and rhythm of movement, you can actually bob up and down for many hours without becoming exhausted.

Use the "drown-proofing" technique to keep from drowning until help comes.

It is essential to get the breathing right, so practice whenever you go swimming. Exhale through the nose, never through the mouth, just as your nose breaks the surface of the water. Be careful not to do it too soon. Blow out hard. If you don't, your nostrils will retain water and you may choke from the water dripping down your throat. You must keep your lips squeezed tightly together when you exhale. Raise your head above the water. Inhale, and then relax and let yourself sink under water again. When submerged, purse your lips and spurt out any water that does get in. Exhale through the nose, and continue the procedure described above. You should stay under a minimum of three seconds at a time, and then gradually increase the time of rest while submerged. The average rest is 10 seconds after doing the cycle for an hour.

Swimming safety rules. As soon as your children are able to understand, caution them about the dangers of going near a swimming pool, lake, or shore area without an adult. Make it a rule that no one—including adults—may swim alone without notifying another person. The safest procedure for everyone is to swim with a "buddy"—if one person gets into trouble, the other can help. All family members—even small children—should be taught the techniques of "drown proofing" and first aid (see page 96).

The proliferation of backyard swimming pools presents an increasing danger to toddlers and adults as well. If you or your neighbors have a swimming pool, no matter how small, assume that a child will try to enter it whether it is full or empty. (Some localities require that a pool be completely fenced in to prevent such mishaps.) Roughhousing or running on the wet pavement around a pool should not be permitted. (See also **DIVING ACCIDENT,** page 92.)

DRUG OVERDOSE

A drug overdose can be deadly, so it is important to identify the drug taken and to obtain prompt medical aid.

A relatively rare but critical occurrence is an overdose of heroin. The victim will usually be found unconscious. If breathing is affected, mouth-to-mouth resuscitation should be instituted while medical help is summoned (see page 106). If possible, take the syringe or container that held the heroin along with the patient to the hospital for analysis.

In the case of a "bad trip" from LSD or other hallucinogens or from "speed," a "talkdown" is recommended while medical advice is being sought. Patients may be extremely frightened by their sensations, so talking softly and soothingly to them will help. It is vital to protect an agitated patient from hurting himself or others while under the influence of drugs. A person on a bad trip may try to escape through a window or run into traffic. In severe cases, hospitalization is recommended, and if a physician is not immediately available, it may be necessary to call the police. Even though legal complications from illicit use of drugs may occur, it is important to save the victim's life. (See also **DRUG ABUSE,** page 63.)

EAR PROBLEMS

Earache. Every one should have ear drops prescribed by a physician available for quick relief from middle-of-the-night earaches. However, ear drops should never be used in an ear that is discharging pus, unless a physician recommends it. For temporary relief, have the patient lie down and elevate his head on several pillows. Place a hot-water bottle, a heating pad, or several folded squares of flannel over the ear. Chewing gum may help relieve an earache and aspirin may ease the pain, but a physician should always be consulted. Be aware that blowing the nose may make an earache worse.

If ear drops can be used, they should be warmed. Heat the bottle of drops by immersing it in warm water, but do not get it too hot. Test the drops on your wrist before using. Instill 2 to 4 warmed drops into the ear, tugging gently at the upper part of the ear to straighten the canal. Ask the patient to keep his head turned to the side for two or three minutes to allow the drops to move down the ear canal.

Insect in ear. If an insect has crawled into the ear, stop the distressing buzzing by applying a little lukewarm salad oil or mineral oil with a medicine dropper. The oil will still the insect and may wash it out. You may also put a flashlight to the ear; insects are attracted to light and may be lured out.

Object in ear. Do not try to dislodge a marble or button or any foreign object in the ear. That's a physician's job. If you tamper with it, you may only make matters worse.

ELECTRIC SHOCK

Every second counts when a person is in contact with a source of electricity—the longer the contact, the less the chance of survival. Never try to pull the victim away from the contact with your bare hands! If you do, you'll become the second victim, because the human body is an excellent conductor of electricity. If you are indoors, disconnect the plug or pull the main switch at the fuse box. Outdoors, use a dry pole, branch, or board that will not conduct electricity. Push or pull the wire off the victim or the victim off the wire. Be sure you are standing on a dry surface when you do it. It is likely that the victim will not be breathing when freed, so begin mouth-to-mouth resuscitation (see page 106) and send someone for medical aid immediately. Continue the mouth-to-mouth resuscitation until someone else takes over or until a doctor arrives to handle the emergency. (See also **LIGHTNING,** page 209.)

EYE INJURIES OR IRRITATIONS

If you suffer a serious eye injury, both eyes should be covered and you should be taken to a physician immediately. Remember, an eye is a delicate organ and must be treated gently.

If you feel "something," such as a cinder or an insect, in your eye, do not rub it. This only adds to the irritation. Close the eye in the hope that tears will wash out the offending object. If this does not work, wash your hands with soap and water and bring the upper eyelid down over the lower for a moment or two while the eye is turned upward. This causes tears to flow, which may wash the speck out of the eye. If the speck remains, wash the eye, using a medicine dropper or an eyecup filled with a solution of boiled water cooled to room temperature. If you have failed to get the speck out at this point, cover the eye and seek professional help.

FAINTING

Fainting may result from fatigue, hunger, sudden emotional shock, a poorly ventilated room, or from a variety of illnesses. When a person feels faint, his breathing is usually shallow, his pulse feels weak, his face is pale, and his forehead is covered with perspiration. He should sit down immediately, place his head between his knees, and breathe deeply. If the patient becomes unconscious, lay him down with his head turned to the side. Loosen his clothing and wave ammonia or smelling salts under his nose. When the patient returns to consciousness, keep him lying quietly for at least 15 minutes.

If the faint lasts more than a few minutes, summon medical help immediately.

FEVER

A fever is a symptom of many illnesses, usually involving a virus or a germ. If an adult's fever goes over 101 degrees F. and a child's over 103, immediately take measures to reduce the temperature. Sponging the body with cool water or rubbing alcohol, if available, will help reduce body temperature and make the patient more comfortable. Ice packs under the arms will often bring a high fever down rapidly. All high fevers, persistent fevers, or fevers accompanied by other symptoms, such as nausea, sore throat, pain, swelling, or rash, should be reported to a physician.

FISHHOOK INJURY

The most common form of fishing accident is getting a fishhook and barb embedded in the flesh. The hook should never be backed out of the wound, because the barb would rip the flesh. Push the hook through the skin until the point and the barb protrude. With a pair of cutting pliers, cut the barbed end off the hook. Then remove the shank and curve at the original point of entry. Or, cut the looped end with pliers and pull through from the other side. That way you don't have to back the curve out. Let the wound bleed for a short time, and then wash it with soap and running water, and bandage with a sterile compress. Get the injured person to a doctor as soon as possible to avert infection and to obtain a tetanus shot, if necessary.

FOOD POISONING

Rapid and effective treatment of food poisoning depends upon identi-

99

fying the food eaten and the toxic material in the food. Often, just identifying the food eaten and describing the symptoms enables the physician to make a diagnosis.

Because the victim of food poisoning is often one of a number of persons affected, you can determine the source of contamination by calling companions who were at the suspected meal or who shop in the same place or patronize the same restaurant.

Bacterial food poisoning. Symptoms of bacterial food poisoning may occur from 6 to 72 hours after ingestion, but they usually strike in about 12 hours. These symptoms include aches and pains, chills, fever, nausea, vomiting, abdominal cramps, and severe diarrhea. Illness ordinarily lasts from 24 to 48 hours. In some cases, it is so mild, it does not affect the daily living pattern and, at the other extreme, it is fatal.

A person ill with bacterial food poisoning should be put to bed, kept quiet and given fluids, as soon as it is possible to retain them (see **VOMITING,** page 118). In all but very mild cases, consult a physician. The victim may require a prescription for antibiotics.

Chemical food poisoning. Chemical food poisoning, which occurs less frequently than the bacterial type, may result from eating mushrooms, immature or sprouting potatoes, contaminated fish and seafood, mold, or chemically contaminated fruits, vegetables, and packaged products. In chemical poisoning, the symptoms often occur more rapidly than in bacterial poisoning and are more severe. If chemical poisoning is suspected, a physician should be contacted at once or the victim taken to the emergency room of a hospital.

Any incident of food poisoning should be reported to the local department of health and to the U.S. Food and Drug Administration, if it involves a product in interstate commerce. The source of the problem can then be traced and corrected.

Precautions. To prevent food poisoning, there are a number of precautions a consumer can take:

> Shop for groceries after doing all other errands, and take any perishables straight home.
>
> Always wash your hands after touching meat and before preparing other food, especially produce that will not be cooked.
>
> After each use, scrub the meat-cutting board, or the counter where raw meat has been placed, with hot water and soap.
>
> Don't allow anyone with an infection, including yourself, to prepare food.
>
> Purchase—and use—an accurate thermometer for the refrigerator and one for meat.
>
> Because bacteria grow between 45 and 120 degrees F., be sure that all leftover foods are refrigerated immediately.

Keep hot foods hot. Use a meat thermometer to check pork and other meats. In general, foods should be kept at a temperature above 140 degrees F.

Keep all homemade salad dressing in the refrigerator. Purchased mayonnaise and other ready-made salad dressings should be refrigerated after opening.

Ground meats, such as hamburger and fresh bulk sausage, are more likely to spoil than roasts, chops, or steaks because they have been exposed to contamination from air, food handlers, and mechanical equipment. Store loosely wrapped in the coldest part of the refrigerator and use within one or two days.

Do not buy a broken package or sticky jar.

Keep custard-filled eclairs, synthetic custards, and other custard-filled desserts in the refrigerator until just before serving.

Chill main-dish salads for large groups in shallow bowls or on trays in the refrigerator. Keep sandwiches or sandwich fillings in the refrigerator until served.

If you use a dishpan for washing dishes, keep it separate and use it only for this purpose. Dishwater should be 130 degrees F. or above. Be sure rinse water is clean and hot and that the towels are clean.

Don't empty the turtle's bowl or clean the dog's dish in the same sink you use for washing dishes and preparing the family's food. The turtle's bowl is full of its waste, and your pet's dish may be contaminated with harmful bacteria.

Don't buy or use canned foods if any of the following signs are present: bulging of the top or bottom of the can, dents along the side seams, or any signs of seepage, off-odor, or foaming when the can is opened, or any unusual milky quality of the liquid.

Don't use leftover food if discoloration, off-odor, or mold is apparent. Any perishable food that has not been refrigerated below 45 degrees may be considered spoiled. Recook any leftover food that has been kept in the refrigerator 36 hours or longer.

To be safe: When in doubt, throw it out.

Fractures. See **BROKEN BONES,** page 89.

FROSTBITE

Just before frostbite appears, the skin turns pink; then, as freezing progresses, it turns white or greyish yellow. There may be initial pain, but this quickly subsides as the skin becomes numb. Cover the affected area

101

with a warm hand, clothing, or blankets but do not rub it or apply snow. If fingers or hand are frostbitten, hold the affected hand under the armpit and go indoors as soon as possible. If possible, immerse the frozen part, in warm, not hot, water (about 108 degrees). When nose or ears are involved, use warm compresses. Never apply hot-water bottles or heating pads or stand near a radiator or stove. Excessive heat increases tissue damage. After soaking, gently wrap the frostbitten part in a blanket or scarf, and let circulation reestablish itself naturally. Keep comfortably warm with blankets (not electric blankets) until medical help arrives. Movement of fingers and toes and warm, nonalcoholic drinks are recommended.

HANGOVER

The headache of a hangover is caused by dilated blood vessels. The caffeine in coffee and tea helps to contract blood vessels, so if the victim can take it, offer a cup of coffee or tea. An ice pack applied to the head is also recommended as an aid in constricting the blood vessels. Because the body loses salt as a result of alcohol intake, slowly sipping a salty beef broth can do much to decrease nausea. Orange juice is also a good source of the water, minerals, and calories necessary to increase blood sugar quickly. If the person is nauseous, however, citric acid can further irritate the stomach, and should not be taken.

A slice of toast well spread with honey, taken prior to bedtime after an evening of drinking, may help to ward off a hangover. The fructose in honey or vegetable juices, including tomato juice, helps to metabolize alcohol and therefore ease the pain.

HEADACHES

The occasional tension headache is easily treated by rest, aspirin, a warm bath, and a cold compress on the forehead. When a headache occurs after a head injury, or if it is sudden and severe and accompanied by nausea or vomiting and eye symptoms, it may be a real emergency. These symptoms could be due to a ruptured blood vessel in the brain, a blood clot on the brain, or an injury. Prompt medical attention is indicated. If a person complains of headache and then lapses into unconsciousness, your first concern should be respiration. If breathing has stopped, begin mouth-to-mouth resuscitation (see page 106), while medical help is being summoned.

Almost everyone has occasional headaches, but if headaches occur frequently or are severe and unrelenting, consult a doctor. (See also **HEAD INJURY,** below.)

HEAD INJURY

When a person is found unconscious or has been hurt in a fall, traffic accident, or other violent mishap, it is very possible that the victim may have sustained head injuries. Symptoms may include rapid but weak pulse, pupils unequal in size, paralysis of one or more limbs, headache, dizziness, or confusion. Keep the victim lying down and warm while medical help is summoned. Do not leave the victim of a head injury unattended. Do not administer alcoholic beverages or other stimulants such as coffee or tea if the person is awake. Never give anything by mouth if the patient is unconscious or semiconscious.

Make sure the neck and back are not broken. If the person is conscious, ask if he can move his fingers or toes easily; whether there is tingling or numbness around his shoulders, or if there is a neck or back pain. If there is no tingling or pain and the fingers and toes can be moved, turn the victim on his side so that the tongue does not fall back into the air passages and the airway can be drained of blood, vomitus, or other fluids. Tilt the head back slightly. Control bleeding from a head wound by applying a pressure dressing. If no sterile dressings are available, use a handkerchief, or if need be, your hand.

Head injuries can be deceiving. They may seem slight at first, and then develop into something more serious later. If someone has received a head injury and subsequently shows signs of undue sleepiness, headache, vomiting, or unusual irritability, seek medical aid at once. Such symptoms may occur up to 30 days after an injury.

HEART ATTACK

Any person suspected of having a heart attack, no matter how mild the symptoms, should have prompt medical attention. Common symptoms of a heart attack are extreme shortness of breath and pain or pressure in the upper abdomen or chest, sometimes spreading down the arms or into the neck and head. The victim may cough and bring up foamy, pink fluid. When any of these symptoms appear, call for a physician or the police. Have the person lie down and prop him up with pillows, or sit him in a chair. Loosen his belt and collar. (If it is a woman, open her bra and girdle as well as her collar and belt.) Keep the victim warm but not warm enough to induce sweating. Do not give anything to eat or drink. If the person is conscious, your most important function, after making him comfortable, is to keep him calm and to reassure him. Ask him to breathe deeply through his mouth. Do not attempt to lift or carry the patient without a doctor's supervision. (See also **CHEST PAIN,** page 93.)

Heat Cramps. See **CRAMPS,** page 95.

HEAT EXHAUSTION

Heat exhaustion may be mild or severe. In mild cases, the person usually feels tired and may experience headache, dizziness, and nausea. In severe cases, the victim is pale and clammy, his pulse is rapid and weak, and he complains of weakness, headache, or nausea. He may vomit and have painful cramps in his stomach or limbs. His temperature is usually normal or subnormal, and he may lapse into unconsciousness. The patient should be lying down, feet elevated. Loosen his clothing. If he is conscious, give him a salt solution—1 teaspoon of salt to 1 quart of water—every 15 minutes. If he feels cold or shows other signs of shock (see page 113), wrap him warmly in blankets and massage his skin to help stimulate circulation. Call a physician.

HEAT STROKE OR SUNSTROKE

This is more serious than heat exhaustion. The patient has a high fever, 105 degrees F. or higher, and has no evident perspiration. His skin is hot and dry. He is weak, irritable, dazed, and nauseated. He may become unconscious. Cool him off quickly. Place him in the shade with his head and shoulders slightly elevated, and pour buckets of cold water over him. Wrap his head in cold, wet towels and his body in cold, wet sheets. Massage his legs upward toward the heart. If he is conscious, give him a glass of salt water—1 teaspoon of salt to 1 quart of water— every 15 minutes. Do not give stimulants of any kind! Call a physician immediately.

HICCUPS

Babies. Babies who are hicupping may be held over the shoulder and burped. If this doesn't work, give the baby a bottle of tepid water. If the baby is still hicupping, moisten the nipple of a bottle (or a spoon), dip it in sugar, and give it to the youngster to suck.

Children and adults. A victim of the hiccups should take a deep breath and hold it as long as possible. If the hiccups don't stop, then sipping a glass of cold water or gargling with plain warm or cold water for a minute or two may help. Another remedy is to swallow a teaspoon of sugar—allow it to melt on the tongue, but don't use water to wash it down. If the hiccups continue, breathing in and out of a paper bag to accumulate more carbon dioxide in the system can be therapeutic. If the hiccups persist for an hour or more, consult a physician.

INSECT STINGS OR BITES—ALLERGIC OR POISONOUS

The sting or bite of a scorpion, black widow, brown recluse spider, or bee should receive immediate attention. Have the victim lie down at once. If the bite is on a limb, apply a constricting bandage above the wound. The bandage should not impede circulation, so do not twist it so tight that there is a throbbing sensation below the tie or the pulse in the blood vessels disappears. If the bite contains a stinger, remove it carefully with tweezers or fingernails. Apply an ice pack over the bite, if possible, and carry the victim or have him carried to a physician or hospital. Do not let the person walk or take alcohol in any form (See also **ALLERGIC ATTACK,** page 86.)

INSOMNIA

Everyone has occasional incidents of sleeplessness, but when insomnia occurs frequently or persistently, a physician should be consulted.

Sleep inducers for insomniacs are many and varied. Over-the-counter sleeping drugs are usually antihistamines that produce drowsiness as a side effect. Among the nonchemical recommendations for inducing sleep are a walk in the fresh air before bedtime, a warm bath, a glass of warm milk, soothing music, or a boring book. Still another technique is to concentrate on flexing and relaxing all voluntary muscles one at a time, starting with the toes, and working up to the eyebrows.

ITCHING

An itch may be due to dry skin, local irritation from soaps, detergents, or cosmetics, skin infections, drugs, parasites, foods, emotions, or a host of other things. Scratching, and applying heat or ice, usually make an itch worse. Soaking for at least ten minutes in bath water to which a cup of oatmeal, corn starch, or baking soda has been added, may relieve an itch. Your physician, of course, will try to determine the cause of a persistent itch and then will probably advise that you avoid the irritant. He may prescribe antihistamines or soothing salves as well. Sometimes rubbing the itch lightly with a very soft brush or taking your mind off the itch with a distracting project may be helpful. (See also **POISON IVY, POISON OAK, AND POISON SUMAC,** page 107.)

Leg Cramps. See **CRAMPS,** page 95.

MISCARRIAGE

If a pregnant woman shows signs of bleeding, her physician should be called, and she should go to bed immediately.

If a miscarriage should occur, elevate the foot of the bed from 12 to 18 inches to retard vaginal bleeding. A fast way to do this is to place books or magazines under the mattress at the foot of the bed. Keep the woman warm and quiet, and give her nonalcoholic liquids until a physician arrives.

MOTION SICKNESS

Motion sickness is caused by exposure to excessive movement, acceleration, or deceleration in a plane, train, car, ship, or bus. Anyone may be affected, but people with a history of ear trouble are most susceptible. The cardinal symptom is nausea, occurring in waves, and frequently ending in vomiting. Early symptoms include yawning, rapid breathing, a greenish pallor, a cold sweat, and sleepiness. Then feelings of suffocation, dizziness, and nausea set in.

Preventing motion sickness is, of course, better than trying to cure it. If you suspect you are susceptible, ask your physician for anti-motion-sickness medication. Before you travel, do not drink much. Avoid alcoholic beverages en route. When choosing a seat on a plane, ship, car, train, or bus, try to sit where the motion is at a minimum. A midship cabin on a lower deck on shipboard, a seat between the wings of a plane, the midsection of a train or bus, and the right front seat next to the car's driver are all best for the sensitive traveler. When you begin to feel queasy, lie down or semi-recline if possible. Do not read or play cards. Fresh air will often help relieve nausea, so take a breath of fresh air or oxygen, if it is available. Eat simple foods such as dry crackers or rolls in small amounts at frequent intervals.

MOUTH-TO-MOUTH RESUSCITATION

Mouth-to-mouth resuscitation (see illustrations below) is the emergency treatment that is recommended when a person has difficulty breathing or stops breathing altogether. If you feel squeamish about putting your mouth on a stranger's, place a hankerchief or paper tissue on the victim's mouth first.

Mouth-to-mouth resuscitation

Tilt the victim's head back and pull or push the jaw into a jutting position.

If the victim is a small child, place your mouth tightly over his mouth and nose and puff lightly about 20 times a minute.

If the victim is an adult, cover his mouth with yours, pinch his nostrils shut and blow vigorously about 12 times a minute.

Blow until you see his chest rise, and then remove your mouth.

Listen while the victim exhales, and then replace your mouth and repeat the procedure.

If you are unable to get air into the lungs, foreign matter may be blocking the throat. (See **CHOKING,** page 94.)

Do not stop resuscitation efforts until someone else takes over or a physician arrives to handle the case.

When the victim starts breathing on his own, do not let him get up and walk around. Keep him lying quiet and warm.

Because complications may occur later, a physician's examination is always in order after a breathing difficulty, even in the case of a normally healthy person.

NOSEBLEED

Nosebleeds can occur spontaneously as a result of injury, from a disease such as high blood pressure, from strenuous activity, colds, or exposure to high altitudes. Reassure the person and keep him quiet. Walking about, talking, laughing, or blowing the nose may cause increased bleeding or restart the bleeding. It is best to sit quietly or lie down with head and shoulders slightly raised. Pressure on the upper lip just below the nose with one or both thumbs may stop a mild nosebleed. If this doesn't work, pinch the nostrils together for a full five minutes without release. This may cause a clot to form over the ruptured blood vessel, and the bleeding will stop. You may have to pack the nostrils with plugs of sterile gauze or cotton. Be sure to leave one end of each nostril plug outside so that it can be removed easily. If the bleeding continues, call a physician. If nosebleeds are frequent and heavy, a doctor should be consulted.

POISON IVY, POISON OAK, AND POISON SUMAC

Poison ivy, poison oak, and poison sumac all contain the same toxic skin-irritating agent, urushiol. This agent remains active even after the plant has died and can be carried on any article that has been in contact with it for several months.

The growth and leaf forms of poison ivies and oaks vary greatly and may not be easy to recognize. However, their leaflets always grow in groups of three and usually have a shiny, reddish appearance. Posion ivy grows as a woody vine, poison oak as a low-growing shrub, and poison sumac as a coarse woody shrub or a small tree.

The first sign of poisoning is a mild itch, followed by a slight reddening of the skin. The itching increases, and tiny watery blisters may appear within a few hours. An acute attack may cause extreme discomfort depending upon how allergic the person is and how extensive his contact with the leaves. Soap destroys the allergen, so wash carefully all over with soap, and then sponge with alcohol. Wash anything that may have come in contact with the plant, such as garden tools, bikes, baseball gloves, and dogs. Bathing will not spread the rash. Cold compresses reduce inflammation, and calamine lotion applied early will hasten the drying of small blisters. Milk of magnesia applied with cotton swabs is an old and widely used remedy to relieve the itching. If the rash spreads over a large area, a physician should be consulted. He may prescribe medication to relieve the inflammation and to ward off any complicating infection.

POISONS—INHALED

One of the most common inhaled poisons is carbon monoxide, a colorless, odorless gas that can kill without warning (see page 41). It accumulates to a dangerous degree when a car motor or an indoor heater gives off fumes in an improperly ventilated, closed space. Symp-

107

toms of carbon monoxide poisoning are headache, dizziness, weakness, difficulty in breathing, and possibly vomiting, followed by collapse and unconsciousness. Skin, fingernails, and lips may be light red.

Other fumes that commonly produce inhalation poisoning are smoke, hydrogen sulfide (smells like rotten eggs or sewers), petroleum vapors, ammonia, carbon tetrachloride, naphthalene, and acetone. All may cause symptoms similar to carbon monoxide poisoning except for the red coloring.

A word of caution. Do not mix chlorine bleach or ammonia with each other or with other household chemicals such as toilet-bowl cleaner, lye, rust remover, vinegar, oven cleaner, or anything else. In an effort to get things sparkling clean, a number of people have mixed household cleansers and, as a result, have released deadly gases. Use all chemicals around the house only as the manufacturers direct on the labels.

When a person has been overcome by any of the fumes mentioned above, carry or drag him—do not let him walk—to fresh air immediately. If you cannot move him, open or smash the windows to let in fresh air. Do not give alcohol in any form. Loosen the victim's clothing, and if he is not breathing, begin mouth-to-mouth resuscitation (see page 106). Call the fire department, police rescue squad, or poison control center (see page 83). When you send for help, be sure to say inhalation poisoning is involved so they will have oxygen and a respirator available. Keep the victim warm and lying on his back until help arrives.

POISONS—SWALLOWED

Curiosity may kill cats, as the saying goes, but it also kills many children every year. There are thousands of chemicals in such common household products as cleaning preparations, cosmetics, medicines, pesticides, and hobby materials. If left within the reach of children, these products are potentially lethal. Even adults mistakenly ingest them.

Precautions. With just a little effort you can poison-proof your home and avert potential tragedy. Here's what to do and what not to do:

Do not leave cleaning preparations, such as dishwasher detergent or abrasives, under the sink, on counters, or anywhere a toddler can reach even using a chair.

Keep foods and cleaning preparations, pesticides, and hobby materials in separate locations.

Never transfer chemicals into food containers such as pop bottles or drinking glasses.

Keep all medicines in a locked medicine cabinet or one that is absolutely out of reach of children.

Whenever possible, buy medicines with childproof caps and even then do not assume that such caps are absolutely childproof.

Keep all medicines in their original containers.

Throw away out-of-date medicines by first dumping the

contents down the toilet and then putting the empty containers in the trash can.

Never awake from sleep and take medicines without turning on the lights and putting on eyeglasses, if needed. Many dangerous mistakes have been made by drowsy people.

After you have taken medicines, do not leave the containers laying around. Return them to a safe place immediately. Be careful about your purse or pockets if they contain medicines.

Do not tell a child medicine is candy.

Always read a label before giving or taking a dose of medicine and before using a household chemical.

Keep the number of your nearest poison control center readily available (see page 83).

Signs of poisoning. You can suspect poisoning if:

There is a strange odor on the breath

There is discoloration of lips and mouth

There is pain or a burning sensation in the throat

Bottles or packages of drugs or poisonous chemicals are found in the presence of children or emotionally upset adults

There is evidence that wild berries or plants have been eaten

There is unconsciousness, confusion, or sudden illness when access to poison is possible

What to do. If you discover that someone has indeed been poisoned, there are several things that you can do:

If the container of the suspected poison is nearby, read the label for the antidote and proceed at once to follow the directions while someone else summons help.

If you know what the person has swallowed but no antidote is printed on the container, try to identify the poisonous ingredient by referring to the list of *Common Household Products with Ingredients That Are Poisonous If Swallowed* on page 111. Once you have determined what poison you have to deal with, find the proper antidote in the list of *Common Poisons Found Around the House and Their Antidotes* on pages 111 f.

If you don't know and can't find out what antidote to administer, attempt to dilute the poison immediately if the victim is conscious. Give several glasses of water or, if possible, at least 4 glasses of milk. Rush the patient to the nearest poison control center.

Administering the antidote. Once you discover what the correct antidote is, administering it usually means making the victim drink a liquid that will neutralize the action of the poison. In many cases, vomiting is recommended in order to remove as much of the swallowed poison as possible before it is absorbed. There are instances, however, in which vomiting is *not* recommended (see below), so be sure vomiting is required as part of the antidote before you try to induce it. In cases where vomiting is recommended, the following procedures are suggested:

To induce vomiting. If you have syrup of ipecac available, and your doctor prescribes it (it is not recommended for children under one year of age), give 1 teaspoonful and at least 1 cup of water. If no vomiting occurs after 20 minutes, this procedure may be repeated, *but only if your physician recommends it.*

If you do not use syrup of ipecac, give milk or warm water and induce vomiting by placing the blunt end of a spoon or your finger at the back of the patient's throat. When vomiting begins, patient should bend forward, with head lower than hips. If patient is lying down, turn head to one side to prevent vomitus from entering the lungs.

After the person has vomited, a glass of milk or water will help dilute any remaining poison.

Always save the container from which the poison was taken and the vomitus to bring to the physician for analysis. Remember, in cases of poisoning, time is essential to prevent absorption and permanent damage or death.

Do not induce vomiting if the victim:

Is unconscious

Is having convulsions

Has symptoms of severe pain

Has a burning sensation in the mouth and throat

Do not induce vomiting if the victim has swallowed any of the following substances:

Acids such as sulfuric, nitric, hydrochloric, oxalic, or hydrofluoric (rust removers); iodine; or silver nitrate (styptic pencil)

Ammonia

Drain cleaner

Household bleach

Petroleum products such as kerosene, gasoline, lighter fluid, furniture and metal polishes, turpentine, oven cleaners, insecticides

Washing soda

Do not induce vomiting if the poison is unknown.

I. COMMON HOUSEHOLD PRODUCTS WITH INGREDIENTS THAT ARE POISONOUS IF SWALLOWED

Ant poison (thallium)
Antifreeze (ethylene glycol)
Antifreeze, nonpermanent (wood alcohol)
Antiseptics (mercury)
Aspirin (salicylates)*

Brass polish (acid, cyanide)†

Camphor (arsenic)
Canned heat (wood alcohol)
Carbonates (alkali)
Caustic soda (alkali)
Cleaning fluid (petroleum)
Cleaning products (ammonia)
Cleansers (alkali)
Codeine (opium derivative)*
Copper polish (acid)
Cough medicines (opium derivative)*
Cream hair remover (thallium)

Deodorizer (acid, chlorine)†
Detergents (alkali)
Disinfectants (acid, chlorine, mercury)†
Drain cleaner (alkali)
Dye (arsenic)

Fingernail polish (acetone)
Fingernail polish remover (acetone)
Fuel oil (petroleum)
Fumigants (cyanide)
Fungicides for molds, mildew, garden rust (mercury)
Furniture polish (petroleum)

Garden sprays (petroleum)
Gasoline (petroleum)

Insect poison (arsenic, cyanide)†
Insecticides (petroleum)

Kerosene (petroleum)

Laudanum (opium derivative)*
Laundry bleach (chlorine)
Lighter fluid (petroleum)
Lye (alkali)

Medication for allergies, colds, or motion sickness (antihistamines)*
Medication for anemia (iron)*
Morphine (opium derivative)*
Mothballs, flakes (naphthalene)

Oil of wintergreen (salicylates)
Oxides (alkali)

Pain killers (opium derivatives)*
Paint (wood alcohol)
Paint remover (alkali, wood alcohol)†
Paint thickener (petroleum)
Paint thinner (turpentine)
Permanent-wave solution, home (ammonium, sodium, or potassium thioglycollate)
Peroxide (alkali)
Potash (alkali)

Rat poison (arsenic, cyanide, fluoride, thallium)†
Rat poison, potent (strychnine)
Roach powder (fluoride)

Silver polish (acid)
Sleeping pills (barbiturates)*
Stain removers (acid)

Varnish (wood alcohol)

Weed killer (arsenic)

† Check label to see which poisonous ingredients the product contains—each requires a different antidote.

* Poisonous only if overdose is taken.

II. COMMON POISONS FOUND AROUND THE HOUSE AND THEIR ANTIDOTES

(See page 110 for instructions to induce vomiting.)

ACETONE (in fingernail polish and fingernail polish remover): *Induce vomiting only.*

ACIDS (brass, copper, silver polishes, stain removers, laundry bleach, disinfectants, deodorizers): Give 1 cup of milk or 2 tablespoons of milk of magnesia to 2 cups of water, and large quantities of water. Wash burned area around mouth with soap and then give ¼ cup to 1 cup of olive oil, mineral oil, melted butter, or 4 tablespoons corn starch to 1 cup of water. *Do not induce vomiting.*

ALKALIS (caustic soda, lye, potash, oxides, peroxides, carbonates, drain cleaners, paint removers, strong washing powders and cleansers): Give 1 cup (to child under 5) to 1 quart (to patient over 5) citrus fruit juice or diluted vinegar. Then give as much milk or water as the victim will drink. *Do not induce vomiting.*

AMMONIA (in cleaning products): Give 1 cup to 1 quart fruit juice or diluted vinegar, and then give ¼ cup to 1 cup of milk or olive oil. *Do not induce vomiting.*

AMMONIUM, SODIUM, OR POTASSIUM THIOGLYCOLLATE (in home permanent-wave solutions): Give 1 quart of citrus fruit juice or diluted vinegar. Then give as much milk or water as the victim will drink. *Do not induce vomiting.*

ANTIHISTAMINES (medications for allergies, colds, or motion sickness): Give strong tea or coffee or 1 teaspoonful of baking soda in 1 quart of warm water. *Induce vomiting.* Keep victim quiet in a dark room.

ARSENIC (in dyes, camphor, insect and rat poisons, weed killers): Give 2 tablespoons baking soda to 1 glass of water, or as much plain water as the victim will drink. *Induce vomiting.*

BARBITURATES (in sleeping pills): *Induce vomiting.* Give strong tea or coffee and keep the victim awake. Force him to walk and get him talking.

BORIC ACID: *Induce vomiting only.*

BROMIDES AND TRANQUILIZERS: *Induce vomiting.* Give 2 tablespoons of epsom salts in 2 glasses of water (except when diarrhea is severe), and then plain water. More specific treatment depends upon the drug ingested.

CHLORINE (in laundry bleach, disinfectants, deodorizers): Give ¼ cup to 1 cup of milk, or 4 tablespoons cornstarch to 1 cup of water, or 1 tablespoon of milk of magnesia to 1 cup of water. *Do not induce vomiting.*

CYANIDE (in insect and rat poisons, fumigants): *Induce vomiting only.*

ETHYLENE GLYCOL (in antifreeze): *Induce vomiting only.*

FLUORIDE (in ant and roach powder): Give 1 cup of milk and 2 egg whites or 2 teaspoons liquid antacid or 2 antacid tablets dissolved in a glass of water. Then *induce vomiting.* If the victim has any form of kidney disease, do not give antacids. Use milk and egg white antidote instead.

IODINE: Give 4 tablespoons of cornstarch or flour to 1 cup of water, or give 1 cup of milk and 2 egg whites. *Induce vomiting.* Give 1 glass of milk.

IRON (medicine for anemia): *Induce vomiting.* Give 1 glass of milk, or 2 tablespoons of milk of magnesia, or 2 teaspoons of baking soda in 1 glass of warm water.

MERCURY (in fungicides for molds, mildew, garden rust, and also in antiseptics and disinfectants): Give 1 slice burnt toast crumbled in 1 glass of milk (do not use syrup of ipecac if burnt toast is given), or 1 cup of milk, or ½ cup of egg whites. *Induce vomiting.* Repeat procedure after vomiting has stopped. Finally, give 2 tablespoons of epsom salts in 2 glasses of water.

NAPHTHALENE (in mothballs, flakes): Give ¼ cup to 1 cup milk, or ½ cup egg whites. Do not give any fats or oils. *Induce vomiting.*

OPIUM DERIVATIVES (morphine, codeine, laudanum in pain killers and cough medicines): *Induce vomiting.* Give glass of milk or 1 slice of burnt toast crumbled in 1 glass of milk. Give 2 tablespoons of epsom salts in 2 glasses of water. Keep patient awake.

PETROLEUM (in gasoline, kerosene, fuel oil, cleaning and lighter fluids, polishes, paint thickener, insecticides, and garden sprays): Give water only, as much as the victim will drink. *Do not induce vomiting.*

SALICYLATES (aspirin or oil of wintergreen): Give milk. *Induce vomiting.* Give tablespoon of baking soda in 1 quart of warm water. Sponge with cool water.

STRYCHNINE (a potent rat poison): Give 1 glass of milk or 1 slice burnt toast crumbled in 1 glass of milk. *Induce vomiting if not convulsing.* Do not give syrup of ipecac if burnt toast is given.

THALLIUM (in ant and rat poisons and in cream hair removers): Give 1 glass milk or 4 tablespoons cornstarch to 1 cup of water. *Induce vomiting.*

TURPENTINE (in paint thinner, waxes, polishes, deodorizers): Give 2 ounces of mineral oil or vegetable oil, then give 1 cup of milk followed by plenty of water, as much as the victim will drink. *Do not induce vomiting.*

WOOD ALCOHOL (methanol or methyl alcohol in paints, varnish, paint remover, canned heat, nonpermanent antifreeze): Symptoms may resemble drunkenness. Give 1 glass of milk or 1 tablespoon of baking soda in 1 quart of warm water. *Induce vomiting.* Repeat until medical help arrives.

RABIES

Rabies is a deadly viral disease transmitted to man through the bite of a rabid animal. Pets can and should be protected against the virus through periodic vaccination. Although human illness from rabies is relatively rare, any bite by a pet or wild animal must always be considered and treated at once as a potential cause of rabies. Once symptoms of this disease occur, the illness is usually fatal.

In deciding whether a victim must be vaccinated, a physician will consider the species of the biting animal, local prevalence of rabies, the apparent health of the animal at the time of the bite, and the vaccination history of the animal. It is of utmost importance to determine whether or not the animal was vaccinated against rabies, for this reduces by 95 percent the probability that a biting animal is rabid. Because the vaccine can cause serious side effects in the victim, it is not given unless absolutely necessary.

In the United States, rabies is reported most frequently in the following animals: skunk, fox, coyote, raccoon, bat, dog, cat, and cattle. Because skunks shed the virus in their saliva at an extremely high level, the bite of a rabid skunk is considered especially dangerous. If a rat, mouse, squirrel, chipmunk, hamster, gerbil, or guinea pig bites, doctors are less inclined to administer antirabies vaccine.

Bites on the head, neck, shoulders, and hands are more likely to result in rabies than bites on the trunk or legs, but all bites should be examined by a doctor.

Doctors emphasize that treatment should never be delayed pending the results of laboratory tests on the animal—even a six-hour delay in administering vaccine to the victim makes a marked difference in the survival rate.

The injections are usually given daily for two weeks. If the animal is captured and remains healthy for from 5 to 10 days, vaccination of the victim can be discontinued. (See also **RABIES,** page 157, for treatment of a rabid animal.)

Scorpion Bites. See **INSECT STINGS OR BITES—ALLERGIC OR POISONOUS,** page 104.

SHOCK

There is always a possibility of shock in every major injury or severe emotional upset. It results from a lack of sufficient blood circulation and may accompany heavy bleeding, stoppage of breathing, poisoning, burns, fractures, strokes, heart attacks, heat exhaustion, and other emergencies. A person who is going into shock exhibits the following symptoms: cold, damp skin; perspiration beads on forehead and palms; shallow breathing; and a pale face. Complaints of feeling chilly and nauseous are frequent, and vomiting may result. Call a physician immediately and in the meantime do the following.

Correct the cause, if possible. If bleeding is profuse, apply a pressure bandage.

Keep the victim lying down and open tight clothing.

Cover the victim with a blanket or coat.

If there is vomiting, turn the head to one side to prevent suffocation.

If there are signs of head or chest injuries, elevate the head just enough to prevent the blood from gathering in the upper part of the body.

If it appears that there are no broken bones and the person does not have a head or chest injury, keep the head lower than the rest of the body. Put the victim on a board or door and use bricks or any other prop to elevate the feet 12 inches or more (see illustration below). If there is no board or door available, invert a chair and put the back under the victim's feet for elevation. If a chair is not available, use any prop under the legs.

When there are no signs of broken bones, head or chest injuries, elevate the feet of a shock victim.

If the victim is conscious and no abdominal injury is suspected, give fluids. A mixture of 1 quart of water to 1 teaspoon of salt and ½ teaspoon of baking soda is recommended.

Reassure the person and keep him warm until the physician arrives.

SNAKEBITE

Poisonous snakes are found in every state except Alaska, Hawaii, and Maine. Pit vipers—including rattlesnakes, cottonmouths, and copperheads—are responsible for about 99 percent of all venomous snakebites in the United States, and coral snakes and foreign venomous snakes in captivity account for the remaining accidents.

A pit viper bite is diagnosed primarily by the type of puncture wound and pain as well as the extent of swelling around the site of the bite. There may be from one to four or more fang punctures depending on the nature and number of bites. Swelling and redness are always present in victims of pit viper poisoning.

Other symptoms of pit viper bites are nausea, vomiting, shock, diarrhea, numbness and tingling around the bites, muscle twitching in the bitten area, coma, abnormal bleeding, and kidney failure.

The victim of a coral snake may have only slight pain and mild swelling.

The first thing to do when a person has been bitten by a poisonous snake is to have the victim lie down to slow the circulation and the spread of venom. Then tie a belt, necktie, folded scarf, or any other length of material several inches from the fang mark between the bite and the heart. Do not tie it tight enough to stop circulation completely.

Experiments have shown that incision and suction can remove venom up to and even after 60 minutes. If you cannot get to a doctor within this period of time, sterilize a knife or razor blade with the flame of several matches. Then make an x-shaped incision ⅛ to ¼ inch deep over the fang punctures. If no suction cup is available, use your mouth to suck the venom from the wound. There is no danger of poisoning yourself if you should happen to swallow any; snake venom is not a stomach poison. The suction should be applied continuously for at least an hour.

Do not pack the wound with ice as is sometimes recommended. It may cause additional harm.

Do not give the victim alcohol in any form. Carry him to a physician. Do not let him walk.

If possible, kill the snake that bit the victim and bring it to the physician for identification.

Nonpoisonous snakebites should be treated like any other superficial wound (see page 119).

Spider (Black Widow or Brown) Bites. See **INSECT STINGS OR BITES —ALLERGIC OR POISONOUS,** page 104.

SPLINTERS

Wash the skin around the splinter with soap and water. If the splinter is difficult to see, apply a drop of iodine, mercurochrome, or food coloring to the affected area. The sliver will darken and show through the skin. An easy way to remove a superficial splinter in a finger or toe is to hold the affected area over the opening of a pop bottle filled with hot water. The steam will soften the skin and you may be able to press the splinter out with your fingers. If the splinter is more deeply embedded, sterilize a needle and tweezers by boiling them for ten minutes or by holding them over the flame of several matches. If you feel the need to anesthetize the skin, place an ice cube on the spot until it feels numb. Then loosen the skin around the splinter with the needle, and remove the splinter with the tweezers. Let the wound bleed to help cleanse it, and then wash again with soap and water, and cover with an adhesive bandage.

SPRAINS

Sprains are injuries to the soft tissues around a joint—ankles, fingers, wrists, and knees are most often affected. Ligaments, muscles, tendons, and blood vessels are stretched and occasionally torn. Because there is always the possibility that both a sprain and a broken bone have occurred, treat a major sprain like a broken bone. The injured joint should be splinted, or the joint placed on a pillow and tied there for support. Consult a physician.

An ice bag or cold compress should be placed over the sprain and the limb elevated to reduce swelling. When the joint can be moved without pain, hot compresses and gentle massage may help to increase blood circulation.

STINGRAY AND JELLYFISH STINGS

Stingrays, which have one or more stingers depending upon the species, frequent the coastal waters of North America, particularly California, the Gulf of Mexico, and the southern Atlantic coast. They usually inject venom into a bather's leg or arm causing severe pain and lacerations. To treat stingray stings, place a constricting bandage above the wound (it should not be so tight that it impedes circulation completely). Then, as quickly as possible, immerse the affected part in hot water and leave it there for 30 minutes to one hour. Because the venom is detoxified by heat, the water should be as hot as can be tolerated.

After the first aid has been administered, a doctor should examine the wound to see if it is clear of irritating debris from the marine animal.

Jellyfish, including the Portuguese man-of-war, have tentacles containing stingers that inject poison into a victim's skin, causing pain, itching, and sometimes collapse. The wound should be flushed with fresh water. If a severe reaction occurs, first aid should be given according to the symptoms. If breathing is impaired, mouth-to-mouth resuscitation may be necessary (see page 106). If shock occurs, treat accordingly until medical help arrives (see page 113).

Stomach Cramps. See **CRAMPS,** page 95.

STOMACH PAIN

Abdominal pain can be a symptom of a great number of illnesses that range widely in degree of severity. Appendicitis should always be considered if the appendix is still present. Do not give the patient a laxative. Take his temperature, and feel his abdomen when he is lying down with abdominal muscles relaxed. If there is any fever, and if the abdomen feels hard or is sore or painful to the touch, especially on the lower right side, call a doctor at once. Other appendicitis symptoms are nausea, vomiting, and persistent pain.

When there is unexplained abdominal pain, do not let the patient eat anything. Food only increases the possibility of the appendix rupturing and further complicates an intestinal block. Never apply heat even if the appendix has been removed. If any abdominal pain persists or grows increasingly worse, seek prompt medical attention.

STROKE

A person who suffers a stroke may first complain of severe headache, or may suddenly develop paralysis on one side of the body, with weak-

116

ness in an arm or leg. He may be difficult to awaken as well. If any of these symptoms are apparent, have the person lie down immediately. Loosen clothing about the neck and waist to permit easier breathing.

If he is conscious, you may place a pillow under his head for comfort. If he is unconscious, do not use a pillow, but turn his head to the side so he does not choke if he vomits. Call a physician. If none is available, summon help immediately from the emergency squad. Do nothing else unless the individual stops breathing, in which case, give mouth-to-mouth resuscitation. (See page 106.)

If the patient is conscious, talk reassuringly to him. Try to keep him calm while medical help is being summoned. Do not give anything to eat or drink.

SUNBURN

If the skin is just reddened, a cool bath with half a cup of baking soda added to the tub water is soothing. After patting the skin dry, apply cold, whole milk compresses. Do not use butter or margarine because they may cause irritation and introduce infection.

If the skin is blistered or extensively burned, cover it with a sterile dressing soaked in a weak solution of baking soda—2 tablespoonfuls of soda to 1 quart of water—or a weak solution of cold tea. The victims of sunburn should not expose themselves to the sun until healing is complete. Severe sunburn, accompanied by chills and nausea, should be treated by a physician.

SWALLOWED OBJECT

Something small and smooth that is swallowed, such as a fruit seed, button, or small coin, will probably pass uneventfully through the system in a few days, Check the stool each day. If the object has not passed within two days, consult a physician. When a sharp object such as a pin or needle has been swallowed, consult a physician immediately.

Swimming Cramps. See **CRAMPS,** page 95.

TEAR GAS

Tear gas causes an acute "instant cold"—tearing red eyes, stuffy nose, coughing, and hoarseness. When the victim has been exposed to only a small amount of tear gas in the open air, the symptoms usually clear within a few hours, although redness of the eyes may last for half a day. Exposure in a confined area may cause symptoms that last for a day or more. Prolonged contact with a high concentration of the gas may result in damage to the respiratory system.

Once out of the area of exposure, wash the eyes freely with tap water. A drinking fountain may serve the purpose well. Wash out the mouth, and gargle to remove any chemicals. Clean the skin thoroughly with water. If rubbing alcohol is available, mix it with water—about half a cup to a quart of water, and wash the skin. If symptoms persist or if any chemical came in direct contact with the eye, obtain medical attention.

Ticks. See **CHIGGERS, TICKS,** page 94.

TOOTH TROUBLE

Toothache. No matter how comforting you think it might be, do not put heat on an aching tooth or jaw. If there is an abcess, heat could spread the infection. Ice will not harm a toothache and might be helpful. If there is a large, exposed cavity, swab it clean, and then stuff it with cotton dipped in oil of cloves. If the pain is severe, and a visit to the dentist is not immediately possible, a pain killer recommended by a physician or dentist to ease suffering may be taken until proper attention can be obtained.

Tooth knocked out. Chances are the tooth can be reimplanted successfully if a dentist is visited within 24 hours, so save the tooth and wrap it in a clean handkerchief. Contact a dentist at once.

Tooth broken. Until a dentist repairs it, put sugarless chewing gum or a soft ball of paraffin wax on top of the broken tooth so the sharp edges won't hurt the tongue, and cold, hot, or sweet foods will not shock the nerve.

UNCONSCIOUSNESS—UNEXPLAINED

When a person is found in an unconscious state, it is difficult, sometimes even for a doctor, to diagnose the cause of unconsciousness. The first thing to do, therefore, is to observe whether the person has stopped or is having trouble breathing. If so, apply mouth-to-mouth resuscitation (see page 106). Next, check for hemorrhaging (see page 88). If the victim's face is red or flushed and the pulse is strong, raise his head slightly. Apply a cold cloth to the head, loosen clothing, and cover for warmth if necessary. If the victim's face is pale and his pulse weak, lower the head slightly and apply heat. If his lips are blue, keep an eye on his breathing and be prepared to give mouth-to-mouth resuscitation if it becomes necessary.

If the unconscious patient vomits, turn his head to the side to prevent choking.

Even if he should regain consciousness, keep the victim lying down and quiet until he is transported to a hospital or until a physician arrives.

Consider anyone found unconscious as a victim of a head injury. *Do not* move the head or any part of the body if there is bleeding from the nose, mouth, or ears unless you can determine that the victim will suffocate from blood or vomit if his head is not turned to the side.

VOMITING

Severe forms of vomiting may be a symptom of serious internal disturbance or brain involvement. If the person is lying down and cannot reach the bathroom or vomit in a bowl, turn his head to the side and slightly arch the neck to prevent strangulation. When the symptoms persist, or if vomit is emitted with great force, call for immediate medical help. In less severe forms, when a person vomits once or twice, do not give anything by mouth for several hours. If the patient asks for water, give small sips or a teaspoon of chopped ice. Wait at least 15 to 20 minutes to see if it stays down. Consult a physician.

WOUNDS

When something goes deeper then just the superficial surface of the skin, it is usually considered a wound. It can be minor, and require nothing more than first aid, or it can be life-threatening. For any wound, major or minor, there are certain don'ts. Don't breathe on it. Don't allow fingers, used handkerchiefs, or any other soiled material to touch it. Keep it dry and clean.

Here are some steps to take for specific types of wounds:

Cut. A cut is usually a wound made with a sharp instrument such as a knife, razor, saw, or piece of broken glass. If there is not much bleeding, simply wash with soap and water and cover with an adhesive bandage. If the cut is deep, or involves a great deal of bleeding, control the bleeding by placing pressure over the wound with a piece of sterile gauze. If not available, use a clean cloth or, as a last resort, your bare hand. Medical attention should be obtained as soon as possible. A deep wound may require stitches in order to heal properly. A physician may also have to administer a tetanus shot.

Abdominal wound. If professional treatment is not immediately available, gently cover the protruding organs with a damp dressing. If no sterile gauze is available, use any clean material. Hold the dressing firmly in place to control bleeding until help is obtained. However, do not press the bandage so hard that you cause further injury to the internal organs.

Deep chest wound. Until medical help is available, place sterile gauze or a clean cloth pad over the wound. The object is to prevent air from escaping through the wound and causing the lung to collapse. Hold the pad in place with firm pressure. Draw a belt around the chest to hold the wound closed. If a belt is not available, use several ties knotted together, or any length of cloth or rope. Make sure the band is not so tight that it constricts breathing.

Puncture wound. Gently press near the hole to encourage bleeding that will wash out the wound. Cover the puncture lightly with a sterile bandage until a physician can be consulted. Do not try to close the wound with a bandage or adhesive. The doctor will want to cleanse the wound and perhaps administer an injection to prevent tetanus.

life's little emergencies

Hardly a day goes by without some minor emergency cropping up that challenges solution but, with a little experience and ingenuity, most of them can be handled easily. A few that require special treatment are included here with suggestions that may prove useful.

BUGS IN THE HOUSE

Because most pesticides are potentially harmful to humans and pets, heavy infestations of termites, hornets, and other insects are best handled by professional exterminators. Advice on what you can do yourself and when to call professional help may be obtained from the extension service listed in your phone book under U.S. Department of Agriculture. If you do use a pesticide around the house, use only those commercial products marked "nontoxic to humans and pets."

For small problems, an easy and safe method is to hunt bugs with your vacuum cleaner. The suction will pull them out of the baseboards and from under sinks and counters. After you have vacuumed up the pests, empty the container in the garbage can outside. But eggs may still be left in the house, so you may have to use a pesticide or call an exterminating service for additional help.

Here is some advice for specific problems:

Cockroaches seek warmth, moisture, and food, and they hide during the day in dark places, coming out at night to forage. Depriving them of what they need by good housekeeping methods may help to get rid of them, so clean out closets and clutter where they may hide, and check to see that there are no leaks that may provide moisture. Because cockroaches can transmit disease to humans, it is wise to keep a roach killer on hand to get rid of these insects quickly. Always use such commercial preparations cautiously if there are children in the house.

Fleas feed on animal or human blood; they cannot breed or survive without it. Their painful, itchy bites may cause discomfort for a week or longer. Some species are more dangerous than others since they can transmit to man the dreaded bubonic plague and other diseases.

The female flea lays her eggs on a furry pet. The eggs fall off and hatch in places where the pet spends most of its time, such as a chair, sofa, rug, carpet, the pet's bed, or a basement floor. Because the larval fleas that hatch from these eggs develop to maturity in floor cracks and other hiding places, a home may become heavily infested with developing larvae before the infestation is even noticed.

Adult fleas that result from the developing larvae can live several weeks without food. This explains why people who own cats or dogs having fleas sometimes return from a vacation and find their homes overrun with fleas, even though none were detected in the house before.

Fleas in the home can be controlled by a combination of good housekeeping and the use of an insecticide. Clean infested rooms thoroughly with a vacuum cleaner; go over baseboards, floor cracks, carpets, rugs, upholstered furniture, and other places where eggs or larvae may be lodged. Then apply a nonstaining insecticide that you know is harmless to pets and people.

Be sure to treat those places in the home where your pet habitually sleeps. You may need to repeat the treatment in a week.

The best way to prevent flea infestations is to control fleas on the pets. Commercial flea collars, sprays, and powders can be purchased in supermarkets, pet shops, and variety stores.

Houseflies constitute about 98 percent of the flies that invade the home. They are very unwelcome guests because they breed in decaying organic matter and feed on manure, garbage, and the food on our tables. They contaminate everything they touch and spread many human diseases. To keep houseflies out, be sure the screens in your windows and doors are in good repair. See that screened doors swing outward. In humid climates, screens of copper, aluminum, bronze, plastic, or rust-resisting alloy should be used. In dry climates, galvanized screening will do. If only a few flies are present, use a fly swatter instead of an insecticide; but if an insecticide is needed, make sure it is formulated specifically for flying insects.

Mosquitoes are annoying not only because of the noise they make, but also because they inflict itching bites and can transmit deadly diseases.

In most parts of the United States, mosquitoes breed during spring, summer, and fall. In some southern areas, they breed all year round. Females lay their eggs on stagnant water or in places that later become flooded. Therefore, to help eliminate mosquitoes around your house, eliminate standing water. Remove unneeded water containers and dis-carded automobile tires, and clean out rain gutters. Fill tree holes with concrete, and see that cisterns, cesspools, septic tanks, fire barrels, rain barrels, and tubs in which water is stored are tightly covered. You might even look for mosquito larvae (wigglers) in the water in flower vases and in the saucers under potted plants.

If it is necessary to use an insecticide, be sure to get the type made for flying insects.

Pantry pests. There are several kinds of insects that can infest the dry food products you keep in your pantry or kitchen cupboards. Almost all dry packaged foods are susceptible, including spices, particularly red pepper, paprika, and chili powder. Although these pests are usually called ''weevils,'' they can include beetles or moth larvae.

To prevent pantry pests, keep shelves clean and free of spills. Inspect food packages and their contents before you use them. Store dry foods in clean metal or glass containers that have tight-fitting lids.

Spiders may be frightening, but most that are found in the United States are harmless to humans. They destroy many injurious household insects and are therefore useful. The two exceptions are the black widow and the brown recluse spider (see page 104).

To control spiders, remove loose brick, wood, tile, or trash from around the yard or basement where the spiders may live or hide. Use a stick or broom to knock down webs, spiders, and egg sacs, and then crush them underfoot.

If the infestation is heavy enough to warrant it, apply a spray designed especially to kill spiders. Be careful that you do not spray spiders over-head. Although a spider hit by the spray may drop down, it may still be capable of biting for some time.

Ticks. The brown dog tick is the only type of tick usually found in homes. After feeding on the dog, these ticks hide in cracks and crevices, under carpets and rugs, in upholstered furniture, and behind baseboards. There the female lays her eggs. Each successive generation eventually finds the dog, feeds on its blood, and drops off to seek hiding places in which to keep the cycle going. Although brown dog ticks rarely bite humans and do not carry human diseases, their presence in the home is uncomfortable, particularly for the dog.

Treat the dog first (see page 158). Then have a professional exterminator rid the house of these pests.

HOUSEPLANTS NEED FIRST AID

Plants, like people and pets, are subject to illnesses and injuries. Each has its own characteristic temperature requirements and tolerances to heat and cold. The right diagnosis and quick action may save the life of a dying plant and restore its beauty.

Sudden collapse. When a plant collapses suddenly, it may be suffering from too little or too much water or overfertilization.

If the plant has gone without water for several days, a generous watering will almost always bring it back to normal. Soaking a plant with too much water, however, will rot the roots and cause the plant to collapse, so be sure the pots have adequate drainage and that water doesn't pool on top of the soil.

Overfertilization could also be the cause of the problem. Dry fertilizers are not recommended for houseplants because they tend to remain in the soil, build up, and eventually poison the roots. If white deposits accumulate on the surface of the soil, remove all the soil from the pot and replace it with a fresh supply. When clay pots turn white and crusty, it means they are loaded with insoluble fertilizer that is toxic to the roots. Replace such pots and throw them away. Breaking them up and using them as drainage material will still poison the plants, even if you have washed and cleaned the pots thoroughly.

Crooked growth. Houseplants and window-box plants often grow crooked in their effort to reach the light. If you place aluminum foil behind them, the light will be reflected and the plants will straighten out. Or, you can turn them weekly.

Fluorescent lamps, controlled by a time clock, can be used to supplement sunlight for a 16-hour day or to treat crooked plants.

Spindly growth. A plant that is too skinny and frail may be suffering from a sunlight, fertilizer, or oxygen deficiency or from too much heat. Put the plant in the sun or use a fluorescent lamp if lack of light appears to be the cause. Use a water-soluble fertilizer according to directions, and keep the plant away from heat. Night temperatures that are comfortable for people—65 to 70 degrees F.—are also good for plants.

Failure to flower. Proper light and fertilizer are also needed if a plant is to flower. Some blooming plants, such as poinsettia and chrysanthemums, will not bloom if exposed to artificial light all through the night. Blooming plants, such as chrysanthemums and gardenias, like night temperatures of from 60 to 65 degrees.

Attacked by insects. If your houseplants are attacked by insects or aphids, use a nontoxic pesticide that is harmless to humans and pets, or wash the leaves with a mild solution of soap and water.

Drooping, discolored, or spotted leaves. A plant with yellow leaves or a drooping stem is suffering from wet roots so cut down on watering. If the leaves turn brown on top, you may have fertilized the plant too much, or exposed it to the cold. (See also **Sudden collapse,** page 123.)

Freezing or burning will kill the leaf and cause it to blacken. Remember to keep the temperature between 60 and 75 degrees, depending on the type of plant. Blackened leaves can also be caused by insects or by insufficient fertilizer or light.

Splashing leaves with too much water, or with water that is hot or very cold, may cause spots. Sometimes too much direct sunlight will also cause speckling.

Loss of foliage. If there is a loss of foliage, the plant may not be getting enough water, or you may be giving it too much fertilizer. Sometimes, leaves fall off if a plant is subject to sudden changes of temperature.

If you must leave them. To keep plants moist while you are away on vacation, give them a good dousing, then cover each one with a clear plastic bag. (One that comes from the dry cleaner is good for a large plant.) Allow a little air space all around, and close up the end of the bag at the base. Keep the plant out of direct sunlight to avoid excessive heat. The humidity inside the bag will keep a plant moist for about two weeks.

ODORS

Just as pleasant fragrances can create a lovely atmosphere, obnoxious odors can cause an unpleasant one. Some odors can be dispelled easily with an aerosol air freshener. Others are difficult to remove in a hurry, but here are some hints for clearing the air.

Garbage disposer odors. See **GARBAGE DISPOSER,** page 21.

Musty odor is caused by the condensation of warm, moist air on cooler surfaces and by the subsequent growth of mold (or mildew) spores that thrive in dampness.

The first thing to do is to ventilate the area. Open the windows and use an electric fan if necessary, to ensure a brisk flow of air.

Moisture in the air can be removed either by a dehumidifier, heating unit, or air conditioner. If such appliances are not available, there are still ways to dry the area. In closets and other small areas, an electric light burning continuously will be sufficient to remove dampness. (Make sure the light bulb is placed at a sufficient distance from fabrics to prevent the possibility of fire.)

Chemicals that absorb moisture from the air include silica gel, activated alumina, and calcium chloride available in department stores, drugstores, and building supply stores under various trade names.

Scrub cement floors and tiled walls with household chlorine bleach. Use ½ to 1 cup of bleach to a gallon of water. Rinse with clear water and wipe as dry as possible. Keep windows open until walls and floors are thoroughly dry.

Commercial disinfectant aerosol sprays work well and are available in grocery and drugstores. They kill spores and therefore destroy the source of the odor. The area must be kept dry to prevent a recurrence of the problem.

Refrigerator odors. For an instant refrigerator deodorant, fill a small bowl with charcoal—the kind used for potted plants—and place it on a shelf in the refrigerator. It will rapidly absorb odors.

Absorbent cotton saturated with extract of vanilla will do an effective job, too. So will an open box of baking soda.

Skunks emit one of the most pungent odors on earth. If the odor becomes attached to clothes that are washable, dip them in a tub of water to which you have added a small can or bottle of tomato juice. Then rinse and put clothes in the dryer or hang them in the warmest part of the house. The heat will help to dissipate what little skunk odor remains after washing. (For handling skunk odor on pets, see page 157).

PESTS

No matter how great an animal lover you are, there are some pesty creatures you would rather not have around the house. Here are the ones that are most bothersome and a few hints on how to outwit them.

Bats may enter a home and establish a roost in the attic, in a space between the walls, or in an unused part of an upper story. They make annoying night noises, smell terrible, and may be carriers of rabies. At night, when bats leave their nesting place, plug up their reentry holes with sheet metal or ¼-inch mesh hardware cloth. Spread flake naphthalene or mothballs liberally in the infested area. If this fails, call a professional exterminator.

Never handle a live bat. You may be exposed to rabies (see page 113). Wear rubber gloves when picking up and destroying dead bats.

Mice usually migrate from outdoor areas into homes when the weather turns cold in the fall. They are annoying pests because they eat or contaminate human food and damage fabrics, wood, and other materials. They can also transmit several human diseases.

To control mice, first seal any holes in the walls, floors, and house foundations; see that no food is left where mice can get at it.

If there are only a few mice in your home, you can handle the problem yourself by getting traps at a hardware or department store and placing them along walls and near holes. Position them at right angles to the wall so the trigger mechanism will intercept the mouse's probable route of travel.

One of the best baits to use in snap traps is peanut butter smeared over the trigger surface. Other good baits are cake, flour, bacon, nut meats, cheese, and soft candies, particularly milk chocolate and gumdrops. Baited traps are a hazard if there are small children in the house, so use them with extreme care or not at all if you feel there is any danger. For large infestations of mice, get professional help.

Rats are dangerous creatures because they bite, transmit human diseases, destroy property, and contaminate human food. If cornered, they attack people or pets.

They enter homes to find food and shelter, so be careful to leave no food in open places, or even in closed cardboard boxes. Place garbage and refuse in tightly covered metal containers (rats can gnaw through plastic ones).

Keep storage places orderly and clean. In the basement and storerooms, stack lumber, boxes, cartons, and other objects at least 1 foot above the floor.

If your house has double walls and spaces between ceilings and the floors below, make sure these areas are tightly sealed—they are favorite hiding places for rats.

It is very difficult to rid your home of rats. Traps may be used but they require patience and skill, and the bait used may be as dangerous as the rats.

About all you can do is seal all holes in exterior walls and see that spaces around windows, doors, and other openings are no larger than ¼ inch. Call your local board of health, which may have an extermination program, or call a professional exterminator.

Woodpeckers. The constant rat-a-tat-tat of a woodpecker is annoying, and the pecking can cause damage to the roof or siding of a house as well.

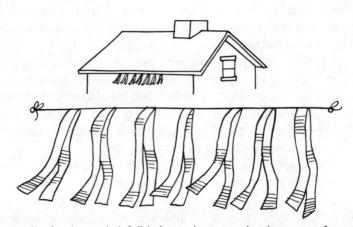

A device made of string and tinfoil helps to keep woodpeckers away from the house.

126

To keep them away, try this device (see illustration on page 126). Take a string about 32 inches long and tear aluminum foil into strips about 2 inches wide and 36 inches long. Fold and twist the strips over the string about an inch apart so that they blow in the breeze. Then tie the string or tack it to the edges of the roof on each side of the house. The fluttering foil should keep the birds away, but if this method fails, call your state extension service for advice.

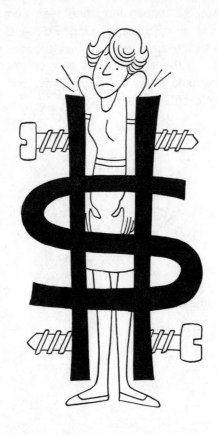

money emergencies

Next to health emergencies, money emergencies are probably the most serious. They can range from the loss of a wallet containing a few dollars to bankruptcy.

A national survey showed that people misplace, destroy, or supply to pickpockets about two billion dollars a year. More than half can't remember how or where the money was lost.

Something that makes money emergencies an ever-increasing hazard, is credit—easy credit. Credit is a service, and as such it costs money. It can be used wisely to buy now and pay later, or it can be used unwisely with the result that you spend more money than you will earn or save in the near future.

This chapter is not meant as a substitute for professional advice. Fortunately, most money emergencies can usually be solved with proper guidance from a lawyer or an accountant. There are also many agencies and institutions, including banks, the Veterans Administration, the Red Cross, and the Federal Housing Administration that will help you cope intelligently with money emergencies.

VITAL INFORMATION

Filling out the following "Family Data Bank" forms will make information immediately available in the event of an emergency such as the serious illness or injury, mental incompetence, or death of family members who normally take care of financial and business matters.

There are also many other situations in which such immediate information would be a convenience—when selling a home or car, for instance, or applying for a loan or insurance coverage; even when someone needs to locate a birth certificate or fill out a form for college.

This record and the lists to which it refers should be updated periodically and kept in a desk or bureau drawer that is accessible to all adult members of the family. As an added precaution, have a photocopy made, and put it with your valuable papers in a bank vault or safe, or give it to your attorney or a relative not living in your home.

FAMILY DATA BANK

HUSBAND'S NAME _____

Legal Address _____

City _____ State _____ Zip _____

Social Security Number _____

Date of Birth _____ Place of Birth _____

WIFE'S NAME _____

Legal Address _____

City _____ State _____ Zip _____

Social Security Number _____

Date of Birth _____ Place of Birth _____

Date of Marriage _____ Place of Marriage _____

CHILDREN'S RECORD

Name	Date of Birth	Place of Birth	Soc. Security No.

money emergencies

Children Not living at Home, Addresses _____

_____

_____

LOCATION OF IMPORTANT FAMILY RECORDS (Birth Certificates, Marriage License, Discharge Papers, Naturalization Papers, if any, Baptismal Certificates, etc.)
If not in the same place, specify location of each _____

_____

_____

_____

BANK ACCOUNTS
Bank (or S&L)   Acct No.   Savings   Checking   Savings Certificate

_____

_____

U.S. GOVERNMENT SAVINGS BONDS:
Registered in the name(s) of _____

_____

_____

Location of the list of these bonds and their serial numbers _____

_____

STOCKS AND BONDS
A record of purchases and a list showing the location of these securities may be found

_____

_____

_____

INSURANCE
Hospitalization   Name of Insured   Company   Policy No.

_____

_____

Medical / Surgical   Name of Insured   Company   Policy No.

_____

Location of these policies _____

LIFE INSURANCE

Name of Insured	Name of Company	Policy No.

Location of these policies _____

OTHER INSURANCE (accident, automobile, personal liability, etc.)

Name of Insured	Type of Insurance	Company	Policy No.

Location of these policies _____

EMPLOYMENT AND BUSINESS INTERESTS

Husband's employer is (or was, if retired) _____

Address _____

He is a participant in:

Pension Plan	Yes	No
Profit Sharing Plan	Yes	No
Group Life Insurance	Yes	No

Other (e.g., deferred compensation, stock options, etc.)_____

Wife's employer is (or was, if retired)_____

Address _____

She is a participant in:

Pension Plan	Yes	No
Profit Sharing Plan	Yes	No
Group Life Insurance	Yes	No

Other (e.g., deferred compensation, stock options, etc.) _____

_____

_____

_____

PERSONAL PROPERTY:

Automobile make _____ Year _____

Registered in the name of _____

Location of title papers _____

Automobile make _____ Year _____

Registered in the name of _____

Location of title papers _____

REAL ESTATE:

Own home or apartment   Yes   No

There is a balance on the mortgage of about $_____ at this date _____

Mortgage holder _____

Rent home or apartment   Yes   No

Name of landlord _____

Address of landlord _____

Other property owned   Yes   No

Location _____

_____

There is a balance of the mortgage(s) of about $_____ at this date _____

Mortgage holder _____

_____

OTHER BUSINESS INTERESTS   Yes   No

Whom to contact _____

Address _____

Location of business agreements _____

PERSONAL CREDITORS (if any)   Address

_____

_____

PERSONAL DEBTORS (if any)   Address

_____

_____

Location of copies of loans & agreements, or contracts _____

_____

OTHER ASSETS _____

_____

_____

Location of papers_____

OTHER LIABILITIES_____

Location of papers_____

LOCATION OF SAFE DEPOSIT BOX _____

Holder of second key _____

LOCATION OF RECORDS FOR TAX INFORMATION _____

LOCATION OF HUSBAND'S WILL _____

Date filed _____

LOCATION OF WIFE'S WILL _____

Date filed _____

LOCATION OF DEED FOR CEMETERY PLOT _____

money emergencies

RELATIVES TO BE NOTIFIED IN CASE OF DEATH

Name   Address   Telephone Number

_____

_____

_____

_____

_____

_____

_____

_____

PERSONS TO CONTACT (if for any reason you are unable to act for yourself)

Attorney _____ Address _____

_____ Telephone number _____

Accountant _____ Address _____

_____ Telephone number _____

Banker _____ Address _____

_____ Telephone number _____

Broker _____ Address _____

_____ Telephone number _____

Clergyman _____ Address _____

_____ Telephone number _____

Doctor _____ Address _____

_____ Telephone number _____

Employer _____ Address _____

_____ Telephone number _____

Executor of estate_____ Address_____

_____ Telephone number_____

Insurance agent _____ Address _____

_____ Telephone number_____

CAN'T AFFORD COLLEGE

No one who is qualified needs to be kept from attending college because of lack of funds. The first thing to do is consult the high school counselor and explain the financial situation. The counselor may offer suggestions. In addition, the student should study one of the many directories and choose one or more of the colleges listed. If the school selected offers no free tuition, a letter should be sent to the college explaining the applicant's interest in the school, the lack of funds, and asking what scholarships and loan plans are available. Admissions officials know the ins and outs of financing an education and are very helpful. Some colleges administer their own loan funds, which usually carry low interest rates.

The Federal Guaranteed Student Loan Program offers loans to students, Preference is given to families with incomes under $15,000 a year, although this figure is expected to be liberalized. Having more than one child in college at a time may make a family with an income above the limit eligible. Loans under this program are obtained through local banking institutions participating in the program.

The majority of banks offer special loans for educational purposes. Rates vary from about 6 to 12 percent simple interest. If the loan is made directly to the student and not to the parents, interest charges and repayment usually do not begin until after graduation.

A number of private finance companies specialize in student loans. Many of them are approved by colleges. Such firms pay the college bills as they come due, requiring the borrower to repay in 48 or 60 monthly installments. They are certainly more expensive than most bank and college loans, but they do provide a means of breaking up the usual two or three large bills per year into equal monthly payments. However, the borrower must proceed with caution and make sure the tuition deferment plan doesn't run interest costs way up.

The National Association of College Admission Counselors has a listing of books on financial aid for college educations. The association's address is: 9933 Lawler Ave., Skokie, Ill. 60076.

CHILD LOSES MONEY

When your child loses money, sympathize with him or her, and discuss it calmly even if the cause was carelessness. Think of the loss in the child's terms. Try not to be upset over what it might mean to the

135

family. Find out how it happened. Did it accidentally slip out of a pocket? Was it put in a safe place? Suggest ways to prevent future losses. If the money was for something important such as carfare to school, or money for lunch, replace it without scolding. If it was money that the child would have spent on something of his or her own choice, let the child do without money until the next allowance comes due.

CONDEMNATION OF PROPERTY

When a government agency seeks to condemn your property under the "Right of Eminent Domain," which means the right to build a public facility such as a school, bridge, or park, it may be difficult to fight, but you can try. Hire a lawyer (see page 60) and seek out a local civic group that might have an interest in the situation such as a civil rights or neighborhood association. Watch for the announcement of public hearings and make your voice heard at any hearings that are held. Write to your legislators.

If you find that you will have to accept condemnation, do not agree to the government's offer right away and don't sign anything! Hire at least two reputable real estate appraisers, and ask them to appraise the value of your property. They will charge a small fee. Check on what your neighbors are getting for their property, if they must sell. Should there be a dispute over the price, have your lawyer request a review by commission, which is required in every state. The commission will review your case and place a value on the property. If either you or the government are unwilling to accept the commission's ruling, your case may have to go to court. Get an estimate of the court and lawyer's fees before the case goes to trial. It may be wiser to settle for the government's price.

CREDIT DENIED

Should your application for credit be turned down by a merchant or organization, you have recourse under Federal law. You have a right to ask for a copy of the credit report upon which the turn-down was based. Furthermore, if something is incorrect in the report, you have a right, under the Fair Credit Act of 1971, to a reinvestigation of credit rating. If the agency agrees that the report is not correct, you are entitled to learn the names of everyone who received reports on your credit within the past six months (or within the last two years if the reports were for employment purposes). If you request it, the agency must (at no cost to you) notify those who received the incorrect reports that certain information is erroneous.

Even if the agency who evaluates your credit rating does not agree that a change in the report is justified, it is required, at your request, to send out your version of the disputed information. They must send it to any names you choose from the list of those who received the original report (within the time limits mentioned above). However, you will have to pay a reasonable fee for this service.

For further information, contact the local office of the Federal Trade Commission, which should be listed under United States offices in your phone book.

DEBT

Here is some advice about avoiding credit pitfalls and what to do if you find you have overused credit or cannot, because of some unfortunate circumstance, pay your creditors.

Installment contracts. A little caution before signing a contract can save a lot of trouble later. Keep the following rules in mind:

> Never sign a blank contract or a contract in which there are any blank spaces.
> Never sign a contract if the salesman offers to "hold it" until you make up your mind. In some cases, the contract will be executed before you put your pen away.
> Never sign a contract without reading it, including the so-called "fine print." Check amounts, dates, and terms.

The Federal Truth in Lending Law requires the seller to inform the buyer in writing on the installment contract of all the financial terms involved in the sale. This includes not only the cash price, but also the amount of the finance charge (interest), both as a percent of the total sale price and as a total dollars and cents figure. This amount (deferred payment price) is almost always larger than the original cash price.

Some states have instituted a "cooling off" period of from one to three days to give you a chance to change your mind after you've signed a contract for an installment plan.

The Federal government protects the homeowner who puts up his or her home as security for an installment plan. This often occurs in home improvement deals. However, the homeowner is only protected to the extent that within three business days after signing the contract, he has the right to cancel without penalty.

Installment creditors. Do not expect to erase your debts by returning merchandise you bought on credit. In many cases, you have signed two contracts, one for the purchase of the goods, and one for the loan of the funds to buy it. Your contract may be sold to a bank or finance company at a discount, and you will owe the money to that institution instead of to the dealer. In some cases, you may find that the bank or finance company to whom your contract was sold is under no obligation to make good on faulty merchandise, but you are nevertheless required to pay for the goods. Some states now have laws to deal with this situation and other states and the Federal government have similar laws pending. These laws state that the bank or finance company will not be allowed to collect money from the buyer if the buyer has a justifiable reason for not paying. One objective of the law is to encourage the bank or finance company to put pressure on the seller of the merchandise to make repairs or to allow credits where necessary. If you are not protected by such laws, check contracts before you sign them for the telltale statement "The seller reserves the right to sell the finance contract to a third party," or ask if the contract will be sold. If so, try to have a clause inserted saying that anyone purchasing the contract will be responsible if the merchandise is faulty.

If you are planning to move, and you are about to sign an installment contract, consider that some states will not allow you to take mortgaged goods such as appliances across state lines.

What action the creditor can take. Most installment contracts have the provision that you can be charged an extra fee if you are late or delinquent in paying your debts.

If the seller refers your case to an attorney, you may be charged an attorney's fee plus court costs plus charges of a court officer such as a marshal or sheriff if such services are required for repossession (see below). Some states control the amount of these fees. Check, if you find you are in this predicament. Seek legal advice the moment a summons is received if the seller sues. See page 60 if advice cannot be obtained from a private attorney. A summons to appear in court must be answered even if you think you should not be sued.

Repossession. The holder of the installment contract can, if you default, reposses the item and sell it to satisfy your debt. However, if the money does not cover the original debt plus "repossession" costs, the holder may sue you in an effort to collect the rest.

Garnishment of wages. To satisfy a debt, a creditor may get a court order that forces your employer to turn over a portion of your paycheck until the debt is cleared. The amount that may be taken varies in individual states. The new Federal Truth in Lending Law contains a section that restricts garnishments to a maximum 25 percent of salary and provides that a paycheck of $48 or less, after deductions, cannot be garnisheed by creditors. Unfortunately, the Federal act provides that if states have their own such laws, the creditors are exempt from the Federal provision. Some states allow the creditors to take almost the whole paycheck.

If you believe you have been treated unfairly or defrauded on an installment plan, contact your state attorney general's office.

If you find you cannot pay. First, get expert advice from your banker, accountant, lawyer, loan agency, welfare department, or the Legal Aid Society. (See page 60.) You, or a counselor acting on your behalf, may contact your creditors and ask them to extend the time for payments. Many creditors will agree to such a plan to avoid the expense of collection and court costs. In most states, the lender is entitled to extra payments for extending the time.

Loans. You may be able to consolidate your debts and pay off what you owe in small, monthly payments. When you do, a bank or loan agency lends you enough to pay your bills and then allows you to stretch out the new loan payments so your monthly obligations will be reduced to a point at which you can handle them. A loan company is easier about credit but charges more than a bank. In any event, it will cost you more money in the long run to pay off your debts this way, so don't do it unless it is really necessary.

Bankruptcy. When nothing else can help, a person may declare bankruptcy in federal court. There are two types of bankruptcy—voluntary, in which a debtor files a petition asking to be adjuged bankrupt; and involuntary, in which creditors ask the court to help them recover part of what they are owed. More than 90 percent of all bankruptcies are voluntary.

There is a fee for filing a bankruptcy petition which can be paid in six monthly installments. The moment the petition is filed, the debtor is declared bankrupt, and creditors must stop hounding him. At the end of six months, barring fraud or deception, the court grants a discharge from bankruptcy, and all the debtors debts are wiped out. However, all his property, with exceptions, such as household furniture and clothing, will be sold, and the proceeds apportioned among the creditors.

Bankruptcy laws vary among states. A person should always obtain a lawyer, if possible, although he may act as his own lawyer if he wishes.

A debtor is permitted to file only one voluntary bankruptcy petition within a six-year period.

DISABILITY

When disability occurs, it may affect a family's financial security more than the retirement or even the death of its principal breadwinner.

Private disability insurance is sometimes included in work contracts. An employer or union can supply information on this. If you are self-employed, consult your insurance agent. Certain disability benefits may be included in either your life or health insurance contracts.

In cases of long-term disability, the local social security office should be contacted. Monthly benefits because of disability are available to:

> Disabled workers under 65 years old and their families.
> Children of disabled or deceased workers who are themselves disabled. These children must have been disabled *before* the age of 18 years. When they reach 18 years, they are then eligible for disability payments under social security.
> Disabled widows, disabled dependent widowers, and under certain conditions, disabled surviving divorced wives of workers who were insured at death. These benefits are now payable beginning at the age of 50.

A worker is considered disabled under the social security law if there is a physical or mental condition that prevents him from doing any substantial gainful work, and is expected to last (or has lasted) for at least 12 months, or is expected to result in death.

The amount of the monthly disability benefit is based on average earnings under social security over a period of years.

A person who applies for benefits because of disability will be asked to provide medical evidence to support the claim. The social security office assists applicants in requesting these reports and helps fill out the application.

DISABLED, AGED, OR BLIND

If social security payments do not meet the basic living requirements of the disabled, aged, or blind, there is a federalized program with national standards of eligibility entitled Supplemental Security Income. There is one flat monthly rate nationwide. However, if cost of living is higher in a state, the state may supplement the Federal program. In some states, if you are eligible for Supplemental Security Income, you also automatically become eligible for Medicaid. Since additional benefits vary from state to state, check with your nearest Social Security office.

DISASTER

A disaster—a fire, flood, hurricane, tornado, explosion, or any other sudden, tragic event, can wipe out all your assets. In such a case, immediately report your loss to your insurance company, and notify appropriate community service agencies (see page 204). These organizations offer food, clothing, temporary shelter, and emergency medical and nursing care. They also offer financial assistance in helping people to return to normal living.

Foreclosure. See **MORTGAGE FORECLOSURE, page 145.**

FORGED CHECK

The bank may be responsible when an imposter or forger cashes your check. The bank may also be responsible if the amount on your check is raised by someone and the bank cashes the check. When you examine your bank statement and cancelled checks, if you find a discrepancy and a forged signature or a raised amount on a check, you must appear at the bank and sign an affidavit of forgery. Then the bank will try to correct the situation. If the bank does not accept responsibility, consult a lawyer or the Legal Aid Society. To prevent someone from raising the amount on your check, you should write the amount, and then fill the rest of the space (at the left or right of the amount) with a wavy line.

GI BENEFITS NEEDED

A veteran of the armed services, or a member of a veteran's family who wants to apply for benefits, should contact the Veterans Administration offices. Counselors there offer advice and help in obtaining benefits. The Veterans Administration cooperates with other community organizations and individuals in offering veterans employment counseling and helping them to readjust to civilian life.

LOST BANKBOOK

Although banks vary in their requirements, you should report the loss immediately by phone, so a ban against withdrawals is put on the account. Usually you will have to appear at the bank in person to sign a paper saying that the bankbook is lost. Depending upon the bank's rules, you will then have to wait from two weeks to a month before you receive a new bankbook. Most banks will make arrangements in cases of need, to allow you to withdraw money from the account during the waiting period, but they discourage this practice.

LOST CASH

Report the loss to the police—you may be pleasantly surprised to find that someone has turned in your money.

Check with your insurance agent since you may be covered, or partly covered. If you are not, you will have to take the loss. Any such loss in excess of $100 that has not been repaid by insurance is tax deductible, provided you have properly reported it to the police.

LOST CHECK

If a check is lost or stolen, it is not the same as if money is lost or stolen. Checks can be cashed only when endorsed or signed by the named payee. If the bank cashes a check for an imposter, the bank is liable.

To avoid losing a check, keep a record of those you receive and those you deposit. Write on the back of each check sent to your savings or checking account: "Pay to the order of _____" (give the name of the bank) or "For deposit only." Include your account number and name.

If you lose a check issued to you, ask the person or the firm that issued it to stop payment immediately and request that another be issued.

If you lose a check drawn on your own account, notify your bank and ask that payment be stopped on the check. The bank will probably ask you to fill out a form giving the number and amount of the check, its date, the name of the person to whom it is payable, and the reason for stopping payment. There may be a fee for the "stop payment order." Once the bank has your request, your account record is flagged and bank personnel are notified not to make payment on the check.

LOST CREDIT CARD

The company that issued the credit card must be notified of its loss immediately. Law requires that all credit cards issued since April, 1971, must be accompanied by a self-addressed, prestamped notification form to be mailed by the consumer to the company in the event of loss or theft. Keep these notification forms in a safe place. If your cards were issued before the 1971 date, or if you have lost the forms, make a list of all your credit cards with the name, address, and telephone number of each issuing company, and the account number on the card. Put the list away where you can find it easily. When a wallet or purse is stolen, it may be difficult to remember all the cards.

If you do not have the notification form, notify the company by registered mail, and retain a copy of your notifying letter.

There are credit card insurance companies that will, for a small premium, protect you against loss from unauthorized use of your credit card. This protection is also available as a rider to your regular liability or all-risk insurance policy. You will have to consider whether the premium is worth it since you are responsible for the first $50 on each lost card by Federal law. If you have many cards, it probably is. If you have just a few, it probably isn't.

LOST INSURANCE POLICY

Notify your insurance agent as soon as possible. He will have you sign a "lost policy release," and then the company will issue a duplicate or new policy. To avoid losses, keep insurance policies in a bank vault, or in a fireproof, waterproof box.

LOST OR STOLEN JEWELRY

When jewelry is lost or stolen, report it to the police immediately. If the loss was in a public place, the jewelry may have been brought to police headquarters. If it was stolen, the police may have been notified that an attempt to pawn it was made.

If jewelry is lost or stolen while you are traveling, report the loss to someone in charge where it occurred. Write down the time and place you first noticed the loss and the name of the person to whom you reported the loss.

If the jewelry is insured, notify the insurance agent handling your policy as soon as possible. Phone or send a telegram if you are traveling. The agent will fill out a claim and may settle it if the payment due (above the deductible) is relatively small. Otherwise, he will notify the insurance company and a claims adjuster will investigate the circumstances of the loss and determine the amount to be paid on the claim.

Valuable jewelry should, of course, be insured even though this type of insurance is expensive. If feasible, it should be protected separately beyond the limits of the basic homeowner's policy to recover the full value if it is lost or stolen. If your jewelry is not insured, or not insured to its full value, the uncompensated loss may be tax deductible. Contact your accountant or the local office of the Internal Revenue Service.

LOST STOCK CERTIFICATE OR STOCK OWNED BY A DECEASED PERSON

State rather than Federal laws deal with the loss of stock certificates and the transfer in the event of a death.

142

Generally, a bank acts as the transfer agent. The name of the bank will be written on the stock certificate. If the certificate is lost and you cannot remember the name, the stockbroker or the issuing company can give you the information. If the stock is listed on the New York Stock Exchange, the transfer agent is required to be located in New York City.

If the stock is in the name of a deceased person, contact the transfer agent, and you will be told what forms and proof are needed.

If the stock is lost, the agent will put a "stop" on the certificate to prevent its sale. You may then be required to furnish the company with a perpetual indemnity bond covering any losses it might incur by re-issuing the certificate. This bond, issued by a surety firm acceptable to the company, ordinarily costs approximately 4 percent of the certificate's current market value.

MONEY NEEDED AFTER BANKS ARE CLOSED

On weekends, holidays, or in the evening, it may be difficult to obtain cash in a hurry. If you know your supermarket manager or druggist, or any other business that stays open at times when most banks are closed, you might ask them to cash a check. In some cities there are money dispensing machines that require only a special credit card. You simply put the card in the machine and it will dispense anywhere from $25 to $100 in cash. You will be billed later, just as you are for other credit card charges. It is a wise idea to keep several small-denomination travelers' checks at home. They can be cashed easily, and if they are stolen, you will be compensated for the loss by the company issuing the checks. Be sure to keep a record of the check numbers in a separate place.

MONEY NEEDS TO BE SENT FAST

Money may be sent by telegram for a nominal cost—a money order fee plus telegram tolls. If you have a charge account with Western Union, you may make special arrangements to send telegraphic money orders over the telephone or Western Union tie-line without a cash deposit. Otherwise, you will have to pay at a Western Union office before the "moneygram" is sent.

Western Union will also send money overseas, but it will take several days and not all offices are willing to make the arrangements.

If you are the person receiving the money, you will be notified by Western Union as soon as the money has arrived or they will deliver the funds within the United States. After identifying yourself, you will receive cash or a check that any bank will honor upon identification.

A bank in which you have an account will also arrange to transfer funds both within and without the United States. If the transfer must be made rapidly, you will have to pay an additional telegram or cable charge. (See also **OUT OF FUNDS OVERSEAS,** page 199.)

MORTGAGES

A home mortgage is an arrangement whereby your home becomes the "collateral" or security for a loan. Mortgage loans are usually repaid in equal monthly installments over a period of from 10 to 30 years. The "principal" is the amount of money you borrow. The "interest" is the charge for borrowing the money, and the "amortization" is that part of each installment applied in reduction of the principal.

Seek legal advice (see page 60) before signing a mortgage contract, and never sign any mortgage deal that has a "demand clause," if you can avoid it. A demand clause calls for payment of the outstanding balance on demand, on 30 to 60 days' notice, or some other forced payment plan. The demand may come when it is impossible for you to meet it, and you can lose your home or suffer other serious financial difficulties.

HOW MUCH OF A MORTGAGE CAN YOU AFFORD?

Experts say that a family may safely purchase a home for a price about double its yearly income. However, such a general figure does not include the family that has a mother-in-law, a maiden aunt, and twelve children to support. Because of extra expenses, a family may not be able to afford such a mortgage.

The staff of the agency from which you seek funds will help you to determine how much of a mortgage you can afford. As with any purchase, however, it pays to shop for the best mortgage deal. Generally, the larger your down payment, and the shorter the term of the loan, the less total interest you will have to pay.

WHERE TO OBTAIN A MORTGAGE

There are at least five types of institutions that provide mortgage money: savings and loan associations, savings banks, mortgage companies, commercial banks, and insurance companies. Rates vary so much among these types of institutions that you would be wise to shop around.

Conventional mortgage. Usually you have to be a better credit risk for a conventional mortgage than for a Veterans Administration loan or a Federal Housing Authority loan, mentioned later in this chapter.

The interest rate of this type of loan may or may not be higher than on FHA and VA loans, so check the terms. Generally, you will have to pay off a conventional loan in 20 or 25 years, whereas government-backed loans may extend over 35 years. Furthermore, government-backed loans require very little or no down payment whereas conventional loans usually require at least 10 percent on new homes, and more on older homes. One advantage, however, is that up to a certain point banks tend to reduce the interest rates on conventional loans in proportion to the size of the down payment; in other words, the higher the down payment, the lower the interest rate may be.

Federal Housing Authority loan. Under an FHA loan, a home buyer makes a small down payment and obtains a mortgage for the rest of the purchase price. The mortgage loan is made by a bank, savings and loan association, mortgage company, insurance company, or other FHA-approved lender, and is insured by the FHA. It is not technically a government loan, although the FHA is a government agency.

The FHA protects the lender against loss on the mortgage. For this reason, the lender may allow more liberal mortgage terms than the home buyer might otherwise be able to obtain, although not always. The FHA requires that the borrower have a good credit record, the cash needed for the down payment at the closing of the home purchase, and enough steady income to make the monthly payments without difficulty. The FHA sets no upper age limit or income level for the borrower.

The FHA states that the property must at least meet certain minimum standards: the house must be livable, soundly built, and suitably located in regard to the site and neighborhood. This is an added protection to the purchaser.

Furthermore, in FHA loans there is no prepayment penalty clause that requires the borrower to pay additional interest if he or she decides to pay off the entire mortgage in advance.

There are mortgage bankers who will locate an FHA-insured loan for you for a fee. Ask your banker about it—he may be a mortgage banker or know where you can locate one.

Veterans Administration loan. A Veterans Administration loan is about equal to the FHA loan in rates. The VA guarantees up to 60 percent of a mortgage loan to eligible veterans (up to a fixed maximum) and in many cases permits a veteran to buy a home without a down payment. Because the VA allows lenders to charge ''points'' (such as a dollar per $100 of mortgage amount), a VA loan can be as expensive as a conventional mortgage, unless the builder absorbs the points, which is frequently done. There is no penalty for prepayment of a VA mortgage.

MORTGAGE FORECLOSURE

Foreclosure of a home is similar to repossession, although it is more complicated. Mortgage holders go to great lengths to allow delinquent homeowners to work out financial problems. If illness or injury have temporarily strapped you financially, ask the mortgage holder to permit you to pay only the interest on the monthly mortgage bill, postponing the payment of principal until you are back on your financial feet.

If you have enough equity in the home, the mortgage holder may suggest refinancing the mortgage (see page 146).

In any case, seek legal advice if you are threatened with loss of your home (see page 60).

Foreclosure proceedings vary among states, and in many, court proceedings are required. The court may order the house sold to satisfy the debt, usually at public auction. If the sale of the house does not satisfy the entire debt, the homeowner may still be liable and may eventually have to pay the difference unless other legal action is taken such as bankruptcy.

In some states, there is a "statutory right of redemption." For a period ranging from a few months to three years, the homeowner may continue to live in the house and may redeem it at any time during the period by paying the original debt plus foreclosure costs.

SECOND MORTGAGES

When you need extra money for home improvements or for a serious financial emergency, you may consider taking out a second mortgage on your home or business.

Before you do, however, consider whether it might be cheaper to re-finance your existing mortgage. If you have no prepayment penalty clause (see page 145) and interest rates have gone up since your original mortgage contract, a lending agency may be willing to give you enough money to pay off the mortgage and take out a new mortgage loan. This technique may be cheaper than taking out a second mortgage while keeping the first.

Many states permit second-mortgage brokers to collect money from investors and provide second mortgages for homeowners who need money. The interest and brokerage rates are usually high.

Before actually taking out a second mortgage, check out the lender and the terms with a local banker, lawyer, or the Better Business Bureau.

Also, be wary of unknowingly signing a second mortgage. Some dealers who sell home modernization plans, reroofing, aluminum siding, and so forth, include a second-mortgage paper unobtrusively among the contracts they ask the homeowner to sign.

The FHA, banks, and savings and loan associations will also provide home improvement loans, so shop around before taking a second mortgage to determine whether it is really necessary.

Out of Funds Overseas. See page 199.

UNEXPECTED EXPENSES

Every family should have a reserve fund to use in case of financial emergencies such as illness, loss of job, sudden need to travel, or unexpected and unreimbursable damage to the home. Just how much you save is up to you and your circumstances, but one rule of thumb suggests keeping a reserve fund equal to two or three times the family monthly income, in a savings account that pays interest. Spend the money only when you face a real emergency.

UNORDERED MERCHANDISE

There are only two kinds of merchandise that can legally be sent through the mails to a person without his consent or agreement: free samples that are clearly and plainly marked as such; articles mailed by a charitable organization asking for contributions. In either case, you can consider the contents of the envelope or package as a gift, if you wish.

In all other instances, it is illegal to send merchandise to anyone unless he has previously requested it. If you receive unordered goods of any kind, you can consider them as gifts and you need not pay for them.

Should you have any problems with unordered merchandise, contact the nearest Federal Trade Commission office or write to:

Federal Trade Commission
6th Street and Pennsylvania Avenue, N.W.
Washington, D.C. 20580

pets

Because pets are members of the family, you will want to know how to take care of all their needs and problems. Major emergencies such as accidents or illnesses as well as minor problems such as rescuing a cat from a tree or ridding a pet of skunk odor all require your immediate attention.

First aid for pets may be even more difficult to perform than first aid for humans. You must rely entirely on your powers of observation, and approach injured animals with caution. Because they are unable to reason or to realize that you want to help when they are sick or in pain, even the most loving pet may unexpectedly turn on you. (See **ANIMAL BITES,** page 87.)

To save a pet's life in an emergency, you should be familiar with the first-aid techniques in this section. To protect yourself, heed the precautions given about handling ill or injured pets.

Also included are helpful hints on caring for ill or injured pets.

ACCIDENT

Always be extremely cautious when approaching an injured animal. Animals react to pain according to their personalities. Some become listless, others move about constantly, continually getting up and lying down. They moan or whimper. Some will have a frightened expression, and others will look vague. Some will want continuous affection, and still others will resent any attempt to touch them. Most will "favor" the injured part, holding up a sore leg, keeping a painful neck stiff, or tensing abdominal muscles when suffering stomach pain. They will rub a sore ear on the floor or against furniture.

If it is frightened or in pain, an animal is potentially dangerous and may want to escape and hide if it can. Sometimes an animal will play dead out of fear, and may suddenly bite or scratch when you touch it.

If the injured dog or cat is conscious, the first thing to do is to muzzle it with a long piece of cloth—a scarf, a man's tie, or belt.

Never pull an injured animal by the legs, head, or tail because its neck, back, or limbs may be broken.

As with humans, profuse bleeding should be attended to first. Apply pressure directly over the wound with a piece of sterile gauze, if possible, or a clean piece of cloth (see page 88).

If breathing has stopped, apply artificial respiration by gently compressing the chest and releasing it repeatedly or give mouth-to-mouth resuscitation as you would for humans (see page 106).

To avoid further injury, improvise a stretcher (see page 91). If the pet is small, a box will serve as a stretcher. If you cannot use a box or make a stretcher, wrap the animal gently in a coat or blanket to keep it immobile. Hold the animal in place gently to prevent it from falling off the stretcher or trying to climb out of the box during transportation. Don't delay in getting the injured animal to a veterinarian; life-threatening shock can occur quickly.

BIRDS

To control a bird while cleaning its cage. Spread a piece of paper on a nearby surface and sprinkle some gravel over it. When the bird goes to peck at the gravel, cover it with a large colander or strainer. It will usually be content in that spot until the cage is clean.

If you need liners for the bottom of the cage, trace the bottom of the cage on a piece of newspaper and cut several liners at one time. When you clean the cage, you will have liners ready to fit into place.

Your bird won't get back in the cage. If you have a feather duster, place it nearby. The bird will think it is a long-lost relative and nestle deep within it. Then place the feather duster at the door of the cage, and the bird will hop into its home. If you do not have a feather duster, place a colander, strainer, or hat over the bird. Then gently slip a cardboard under the container, carry the bird to the cage, and gently ease it through the door.

BIRTH

Normally, animals do not need help when giving birth. In fact, people often interfere in misguided attempts to serve as midwives.

For a household pet, however, it would be a kindness to provide a whelping box large enough for the pet to lie down comfortably with its litter. There should be a lip around the edge of the box about three inches wide, to prevent the mother from pressing the babies against the side. Put several thicknesses of newspaper in the box. Don't use torn or shredded paper as it may cover the babies and obscure the mother from them.

If your pet is obviously trying to whelp—the water bag breaks or contractions are occurring—and nothing appears for more than one-half to one hour, contact a veterinarian. If the puppy or kitten protrudes from the pelvis of its mother for more than 1 to 15 minutes, the mother is obviously having trouble. By wrapping a clean cloth around the protruding baby and gently easing it into the world, you may save the mother's life. If a baby's hind feet appear first, the mother may have difficulty, and you should watch carefully to determine whether the baby is being forced out by the mother. If not, call a veterinarian.

If the baby is born with a sac over its head, tear the sac with your fingers and remove it quickly. Then place the baby where the mother can clean it. Usually the mother can take care of everything herself, unless the litter is too large, or a young one is in a position that prevents normal passage through the birth canal.

BLEEDING

Apply pressure directly over the wound with a piece of sterile gauze, if available, or the cleanest cloth you can find, such as a freshly laundered handkerchief or hand towel. If the bleeding does not stop, or you must transport the animal to a veterinarian by yourself, make a tourniquet (see page 89) from a strip of cloth, necktie, bandage, or belt. Tie it around the animal between the wound and its heart. Loosen every five minutes, and then reapply.

BURNS

Most pets are burned by hot water, grease, hot tar, or other scalding liquids, but chewing wires or being trapped in a burning building can also cause bad burns.

Burns on the head or joints are most serious because the formation of scar tissue in these areas causes severe pain. Burns affecting more than 15 percent of the body are also very serious. When the percentage goes above 50 percent, nearly all victims suffer acutely and die within two weeks. Veterinarians therefore suggest prompt euthanasia for severely burned animals.

If you know the burn was caused by a chemical, flush the area immediately and copiously with water. Then look at the directions on the container, which usually describe the next action to take. If there are no instructions, and the substance was a caustic such as drain cleanser or strong detergent, apply vinegar to neutralize it. If the substance was an acid such as stain remover or laundry bleach, apply baking soda mixed with a little water or milk.

For small burns caused by boiling water, hot fat, fire, or electricity, the best treatment is cold water or ice. Afterward, a compress soaked in cold tea may be soothing.

Remember: A pet will try to return to a burning home because it thinks it will be safe there. So if the house is on fire, take your pet out of the house and restrain it.

Burrs. See **TICKS AND BURRS,** page 158.

CAT IS ANGRY

If a cat seems angry, it is usually because it is injured or sick. Try to grab it by the scruff of the neck and lift it up. This will usually subdue the animal, which then curls up like a kitten being carried by its mother.

If you cannot safely get your hand on the cat, fold a blanket, drop it over the animal, and scoop it up. Don't smother it. Drop the cat and the blanket gently into a clothes hamper or in a closet and shut the door until the cat calms down.

If the cat needs professional help, take it to the veterinarian in a hamper or another container. If a container is not readily available, pin a blanket around the cat like a straitjacket. Cover its feet (claws), but make sure that the animal can breathe easily.

CAT UP A TREE

A cat up a tree is really no laughing matter. It can starve to death or injure itself by falling from a branch. If your pet has found its way up and doesn't want to come down in a reasonable time, it is wise to attempt to coax it down.

The first approach is to tempt it with its favorite food. If your cat has a tendency to get itself up a tree often, there are special cat forceps made just for such occasions that can be purchased from veterinary supply houses. Ask the veterinarian about them.

Firemen are often willing to use their time and equipment to retrieve a cat from a high place, so if you cannot get the animal down yourself, call your local fire department and ask for assistance.

CHEWING PUPPY

If a new puppy is damaging rugs and shoes by chewing, give it an empty, thoroughly washed out plastic bleach bottle. The puppy can chew and gnaw to its heart's content because the bottle is practically indestructible. And it may save your belongings.

CHOKING

If a pet is choking or pawing at its mouth, it probably has a foreign body caught in its mouth or throat. Have someone hold the struggling pet while you pry open its mouth, holding the jaws firmly so it cannot bite. If you are trying to help a cat, wrap it in a towel or blanket so it cannot scratch.

Should there be no help available, straddle the pet and grasp its head firmly between your knees.

Try to remove the object with pincers or with your fingers. If you are not successful on the first attempt, get the animal to a veterinarian or hospital quickly.

DANGEROUS DOG

If a dog growls and appears to be about to bite, stand perfectly still. Dogs do not see nonmoving objects very well. Stand with your legs together and your arms folded on your chest. Most bites are on extremities. Be sure, however, that you make no sudden motion, particularly when you raise your arms to fold them. Talk to the dog in a firm steady voice. After it calms down, take one tentative step forward to see if the animal objects. If it does not, proceed slowly on your way, pausing after each step. If the dog threatens, move backward, still facing it, one step at a time.

Should the dog crouch and bare its teeth, prepare for an attack by crossing your arms and gripping your elbows firmly. When the animal leaps, try to knock it off balance by giving it an uppercut with your arms or knee. Since the dog's legs are off the ground when it first attacks, its balance is precarious and the animal can usually be pushed off. While the dog is regaining its balance, make your escape.

If the animal's attack knocks you over, do not attempt to fight it off. Instead, fold your arms over your face and lie perfectly still. Even dogs use this psychology. When a big dog attacks a smaller one, the little dog will just lie on its back with its feet up in the air and surrender. The attacker loses interest and walks away. If you lie still and cover your face with your arms, the dog will probably stop attacking.

DEATH

The death of any pet—a cat, dog, or even a mouse, turtle, or hamster —can be very upsetting to a family. If the pet is small and you have an ample backyard, you may want to bury the pet there. Make a hole at least four feet deep and large enough to place the animal in it easily. Planting a new tree as a marker is a nice idea and it discourages other animals from digging at the grave.

If you want to have a cat or dog removed, call the local dog warden, or the American Society for the Prevention of Cruelty to Animals. The warden will usually come only if the animal is in the street, and not all branches of the A.S.P.C.A. offer this service.

Veterinarians will remove a dead animal for a fee, and some have a cremator, in which case, the owner can request the pet's ashes.

Pet cemeteries will make arrangements to transport a deceased pet, but this service is expensive.

DOG FIGHT

Never allow yourself to get between two fighting animals. Instead, if you are strong enough, or the dogs are small enough, concentrate on the end that doesn't bite. Grab the hind leg or tail (if it is long) of one of the dogs, pull back, and toss the animal behind you. Once separated, the dogs are less likely to start the battle again, especially if you admonish them sternly. But be prepared to repeat this procedure. If you are alone and the dogs are too large or too fierce, get a bucket of cold water and throw it at the dogs. This usually cools things off. As they stop fighting, even temporarily, grab one and hurry it away to prevent recurrence. (See also **ANIMAL BITES,** page 87; **DANGEROUS DOG,** page 152.

EYE INJURIES

Eye injuries are very common in pets. When they occur, don't delay seeking professional help to prevent permanent damage. Even if an accident causes the eye to protrude out of the socket, sight may be saved by prompt action. The most important thing to remember is to keep the eye moist. Apply pads soaked with water, or drop mineral or salad oil into the eye until you can get the animal to a veterinarian.

GAS OR SMOKE POISONING

An animal poisoned by gas or smoke will usually be prostrate. Other symptoms are shallow breathing and glassy eyes. Take the pet into the fresh air immediately. If breathing has stopped, apply artificial respiration by gently compressing the chest and then releasing it repeatedly, or give mouth-to-mouth resuscitation as you would for a human (see page 106).

If a veterinarian is nearby, rush the pet there. Otherwise, take the pet to the nearest fire house, and ask the firemen to apply a respirator.

HAIR BALLS

During shedding season, many cats, especially the long-haired ones, accumulate hair balls in their stomachs. This can cause such symptoms as loss of appetite, vomiting, coughing, sneezing, and bad breath. To prevent or cure hair balls, give the cat some oil to lap at least once a week. The oil from a can of tuna fish or sardines will not only be therapeutic, but a treat for the cat. Cod liver oil is also suitable. Adding it to the food in small amounts—½ teaspoonful—is usually a good method. As a preventive, comb the cat at least twice weekly with a stiff, fine-tooth comb, the kind used for babies' hair. Collect the loose hair and dispose of it.

HEART ATTACK

Pets, like people, may have heart attacks. If your pet seems to be overcome with extreme weakness, lapses into unconsciousness, or appears to have a brief fainting spell, it could be having a heart seizure. Allow the animal to lie quietly while you call the veterinarian for further instructions.

HEAT STROKE

Although cats love to sun themselves, they rarely have heat stroke. Dogs do—especially those with thick coats and short noses, or other characteristics that impede breathing. A dog suffering from heat stroke may appear to have difficulty breathing, drool, or have a dry or blue tongue. It may pant very rapidly as well.

If the weather is hot and your dog displays any of the symptoms described, plunge it into a tub of cold water to reduce its temperature quickly. Then place it out of the sun, and circulate the air by fanning. If the dog is too large to do this, lay it on a flat surface and fan it, or rig up an electric fan to blow over it while you soak the animal with water.

HOUSEBOUND PETS

Do you have a puppy, small-breed dog, or kitten that must be kept in the house all day when you aren't there? To prevent damage and to keep your home neat, set up a child's playpen in one of the rooms. Line the bottom with a sheet of heavy plastic and several layers of newspaper. If the openings around the sides of the pen are large enough for a puppy or kitten to push through, line the sides with chicken wire or tie on old window screens.

Before you leave, put a weighted pan of water in the pen. If you will miss the animal's feeding time, put down a pan of food as well. When you come home, your house will be exactly the way you left it, and your pet will be content.

IN HEAT

Female dogs come into heat for the first time between 6 and 12 months of age and then every 6 to 8 months thereafter. If breeding is not wanted, keep the dog in the house for the entire three-week period except to walk it on a leash. The animal is normally receptive to breeding from about the 9th to the 16th day after heat begins. Unplanned pregnancies may be interrupted safely with hormone treatments within 24 to 48 hours after conception occurs. Ask your veterinarian for information.

Cats have erratic heat periods, usually beginning at 6 months of age. Some stay in heat constantly until conception. Others come into heat every 2 or 3 weeks and some only every 6 to 12 months.

The only visible sign to indicate that a dog or cat is in heat may be general excitability.

Female dogs and cats can be spayed, an operation in which the ovaries are removed, to prevent conception. Male cats kept as house pets may also be altered at about 7 to 9 months of age.

MEDICATION

Like children, pets often get balky about taking medicine, but you don't have to be a contortionist to get the dose down if you follow this advice:

To give a dog a pill. Push on each side of the animal's upper jaw with the thumb and forefinger of one hand, pressing the upper lip against and slightly under the upper teeth. The jaw will be forced open and if the animal tries to close its mouth, it will bite its own lip. Take the pill with the other hand, and push it into the back of the animal's mouth. Withdraw your hand quickly, and as the dog closes its jaw, tap it under the chin. This startles the animal, making it swallow. You can be sure the medication is down when the dog swallows. If that doesn't work, open the animal's mouth again, and place the pill on the back of its tongue. Then force the pill down its throat gently by putting a couple of drops of water from a spoon into the open mouth.

Most dogs like chocolate candy, so if yours refuses to swallow a tablet or capsule, push the pill into a piece of candy, covering it entirely so the dog can't smell it. You can also hide the pill in a meatball or chunk of dog food.

To give a cat a pill. Wrap the cat in a towel or small blanket before you start so it cannot scratch you. Then follow the directions above.

Liquid medication (seldom administered to cats). Give a teaspoonful at a time and pour it into the side flap of the lip (see illustration below). Allow time for swallowing, to prevent the liquid from going into the lungs.

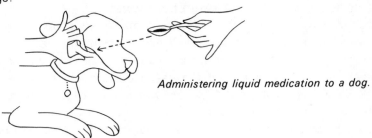

Administering liquid medication to a dog.

PET FOOD SUBSTITUTES

If you find you are out of pet food, table scraps will suffice for dogs and cats. Lacking scraps, any canned meat or fish (with the bones removed) will be eagerly gobbled up by the pet.

Raw chopped meat or tiny bits of other raw meat are good for most salamanders, chameleons, snakes, lizards, and turtles.

When nothing else is available, pet rodents of all sorts will eat corn-flakes. A few pieces of raw potato or carrot are also good.

Parrots, parakeets, and other birds do "want a cracker" when you run out of other food.

POISONING (ANIMALS)

Poisons vary, as do their symptoms, but if your pet trembles violently, vomits excessively, or shows signs of great pain, chances are it has been poisoned. How quickly you can empty its stomach may mean the difference between life and death.

If you know that the animal has swallowed poison and it does not vomit, induce vomiting by pressing your fingers against its upper lip and gum to force the animal's mouth open. When the mouth opens, press the rim of the upper lip over the upper teeth. If the animal tries to close its mouth, it will bite the upper lip. Gently drop a swallow or two of hydrogen peroxide (3 percent) into the mouth until ½ cup has been given. (See **LIQUID MEDICATION,** page 155.) Usually, vomiting occurs quickly.

After vomiting, give a solution of 2 tablespoons of sugar and a pinch of salt in 1 pint of water. This will dilute the poison and prevent dehydration.

Should the animal be highly excited or convulsing, try to make sure it does not harm itself. Carefully avoiding its jaws, wrap the animal in a blanket. Rush the pet to the veterinarian with a sample of the poison, if available, or with a sample of the vomitus.

POISONING (FISH)

There are several ways fish can be poisoned, so keep a close watch over tank conditions. An excess of chlorine in the water may kill fish quickly, causing them either to sink to the bottom, or float to the surface on their sides. All you can do is remove the fish that are still alive and put them into fresh water. Clean the aquarium with vinegar (do not use soap or detergent). Then fill it with fresh water.

Lack of oxygen which results from too many fish in one bowl or from dirty water can also be poisonous. When the fish stay near the surface of the bowl and seem to gulp for air, you can make this diagnosis.

Green water in a fish bowl means an overgrowth of some form of algae. Clean the bowl, and move it out of the light for most of the day. In the meantime, separate fish into bowls or jars if you don't have an adequately large container. Keep them there until the aquarium has been cleaned and filled with fresh water.

Cloudy water is probably due to overfeeding, so stop giving food and siphon off all decomposed food from the bottom of the tank. An antibiotic may be added if your veterinarian or pet store recommends it. To avoid cloudiness, feed only as much as the fish can eat within five or ten minutes.

RABIES

Rabies is a viral disease of the central nervous system to which all warm-blooded animals are susceptible. The virus is transmitted to man through saliva from a bite or through a break in the skin. Once the symptoms of the disease appear in man, death usually follows. Although cases of human illness caused by rabid animals are relatively rare, precautions must be taken.

If your dog suddenly has a change in personality, becomes sullen, or even overly affectionate, if it begins to chew strange things and then seems unable to swallow, and begins to froth at the mouth continuously, the dog may have rabies. If your cat hides, acts strangely, and refuses to eat or drink, it may have rabies.

Never handle a pet you suspect may have the disease. Try to back the animal into a room or a closet with a broom or chair until you can summon a veterinarian or a health officer. If you cannot back the animal away, drop a folded blanket over it, scoop it up, and put it in isolation. Be sure to have adequate protection from a bite.

Caution your children always to stay away from any animal acting strangely, and tell them never to pick up a bat they may find on the ground, because this animal is a common source of the disease. Unless a bird or a wild animal obviously has a broken limb or has been wounded by a missile, it is better to leave it alone. It may have a serious disease that could bring illness and even death to members of your family.

By law, any animal that has bitten a person must be kept confined for from 10 to 14 days, so always notify your local health officer. A rabid animal will usually die within 8 to 10 days, confirming the diagnosis.

Rabies is controlled through vaccination of pets. Consult your veterinarian as to how frequently this should be done. (See page 113 for treatment of a person bitten by a rabid animal.)

SKUNK ODOR

If you have ever had a pet that antagonized a skunk, you know it can be an overpowering situation. In a well-ventilated area, wash the pet with tomato juice. If the smell is still strong, wash the animal with shampoo and water, and rinse with a gallon of water to which 1 teaspoonful of ammonia has been added. Then rinse the pet thoroughly with clear water.

STAINS

Liquid pet stains may be removed from the carpet or upholstery by first blotting up as much moisture as possible with paper toweling or facial tissue. Solids should be scooped up with pieces of cardboard. Then soak the stain with club soda straight from the bottle, and blot again. Place a dry white towel or white paper towel over the stain. Weight it down with a heavy object so the moisture can be absorbed from the carpet into the towel, preventing any further spots or rings. Replace the damp towel with a dry one. (See page 186 for carpet stains.)

TAG JINGLING

The jingling of the metal tags on your pet's collar serves to warn birds and squirrels, and it also tells you where your pet is. But if you can't stand the jingling in the house, merely cover the tags with transparent or adhesive tape.

THORN OR SHARP OBJECT IN PAW

When an animal favors a paw and holds it up when walking, a thorn or sharp object is probably causing the trouble. Take a magnifying glass or use your naked eye to try and spot the sticker as you gently spread the paw pads. If you see it and it is large enough to pull out easily with your fingers, do so. If it is too small or fragile, sterilize a pair of tweezers by heating the end with two matches, one after the other, and carefully remove the object. It would be a good idea to have someone hold the animal while you remove the sticker. Soak the paw for a few minutes in warm soapy water, and dry it.

TICKS AND BURRS

Ticks can cause problems for both you and your pet because some carry disease, and all cause skin irritation. If you see a tick attached to your pet's skin, pull it off gently, preferably with tweezers, or use gauze or cotton. A drop of turpentine or oil may cause the tick to dislodge itself and back out. After removing the tick, disinfect the bite with alcohol or some other disinfectant. Never crush a tick between your fingers or fingernails, and do not leave the head of the tick imbedded in the skin. If you cannot remove the tick easily, let it alone and take the animal to a veterinarian.

Burrs may be removed by lifting them from the animal's fur with tweezers. If the burrs are too entangled in the fur for easy removal, hold the burr with tweezers and gently cut around it with small scissors until you can remove it.

TRANSPORTATION FOR PET

The Civil Aeronautics Board allows pets to travel in the plane cabin with passengers under certain restrictions. Only one pet container 18 inches by 12 inches by 8½ inches high is allowed per passenger. Only one pet per first class section and one pet for each tourist section is permitted. The charge for transporting a pet in that manner is 200 percent of the excess baggage rate.

Airlines, however, vary in their acceptance of pets in passenger areas. You must make reservations for birds, dogs, cats, and most other pets even if the airline permits them to travel with you.

Guide dogs are always allowed to travel with their masters.

Kennel sections of the cargo area on planes have oxygen and temperature control. Cardboard carrying cases for small pets are usually available at the ticket counter, and there are large wooden kennels for sale if you do not have a case of your own.

Railroads allow you to travel with your pet in the coach section if the pet is of the household variety and is in a carrying case. If you take a roomette or larger accommodations, the animal may be housed with you, but it must be muzzled while traveling to and from the compartment. Larger animals are required to travel in baggage cars housed in suitable kennels. Not all trains have baggage cars today, so check in advance.

For further information on traveling with a pet, write the A.S.P.C.A., 441 East 92nd Street, New York, New York 10028.

WHINING PUPPY OR CRYING KITTEN

A new puppy or kitten may miss the warmth and comfort of its mother, so make it feel at home with a warm water bottle wrapped in flannel or a towel and a ticking clock (if you have one). Placed in the box or basket, these items will comfort the animal. A radio playing soft music might also help. Oil from a tuna fish can on the paws of a lonesome youngster or a cupful of warm milk may also be soothing.

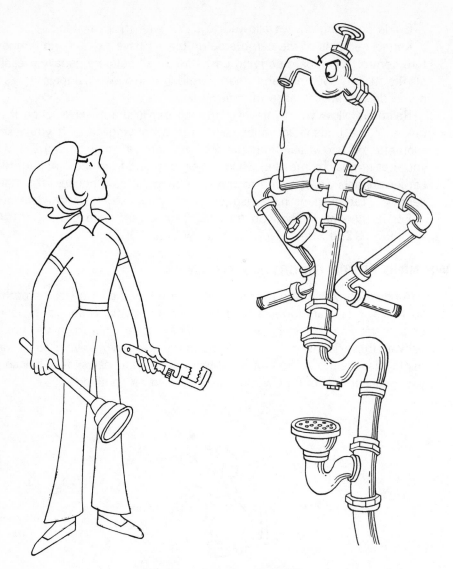

plumbing

Plumbing is a great invention, but like all mechanical devices it doesn't always work, and when something goes wrong, it may be rather difficult to repair. Difficult or not, plumbing problems often require quick action, so it is wise to know how to do certain jobs yourself. You may prevent a major repair job or expensive water damage.

Have a plunger (plumber's helper) on hand for unplugging clogged toilets and drains. Friction tape is invaluable in patching drips and leaks temporarily. Other handy plumbing tools are a pipe wrench, a monkey wrench, pliers, a screwdriver, a hammer, and spare washers.

Don't wait until you have a water pipe emergency to find the location of the main valve that shuts off the water entering the house. City water is usually supplied from a public main under pressure. A cut-off valve is located where the supply pipe enters the house. In homes that have their own supply, water is pumped in from a spring or supplied through a hydraulic ram. Pumps, usually located in the cellar or well house, force water into the home. Local valves are used to control the supply to various fixtures on both hot and cold water lines. When you have a water leak of unknown origin, or a flow that you cannot control with a local, specific valve, you will have to turn off the main valve.

No matter how water is supplied to your home, each fixture such as a kitchen sink or bathtub should have a valve to shut off the water supply to the faucets or bowl.

Label the drain petcocks (faucets) in the basement to indicate what pipes they control. A good way to do this is to turn the water on in sinks, tubs, and appliances, then test to see which petcock controls the drain to each one. If you label them, you will know at once which pipe to drain when a plumbing emergency arises.

In apartments, it is necessary to call the superintendent to cut off the main supply to your rooms. (If you are lucky, a superintendent may take care of the problem for you.)

DRAINS

Clogged drains. There are usually many drains in a home plumbing system, and all of them are susceptible to clogging. If you have a problem in your home and none of the solutions below seem to help, it may be that the main line leading into the house is clogged. If so, do not try to fix it yourself. Instead, call a plumber.

Floor drain. Take off the strainer and clean the drain with a stiff wire and a spoon, or even a straightened coat hanger. Pour in several gallons of boiling water.

Shower drain. Remove cover and clean out the drain with a hooked wire. Again, a wire coat hanger will do. If this doesn't work, use a half cup of ammonia to a gallon of boiling water and pour the mixture down the drain. Use a plumber's helper. Repeat, alternating the ammonia-water and the plumber's helper until the drain is free. When using a plumber's helper and ammonia-water, be sure to protect your eyes— there is always the chance that some of the liquid could fly up at you.

Sink drain. Use a chemical drain cleaner unless you have a disposer or directions warn against using such a product in your type of drain. Be sure to keep the container tightly capped and out of reach of small children. It is also wise to wear rubber gloves when handling such products. Use the drain cleaner sparingly, especially if you have copper pipes, and do not allow it to touch porcelain or enamel surfaces. A funnel is helpful in preventing spillage, but be sure to store it away from other kitchen utensils, and keep it out of the reach of children.

If you cannot use a chemical drain cleaner, pour the boiling water-ammonia mixture down the drain. Let it stand for a few minutes. Then fill the sink with hot water, place the suction cup of a plumber's helper over the drain, and pump up and down. Again, be sure to protect your eyes. To get full suction, stuff the overflow valve in the sink with a rag, and hold in place. If the drain is still clogged, the trap will have to be removed and the drain reamed with a long wire or coiled-spring snake. In a bathroom sink, the drain is often clogged with hair. The best way to clear the drain is to snake out the hair with a wire. Chemical drain cleaners work on grease, but they are not effective in removing an accumulation of hair.

Tub drain. If a tub drain is clogged, try clearing it with drain cleaner or boiling water before taking any other action. Be sure none of the drain cleaner touches your hands. If that doesn't work and your drain is the kind that closes with a mechanical metal stopper, unscrew the protective shield holding the drain control. Then lift out the arm that connects the control handle to the stopper. Clean the bottom end of the arm and replace it.

If you have the type of tub drain that is closed manually with a rubber stopper and the chemical drain cleaner does not clear the blockage, try using a plumber's helper.

Frozen sink drains. If the drain in a sink is frozen, apply heat to the trap. One way to do this is to soak rags in boiling water. Remove a hot rag from the water with kitchen tongs and place it over the trap. As soon as the rag starts to cool, replace it with a hot one. Or, you can apply heat to the trap by using a heat lamp or hair dryer. Avoid using open fire.

FAUCET DRIPS

A dripping faucet can be maddening. If it occurs during the night, you may be able to sleep undisturbed if you wrap a cloth around the opening of the faucet to soak up the water until morning.

As soon as possible, change the washer. Turn off the water either at the fixture or at the main valve. Unscrew the cap nut just below the faucet handle. If it is hexagonal, use a monkey wrench. If it is round, use pliers, but place a cloth between the jaws first, to avoid scratching the metal. Unscrew the handle as if you were turning the water on, and remove it. Unscrew the old washer with a screwdriver, or if the head of the screw is damaged, use pliers. Replace the washer and reassemble the faucet.

If the faucet still drips after you have replaced the washer, the trouble could be in the valve seat or in the faucet. Unless you are an inveterate do-it-yourselfer and have a good home repair book handy, get a plumber to do the job.

PIPES

Burst pipes. If a water pipe bursts and water gushes from it, quickly turn the water supply off at the source. If you can't locate the source immediately, turn off the main valve.

When a sink pipe bursts, turn off the two valves that control the flow. They are usually located directly under the sink.

If the water heater or a hot water line bursts, turn off the valve at the tank. Be extremely careful not to be scalded. Then turn the heat control on the heater to "off." Call a plumber to repair the pipe.

Frozen pipes. To thaw a frozen pipe, fill a bucket with very hot water. Dip heavy cloths in the water. Remove them from the water with tongs, and wrap them around the pipes. As soon as the cloths chill, reheat them and reapply. You may also thaw a frozen pipe with an electric hair dryer by moving it back and forth so heat is not concentrated in one spot. Keep faucets turned on while you are trying these thawing methods. When the water starts to flow you will know that the job is done.

Never use a propane torch to thaw a pipe. Besides being a fire hazard, these torches are a concentrated heat source and too much concentrated heat on a frozen pipe will make it burst by causing the air in the pipes to expand.

To keep pipes from freezing, don't leave windows open near uninsulated pipes during the winter. Wrap all exposed pipes with insulation made for the purpose or with strips of old blanketing. If you are closing up a summer home in an area that is subject to cold winters, turn off the water supply and be sure to drain the pipes thoroughly before you leave. Open all sink faucets and the drain cork in your water supply pipes. Flush the toilets so that tanks are dry. Remove as much water as possible from toilet bowels. Pour a gallon of kerosene into each toilet bowel and into each sink.

In a heated house you may be able to eliminate the job of draining the pipes if you leave enough heat on all winter to keep the temperature just above freezing.

Leaky pipes. Shut off the water at the nearest valve and open the faucet that will drain that section of the pipe. You can control a small leak temporarily by drying the pipe thoroughly and wrapping two or three layers of friction or adhesive tape over the hole or crack. As the adhesive on the tape becomes wet, it will not stick close enough to the pipe to stop the leak, but it will make the drip small enough to contain in a pail until the plumber comes.

If the hole or crack is large enough to cause a considerable drip, cover the break completely with a piece of rubber (from a rubber ball or old inner tube); place one strip of wood on each side of the pipe and use a clamp (preferably, a hose clamp) to hold the pieces of wood together. (Never tighten a clamp *directly* on a metal pipe. You may dent it or cause another crack.) This will keep the pipe from dripping until the plumber comes to repair it.

Noisy pipes. An air lock in a water supply pipe may cause annoying knocks and rattles in pipes and faucets.

Check faucet parts to see if they are worn or loose. If they are not, trace the pipe that leads to the faucet and look for a sag. Perhaps a support that holds the pipe to the ceiling of your basement has come loose or the pipe is weighted down with something heavy. If you find a sag, it is usually easy to repair. Just shore the pipe up to its original position by nailing the loose support back in place, or remove the weight that is bending the pipe out of line.

Should the knock persist, call a plumber for a consultation. Sometimes the only way to eliminate the annoyance is to install an extension on the pipe above the top faucet in each supply line, or near the water meter. The air cushion in the pipe extension will absorb the shock when the flow of water is suddenly stopped, eliminating the noise.

SHOWER HEAD CLOGGED

If the shower head can be removed, take it off and place it in a pan of hot, sudsy water. Scrub with a brush, and if necessary, clean out the sediment with a wire. Rinse thoroughly. If the head cannot be removed, poke a slim wire or a toothpick through the little openings to clean them out.

TOILETS

Clogged. If the toilet drain is clogged, place the plumber's helper over the outlet and pump up and down. If this doesn't work, crank a coiled-spring auger down the drain. If you don't have one, you may try to clear the drain with a straightened coat hanger.

Overflowing. The water supply valve to the toilet is usually under the left side of the tank. If the water is overflowing copiously, first try a simple technique. The water in the tank is controlled by a hollow copper ball that floats. This ball operates a valve on the end of the water inlet pipe through a small lever. When the water overflows from the tank and runs into the bowl, the valve is not closing properly. Take the top of the toilet tank off and lift the copper float ball as high as possible. If this stops the overflow, bend the float rod attached to the copper ball downward slightly to lower the float. If the flow continues, unscrew the float ball. If its is full of water, it must be replaced with a new one.

If you cannot stop the overflow with the copper ball maneuver, you will have to turn off the water supply at the side of the tank, and call a plumber.

Water keeps running. When the tank does not fill, and the water keeps running, the trouble may again be in the float rod. Bend the float arm near the center so that the float will be about ½ inch lower.

stains
and special cleaning
problems

Stains or spots on clothing and upholstery are not only aggravating, but they can also be costly unless you can remove them. Although a stain should be removed as promptly as possible, all is not necessarily lost if you discover it hours or even days later.

In this chapter, you will find a list of various kinds of stain removers, special instructions for using stain-removing solvents and bleaches, directions for removing specific stains from fabrics, and answers to other stain-removal problems. The chart on page 170 tells you which stain removers to use and which ones not to use on specific fabrics.

In some cases, of course, it is better not to attempt to remove a spot yourself, but to let a professional do the work for you. When should you try to do it yourself? When the spots are not numerous, and when they do not cover a large area; when the material is not fragile or heavily sized (treated with a substance that produces a stiff finish); and when you know what the stain is and how to treat it.

Before using any kind of spot remover, make sure it will not harm the fabric. (Consult the chart on page 170.) Then test the material on the wrong side in a place that will not show if it should be damaged. An inside hem or the inside of a pocket are good testing areas. If you discover that the remover recommended for a specific stain will harm the color or the fabric, consult a dry cleaner who may have the skills necessary to remove the spot without damaging the material.

STAIN-REMOVAL SUPPLIES

Here is a list of the various types of supplies and spot removers which can be used to treat a wide variety of stains at home. A kitchen syringe and medicine or eye dropper are useful for applying the liquid cleaners. (Be sure to check the chart on page 170 for fabrics on which specific cleaning agents can and cannot be used.)

Absorbent materials. Included in this category are powders such as cornmeal, talcum, or powdered chalk, which absorb greasy stains. Other absorbent materials are cotton, sponges, blotters, paper towels, facial tissues, and soft cloths, which are used to apply and to blot cleaning agents.

Soaps and detergents. Sometimes these products are all you will need to remove many kinds of stains.

Solvents (see page 167 f. for instructions on use):

Water is, of course one of the most useful solvents since it is effective in removing many non-greasy and even greasy stains when put to work promptly.

Commercial spot removers can be used for a wide range of stains from grass to grease. They usually contain perchloroethylene, trichloroethylene, or trichloroethane, all of which can be purchased in hardware stores and supermarkets under various trade names. (Check ingredients listed on the container.)

Naphtha is the most common grease solvent. It is sold under its own name or under a variety of commercial names at drugstores and supermarkets. Because it is extremely flammable, naphtha is not recommended for use.

Fingernail polish remover (acetone) is a solvent that is effective in removing stains such as fingernail polish, ball-point pen ink, and airplane glue. Buy in small quantities and use with caution—it is flammable and poisonous. Because acetone has an odor that is attractive to children, it should be stored out of their reach.

Amyl acetate (labeled "chemically pure") removes the same stains as does fingernail polish remover. However, it can be used on fabrics that cannot be treated with acetone. Amyl acetate can be purchased in a hardware store, but buy only small quantities as it is flammable and poisonous.

Alcohol (rubbing), if safe for the fabric, is an excellent solvent to use for removing a number of stains such as those caused by medicines and liquor. It can be used full strength, except on acetate, in which case it should be diluted with 2 parts water to 1 part alcohol. Rubbing alcohol is flammable and poisonous.

Turpentine and other commercial paint removers are used to remove paint stains. All these paint solvents are flammable and poisonous.

Bleaches and other chemical spot removers. These are widely used to remove stubborn stains. Because they are powerful, they must be handled with care and fabrics should be tested on a hidden area first (see page 166):

Household chlorine bleach is sold under many brand names. (See instructions for use on page 168.)

Peroxygen bleaches release oxygen as they work. *Sodium perborate* is a powdered peroxygen bleach and *hydrogen peroxide* (3 percent solution) is a liquid peroxygen bleach. Both forms are available in drugstores and supermarkets. Hydrogen peroxide, which is not as strong as sodium perborate, acts slowly on stains and is safe for most fabrics. Because it rapidly loses its strength on standing or when stored, it is best to buy it in small amounts. Do not store it in a metal container. (See instructions for use on page 168f.)

Oxalic acid and other rust removers are available in hardware and variety stores and supermarkets. Oxalic acid is a strong bleach and rust remover, and although it is safe for all fabrics, it may cause a color change. If so, the original color may be restored by moistening the stained area with ammonia. Since it is poisonous, oxalic acid should be kept in its original container and out of the reach of children. Throw out any unused portion. (See instructions for use on page 169 f.)

Ammonia (10 percent household ammonia) is safe for most fabrics but must be diluted with equal parts of water when used on silk and wool. Ammonia is frequently used to neutralize acid stains such as fruit juices, and to restore color that has been changed by other cleaning chemicals;

Vinegar is used to neutralize alkali stains, such as those caused by lye or drain cleaner.

Color removers, sold under various trade names in drugstores and supermarkets, are used when stains cannot be removed with ordinary bleaches. Color removers may fade or remove many dyes. If a test shows that this type of bleach causes a distinct color change rather than a fading, you may be able to restore the original color by rinsing the article immediately and drying it in the air. If it really fades the color, the original color cannot be restored, so be sure to follow the manufacturer's instructions carefully.

INSTRUCTIONS FOR USING SOLVENTS

Place the stained area face down, if possible, on a pad, soft cloth, or other absorbent material, so that the stain can be drawn out of the fabric during the treatment.

Dampen a pad of cotton, paper toweling, or a soft cloth with the liquid solvent and sponge the back of the stain. If the solvent is in spray or powder form, apply accordingly. Repeated treatments with small amounts of solvent are better than a few heavy applications.

Work from the center of the stain outward, using a light, brushing motion. Brush unevenly all around the edge of the stain to avoid a tell-tale ring.

Use a fresh pad for sponging and absorbing as soon as the one you have been using becomes soiled. In this way, the stain will not be returned to the fabric.

When using solvents that are irritating to eyes or lungs (such as acetone or ammonia), be sure to work in a well-ventilated room.

INSTRUCTIONS FOR USING CHLORINE BLEACHES

Mild Treatment	Strong Treatment
Washables	
Mix a solution of 1 tablespoon of liquid bleach to 1 pint of cool water. *Small stain:* apply with medicine dropper. *Large stain:* soak in solution. Leave on fabric for 5 to 15 minutes. Rinse well with water. Repeat, if necessary.	Mix equal parts of liquid bleach and cool water. *Small stain:* apply with medicine dropper. *Large stain:* soak in solution. Leave on stain 5 to 15 minutes. Rinse immediately with water. Repeat, if necessary. Make sure all bleach is thoroughly rinsed out of fabric.
Nonwashables	
Mix a solution of 1 teaspoon of liquid bleach to 1 cup of cool water. *Small stain:* apply with medicine dropper. *Large stain:* soak in the solution. Leave on fabric for 5 to 15 minutes. Rinse well with water. Repeat, if necessary.	Not recommended.

INSTRUCTIONS FOR USING PEROXYGEN BLEACHES

Sodium Perborate (powdered)

Mild Treatment	Strong Treatment
Washables	
Mix solution of 1 to 2 tablespoons to 1 pint of lukewarm water (for wool, silk, or Dynel®) or 1 pint of hot water (for other fabrics). Mix just before using. (Solution loses strength on standing.) Cover stained area with solution, or soak entire article until stain is removed (several hours or overnight). Rinse well. If wool or silk is yellowed, sponge with vinegar, then rinse with clear water.	Sprinkle directly on stain. Dip stain into very hot or boiling water. Rinse well. Repeat, if necessary.

168

Sodium Perborate (powdered)

Mild Treatment	Strong Treatment
Nonwashables	

Mild Treatment	Strong Treatment
Sprinkle on stain, then cover stain with cotton pad dampened with lukewarm water (for wool, silk, or Dynel®) or hot water (for other fabrics). Keep damp until stain is removed. Rinse well. *Alternate:* Mix 1 to 2 tablespoons to 1 pint lukewarm water (for wool, silk, Dynel®) or hot water (for other fabrics). Mix just before using. (Solution loses strength on standing.) Apply to stain with medicine dropper. Keep damp until stain is removed. Rinse well. If silk or wool is yellowed by bleach, sponge with 10 percent acetic acid or vinegar. Rinse with water.	Dampen stain with cool water. Sprinkle powder on stain. With spoon or medicine dropper, pour a small amount of boiling water on stain. Use a sponge or absorbent pad under stain to absorb water. Rinse well. Repeat, if necessary.

Hydrogen Peroxide (liquid)

Mild Treatment	Strong Treatment
Washables	

Mild Treatment	Strong Treatment
Moisten the stain with a few drops of a 3 percent solution. Expose stain to direct sunlight. Add hydrogen peroxide as needed to keep stain moist until stain is removed. *For stubborn stains:* add a few drops household ammonia to 1 tablespoon hydrogen peroxide. Moisten stain immediately, and cover with pad of cotton dampened in same mixture. Keep damp until stain is removed (several hours). Rinse well.	Cover stain with a cloth dampened with 3 percent solution hydrogen peroxide. Cover that cloth with dry cloth. Press with iron as hot as is safe for fabric. Rinse well.

Nonwashables

Same as for washables.	Same as for washables.

INSTRUCTIONS FOR USING OXALIC ACID (CRYSTALS) AND OTHER RUST REMOVERS

Mild Treatment	Strong Treatment
Washables and Nonwashables	

Mild Treatment	Strong Treatment
Dissolve 1 tablespoon in 1 cup of warm water. Keep stain wet with the solution until stain is removed. Then	Dissolve 1 tablespoon in 1 cup of water as hot as is safe for the fabric. Continue as with mild treatment.

stains and special cleaning problems

rinse thoroughly with clean water.

Alternate (for all fabrics except those harmed by hot water): sprinkle crystals on dampened stain. Dip stained area in very hot water. Rinse thoroughly.

STAINS ON FABRICS

On the following pages you will find the methods recommended for treating the most common stains on washable and nonwashable fabrics. Before you start to remove a specific stain, check:

1. The label on the garment or fabric for the fiber content. (Refer to the chart below for stain removers recommended for specific fibers.)
2. Washing instructions for temperature of water and choice of washing products; also whether fabric is machine- or hand-washable.
3. The label on the garment or fabric to see if it is marked "dry clean only." If so, test the fabric before using any cleaning agent that contains water or has to be diluted or rinsed with water.

STAIN REMOVERS RECOMMENDED FOR SPECIFIC FABRICS

	Alcohol	Ammonia (Household 10%)	Amyl Acetate (Pure) Synthetic Banana Oil	Chlorine Bleach	Detergent	Fingernail Polish Remover (Acetone)	Oxalic Acid	Perchloroethylene*	Peroxygen Bleaches	Soap and Water	Trichloroethane*	Trichloroethylene*	Turpentine	Vinegar
Acetate	√†	√	√	√	√	No	√	√	√	√	√	√	√	√
Acrylic	√	√	√	√	√	√	√	√	√	√	√	√	√	√
Cotton (untreated)	√	√	√	√	√	√	√	√	√	√	√	√	√	√
Cotton (permanent press)	√	√	√	No	√	√	√	√	√	√	√	√	√	√
Modacrylic	√	√	√	√	√	No	√	√	No	√	√	√	√	√
Nylon	√	√	√	√	√	√	√	√	√	√	√	√	√	√
Olefin	√	√	√	√	√	√	√	√	√	√	√	√	√	√
Polyester	√	√	√	No	√	No	√	No	√	√	No	No	√	√
Rayon	√	√	√	√	√	√	√	√	√	√	√	√	√	√
Silk	√	√♦	√	No	√	√	√	√	No	√	√	√	√	√
Spandex	√	√	√	No	√	√	√	√	√	√	√	√	√	√
Triacetate	√†	√	√	√	√	No	√	No	√	√	No	No	√	√
Wool	√	√♦	√	No	√	√	√	√	No	√	√	√	√	√

* **Basic ingredient of many commercial spot removers. † Diluted 2 parts water to 1 part alcohol.**
♦ **Diluted (50–50) with water.**

ANTIPERSPIRANTS AND DEODORANTS

Antiperspirants that contain substances such as aluminum chloride are acid and may cause fabrics to fade and to fall apart, so treat the stained area gently.

Washables and nonwashables. Wash or sponge stain with soap or detergent and warm water. Rinse. If stain is not removed, use a chlorine or peroxygen bleach on white or color-fast materials (see charts on pages 168 f. and 170) If the colors have faded, you may be able to restore them by sponging the faded area with ammonia. Household ammonia can be used full strength on all fabrics except wool or silk. For these, dilute ammonia in an equal part of water. Rinse.

BALL-POINT PEN INK

Washables. Although washing removes some types of ball-point pen ink stains, it sets others. To determine whether the stain will wash out, mark a scrap of similar material with the pen and wash it. Another way to remove some ball-point pen inks is to spray the stain with hair spray and allow to dry. Then wash to remove the spray. Test this method on scrap material first.

Washables and nonwashables. Try sponging the stain repeatedly with fingernail polish remover (acetone) or amyl acetate (see chart on page 170 for fabrics on which acetone cannot be used). (See also **HANDS AND FEET,** page 189.)

BLOOD

Washables. Soak in cold water and then wash in warm, soapy water. If the stain has already set, add 2 tablespoonfuls of ammonia to each gallon of water, or strong, salt water. If the stain remains, sponge with hydrogen peroxide. For blood stains on silk or wool fabrics, sponge with cold water—hot water sets the stain.

Nonwashables. To remove a small, fresh blood spot from clothing, put a few drops of water on each spot and powder thickly with cornstarch. When the starch is dry, it can be rubbed off, and the blood stains are likely to have disappeared.

When removing an old blood stain from nonwashable fabric, sponge the spot with cool water, then sponge with hydrogen peroxide, if it is safe for the fabric (see chart on page 170). If not, drying the fabric in the sun may bleach out the stain.

BUTTER

Washables. Washing by machine or by hand will probably remove the stain. However, with some wash-and-wear or permanent press fabrics, or with "old" stains, it may be necessary to dampen the stain first, rub in soap or detergent, and allow it to remain for several hours or overnight. Then rinse the stain and wash by machine or hand.

Nonwashables. Use a commercial liquid spot remover. If a yellow stain remains after solvent has dried, use a chlorine or peroxygen bleach— if it is recommended for the fabric (see charts on pages 169 and 170).

CANDY (Not Chocolate or Syrups)

Washables. Fresh stains may be removed by regular laundry methods. If stain is ''old'' or difficult, sponge with cool water or soak in cool water for 30 minutes or longer. If stain remains, work soap or detergent into the stain, then rinse thoroughly and allow to dry. If stain still remains, use chlorine or peroxygen bleach (see charts on pages 168 f. and 170).

Nonwashables. Scrape off as much candy as possible. Sponge stain with cool water or force cool water through the stain with a small syringe or eye dropper, using a sponge under the stain to absorb the water. If a stain remains, rub soap or detergent on the dampened stain and work it into the fabric. Rinse spot well with water and allow to dry. If a greasy stain remains, use commercial spot remover. Repeat, if necessary. If colored stain remains, use a chlorine or peroxygen bleach (see charts on pages 169 and 170).

CARBON PAPER

Washables and nonwashables. Dampen spot and work in soap or detergent. Rinse well. If stain is not removed, apply a few drops of household ammonia and repeat treatment. Dilute ammonia in an equal part of water for use on silk and wool. Rinse well.

Catsup. See **TOMATO JUICE AND SAUCES,** page 182.

CHEWING GUM

Washables and nonwashables. If possible, fabric should be placed in the freezer in a clear plastic bag. The gum will freeze and be easy to remove. If you can't put the fabric in the freezer, remove surface gum with the blunt edge of a knife. Rub stain with ice and then scrape hardened gum off the cloth. If stain remains, apply commercial spot remover. (See chart on page 170.)

CHOCOLATE AND SYRUPS

Stains of this type are considered combination stains because both greasy and nongreasy substances are involved.

Washables. Sponge stain with cool water or soak it in water for 30 minutes or more. If stain remains, rub soap or detergent into it, rinse thoroughly, and allow to dry. If a greasy stain remains, use a commercial spot remover. Repeat if necessary. If a colored stain remains, use a chlorine or peroxygen bleach (see charts on pages 168 f. and 170).

Nonwashables. Sponge stain with cool water, or force water through it with a small syringe, holding a sponge underneath to absorb water. If stain remains, rub in soap or detergent. Rinse well with water and allow to dry. If a greasy stain remains, sponge with commercial spot remover. Repeat, if necessary. If colored stain remains, use a chlorine or peroxygen bleach if recommended for the fabric. (See charts on pages 169 and 170).

COFFEE AND TEA

Washables. Even when cream or milk is involved, most fresh coffee or tea stains can be removed with regular laundering methods. For old stains, use the following methods:

Stains without cream or milk. Sponge stain with cool water, or soak the stain in cool water for 30 minutes or longer. If stain remains after sponging or soaking, work in soap or detergent and then rinse. If stain still remains, use peroxygen or chlorine bleach (see charts on page 168 f. and 170).

Stains with cream or milk. Follow the procedure above, but before using a peroxygen or chlorine bleach, use a commercial spot remover to remove any grease stain which remains. Then if necessary, use the bleach. (See charts on page 168f and 170).

Nonwashables. *Stains without cream or milk.* Sponge stain with cool water, or force cool water through stain with a small syringe using a sponge underneath to absorb water. If stain remains, rub soap or detergent into stain and work into fabric. Rinse. A final sponging with rubbing alcohol helps to remove the soap or detergent and to dry the fabric more quickly. See page 166 f., especially before using on acetate. If stain remains after rinsing, use a chlorine or peroxygen bleach (see charts on pages 169 and 170).

Stains with cream or milk. Same as above, but if there is a greasy stain remaining, use a commercial spot remover before using bleach. Repeat, if necessary. If a stain persists, use a chlorine or peroxygen bleach. (See charts on pages 169 and 170.)

COSMETICS

The following instructions apply to eye shadow, liquid eyeliner, liquid foundation, mascara, pancake makeup, powder, and rouge. (See also **LIPSTICK,** page 176.)

Washables. Apply undiluted liquid detergent to stain and rub with your finger until thick suds are formed. Work in until outline of the stain is gone, then rinse well. Repeat if necessary. Drying the fabric between treatments may be helpful.

Nonwashables. Sponge with a commercial spot remover until color from the stain no longer comes out. If stain is not completely removed, use method given for washable articles. (See chart on page 170.)

Deodorants. See **ANTIPERSPIRANTS AND DEODORANTS,** page 171.

DYE

Washables. A long soak in warm, sudsy water is often effective for fresh dye stains. If a bleach is needed, use chlorine bleach or a color remover, provided they will not cause further damage to the fabric (see page 167 and chart on page 170).

Nonwashables. Rub detergent into the stain and rinse. If stain remains, allow the fabric to dry, then treat with color remover (see instructions on page 167 and chart on page 170).

EGG

Washables. Scrape away surface spot with a blunt knife. Sponge with cold water—never hot. If stain is stubborn, soak in cool water for 30 minutes. Then work in detergent with your finger, and rinse. If the stain is still there, use a chlorine or peroxygen bleach (see charts on page 168 f. and 170).

Nonwashables. Sponge stain with cold water, or force cold water through it with a small syringe, using a sponge underneath to absorb the water. If stain remains, rub in soap or detergent and work it into the fabric. Rinse. A final sponging with alcohol if the fabric permits (see chart on page 170) will remove the soap or detergent and dry the fabric more quickly. If stain remains, use a chlorine or peroxygen bleach (see charts on pages 169 and 170).

FINGERNAIL POLISH

Washables and nonwashables. Apply fingernail polish remover (acetone) on the underside of the material if it is recommended (see chart on page 170). The polish usually can then be peeled off. For fabrics on which acetone cannot be used, apply commercial spot remover. Then brush lightly with a clean, soft cloth.

Food Coloring. See **DYE,** above.

FRUIT AND FRUIT JUICES

These stains should be treated as soon as possible because some fruit juices (such as citrus) dry invisibly on fabric and then turn yellow as they age or when they are subjected to heat. This yellow stain is very difficult to remove. (See also stains on **HANDS AND FEET,** page 189.)

Washables. Pour boiling water through the stain from a height of one to three feet. You can do this safely by stretching the stained area over a bowl and securing it with a rubber band. (Never do this on silk or wool, which must be sponged with cool water only.)

Nonwashables. First sponge the stain with cool water, then immediately work in laundry detergent. Let stand for several hours. Then

174

pour a drop or two of white vinegar on the spot, and let it remain a minute or two. Rinse with cold water. If this does not remove the stain, try using hydrogen peroxide bleach if the fabric permits (see charts on pages 169 and 170).

FURNITURE POLISH

Washables. If the polish contains wood stain, scrape off as much as possible, then sponge with turpentine, commercial spot remover, or alcohol. Wash in soapy water and rinse.

If the furniture polish does not contain wood stain, wash by normal laundry methods. On some wash-and-wear and permanent press fabrics, you may have to dampen the stain and rub detergent into it. Allow it to stand overnight and then wash.

Nonwashables. Use commercial spot remover. (See chart on page 170.)

GLUE

Washables and nonwashables. For *mucilage,* soak a washable fabric in hot water. Sponge a nonwashable fabric with hot water. If the stain remains, work in detergent, then sponge with water.

For *airplane glue* and *household cement,* use fingernail polish remover (acetone) on the underside of the fabric if it is recommended (see chart on page 170). Pure amyl acetate may be used on some fabrics for which acetone is not safe.

For *plastic glue,* sponge stain with lukewarm water before glue sets, if possible. If the glue has hardened, immerse the spot in warm white vinegar. Allow up to 15 minutes for the treatment to take effect and then rinse fabric thoroughly with hot water.

GRASS AND OTHER FOLIAGE

Washables. Dampen the stain with water, and work in detergent. If it will not affect the color or the fabric (see chart on page 170), sponge the stain with full-strength alcohol. If the stain remains, use chlorine bleach or peroxygen bleach (see charts on pages 168 and 170).

Nonwashables. Use the same methods as for washables, but try alcohol first if safe for color and fabric. (See chart on page 170.)

GRAVY AND MEAT JUICE

Washables. Sponge stain with cool water, or soak in cool water for 30 minutes or longer. If it remains, work in soap or detergent, then rinse thoroughly and allow to dry. If a greasy stain remains, sponge with a commercial spot remover and allow to dry. Repeat if necessary.

If a colored stain remains after the fabric dries, use a chlorine or peroxygen bleach (see charts on pages 168 f. and 170).

Nonwashables. Force cool water through the stain with a small syringe or eye dropper, holding a sponge underneath to absorb the water. If a stain remains, rub in soap or detergent. Rinse spot well with water and allow to dry. If a greasy stain remains, use a commercial spot remover. If it still persists, use a chlorine or peroxygen bleach (see charts on pages 169 and 170).

GREASE

All fabrics. Sprinkle talcum, cornstarch, or powdered chalk on a fresh grease stain. Rub in well, let stand until the grease is absorbed, and then brush off. Repeat several times, if necessary.

Washables. If the stain remains, dampen the spot, and rub in detergent or soap; then rinse with warm water. On some wash-and-wear or permanent press fabrics, it may be necessary to rub soap or detergent thoroughly into the dampened stain, allowing it to stand for several hours or overnight. If the stain still remains, try a commercial spot remover. The yellow stain that may remain after such treatment can be removed with a strong sodium perborate treatment or a chlorine bleach, if safe for fabric (see charts on pages 168 and 170).

Nonwashables. Use commercial spot remover after powder treatment (see chart on page 170). Take same steps as for washables, if necessary.

Ice Cream. See **MILK,** page 177; **CHOCOLATE AND SYRUPS,** page 172.

LIPSTICK

All fabrics. An easy and sometimes successful way of removing lipstick from a fabric is to rub the stain with a slice of white bread. Brush away the crumbs, and the traces of red will probably have disappeared with them. (See also **COSMETICS,** page 173.)

If this doesn't work, try the following methods:

Washables. Pour about 1 teaspoonful of salad oil on the stain, and rub the spot until the fabric is saturated through to the opposite side. Wait about 10 minutes, and wash by hand or machine. The oil will melt the lipstick and the laundering will take out the oil.

Nonwashables. Use commercial spot remover. (See chart on page 170.)

Liquor. See **WINE AND LIQUOR,** page 184.

Makeup. See **COSMETICS,** page 173.

MAYONNAISE AND OTHER SALAD DRESSINGS

Washables. Sponge stain with cool water, or soak in cool water for 30 minutes or longer. If stain remains, work in soap or detergent, rinse thoroughly, and allow article to dry. If a greasy stain remains, apply a commercial spot remover. If a colored stain remains, use a chlorine or peroxygen bleach (see charts on pages 168 and 170).

Nonwashables. Sponge stain with cool water, or force cool water through the stain with a small syringe, holding a sponge underneath to absorb the water. If a stain remains, rub on soap or detergent and work it into the fabric. Rinse spot well with water and allow article to dry.

MERCUROCHROME, MERTHIOLATE, AND METAPHEN

Washables. Soak stained articles overnight in a warm soap or detergent solution that contains 4 tablespoonfuls of ammonia to each quart of water. Rinse thoroughly. If ammonia has changed the color of a dyed fabric, sponge the area with water, then moisten it with white vinegar.

Nonwashables. Sponge stain with alcohol, if it is safe for the dye and the fabric (see chart on page 170). If the stain persists, place a pad saturated with alcohol on top of it. Keep the pad wet until stain is removed.

If alcohol is not safe for the dye, wet stain with liquid detergent and add a drop of ammonia with a medicine dropper. Rinse with water. Repeat, if necessary.

MILDEW AND MOLD

Mildew is a thin, whitish growth produced by molds. It is most common in muggy summer weather and develops most often on cotton, linen, rayon, silk, and wool. Mildew discolors the fabric, sometimes eating into it and giving off a musty odor. It also forms on plastics (especially shower curtains) and between tiles.

The best best way to prevent mildew or mold is to keep the air dry. An air conditioner or dehumidifier takes moisture out of the air as does heat. A lighted electric light bulb is effective in keeping the air dry in a closet, but be sure not to put the light near anything that may catch fire.

Remove any mildew spots the minute you see them, preferably outdoors, to prevent spreading the spores.

Washables. Soap and water will remove fresh stains from washables, including plastics. If the stain is stubborn, try chlorine or peroxygen bleach (see charts on pages 168 and 170). Dry in the sun.

Nonwashables. Have the article professionally dry cleaned as soon as possible.

MILK

Washables. Wash immediately in cool water. If stain remains, work soap or detergent into the fabric, and then rinse. If it's still there, use a chlorine or peroxygen bleach (see charts on pages 168 and 170).

Nonwashables. Sponge stain with cool water, or force cool water through it with a small syringe, holding a sponge underneath to absorb the water. If a stain remains, rub in soap or detergent and rinse. A final sponging with alcohol helps to remove the soap or detergent and to dry the fabric more quickly (see page 166 f. and chart on page 170).

If the stain still remains after rinsing, use a chlorine or peroxygen bleach (see charts on pages 169 and 170).

Mucus. See **VOMIT AND MUCUS,** page 183.

MUD

All fabrics. Allow the mud to dry and then brush off.

Washables. If stain remains, wash in hottest water safe for fabric. If stain still persists, sponge with rubbing alcohol (see page 166 f.).

Nonwashables. Sponge stain with cool water, or force cool water through it with a small syringe, holding a sponge underneath to absorb the water. If stain remains, rub in soap or detergent, then rinse. A final sponging with alcohol helps to remove the soap or detergent and dry the fabric more quickly (see page 166 f.; and chart on page 170).

Stains from iron-rich clays that cannot be removed by the methods above should be treated as rust stains (see pages 167, 169f, and 170).

MUSTARD

Washables. Rub soap or detergent into the dampened stain, and then rinse. If the stain is not removed, soak fabric in hot detergent solution for several hours or overnight, if it won't harm the material.

If stain remains, use a sodium perborate treatment, if safe for the fabric (see charts on pages 168 and 170).

Nonwashables. If safe for the fabric, sponge stain with alcohol (see page 166 f. and chart on page 170.) If alcohol is not safe for the garment, rub soap or detergent into the dampened stain, with a sponge underneath to absorb water. If this doesn't work, repeat, and then force water through stain with a syringe. Sodium perborate, if safe for fabric (see charts on pages 169 and 170), may remove a stubborn spot.

OIL—FISH, LINSEED, MACHINE, MINERAL, AND VEGETABLE

Washables. Conventional washing methods may remove the stain, but if not, dampen the spot, rub in soap or detergent (dry or liquid), and then rinse with warm water. On some wash-and-wear or permanent press, it may be necessary to rub soap or detergent thoroughly into the stain and to allow it to stand for several hours or overnight before rinsing. Very often, however, you will have to resort to a commercial spot remover which is effective even after the garment has been washed.

If a yellow stain remains after the solvent treatment, use a chlorine or peroxygen bleach. If safe for the fabric, the strong sodium perborate treatment is effective (see charts on pages 168 and 170)

Nonwashables. Begin by using a commercial spot remover. Allow it to dry and repeat, if necessary. If a yellow stain remains, use a strong powdered peroxygen bleach treatment, if it is safe for the fabric (see charts on pages 169 and 170). If this is not safe for the fabric, use chlorine bleach or hydrogen peroxide (see charts on pages 168, and 170).

PAINT AND VARNISH

These stains should be treated promptly; dried paint stains are almost impossible to remove. Because there are so many different kinds of paints and varnishes, no one method will remove every stain. Read the label on the container. If a specific solvent is recommended as a thinner, it may be more effective in removing stains than the solvents recommended here.

For oil paint, varnish, and enamel stains, scrape off as much as possible. Then use the following method:

Washables. Work detergent into spot, then launder the fabric. If this does not work, apply turpentine, commercial spot remover, or alcohol. Wash in soapy water and rinse. For rubber-base paints, wash in soapy water. For small spots, and if safe for the fabric, fingernail polish remover (acetone) works well (see chart on page 170).

Nonwashables. Sponge fresh stain with turpentine or commercial spot remover, if safe for fabric. If this does not work, apply commercial spot remover. If the spot remover is a liquid, dampen a cotton pad with it, and cover the stain with the pad for 30 minutes or longer. When the stain seems loosened, reapply the spot remover. If the stain still remains, work in liquid detergent, and apply spot remover. Alternate between applying detergent and spot remover until the stain is removed. Then sponge the area with warm, soapy water, and rinse with clear water. If rubbing alcohol is safe for the fabric, you can finish sponging with alcohol diluted in two parts of water (see page 166 f. and chart on page 170).

PENCIL MARKS

Washables and nonwashables. Lead and colored pencil marks may be removed by rubbing the spot with a soft eraser. If the mark cannot be erased, dampen the spot, and work in soap or detergent. Rinse well. If the stain remains, sponge it with alcohol (see page 166 f. and chart on page 170). If the stain still persists, rub in soap or detergent and rinse with cool water. Repeat if necessary.

PERFUME

Washables. Treat fresh stains by soaking fabric in cool water and then working in detergent. For old stains, sponge spot with alcohol if it won't harm the fabric (see page 166 f. and chart on page 170). On white fabric, if a stain remains, use chlorine or peroxygen bleach (see charts on pages 168 f. and 170).

Nonwashables. Sponge fresh stain with water and detergent instead of soaking fabric. Then follow steps for washables. Remember the alcohol in perfume may cause loss of color or a dye ring around the edge of the stain and the original color cannot be restored.

PERSPIRATION

Washables and nonwashables. Wash or sponge stain thoroughly with soap or detergent and warm water. Work gently, because some fabrics are weakened by perspiration, particularly silk.

179

If perspiration has altered the color of the fabric, try to restore it by treating a fresh stain with ammonia (see chart on page 170), or an old one with vinegar. Then rinse with water.

Remove any yellow discoloration with a chlorine or peroxygen bleach. If safe for fabric, try strong sodium perborate treatment (see charts on pages 168 f. and 170), usually the most effective for this type of stain; otherwise treat with hydrogen peroxide.

If an oily stain remains, use a commercial spot remover.

If perspiration odor still clings to a washable garment after laundering, soak the fabric in a solution of 4 tablespoonfuls of salt to 1 quart of warm water.

RUST

Washables and nonwashables. An old idea, but still a good one, is to remove rust stains from clothing by squeezing fresh lemon juice on the spot and putting salt on top of that. Then hang the article in the sun, or hold the stain over the spout of a steaming kettle. Rinse thoroughly, and repeat if necessary.

Or, if the fabric can take it, boil the stained article in a solution containing 4 teaspoonfuls of cream of tartar to each pint of water. Boil until stain is removed, then rinse thoroughly.

Color removers (see page 167) can be used to remove rust stains from white fabrics.

A commercial rust remover or oxalic acid may be used if necessary, but most are highly toxic, so be careful. (See pages 169, and 170.)

Salad Dressings. See **MAYONNAISE AND OTHER SALAD DRESSINGS,** page 176.

SCORCH

Washables. Regular washing techniques may take out the stain, but if not, try hydrogen peroxide. Use a fresh bottle, because peroxide loses strength when stored. Moisten stain with a few drops and expose it to direct sunlight. Add hydrogen peroxide, as needed, to keep stained area moist until stain is removed.

If the above treatment does not remove stain, add a few drops of household ammonia to about 1 tablespoon of hydrogen peroxide. Moisten stain immediately with this mixture, and cover with a pad of cotton dampened with the same mixture. Keep damp until stain is removed (it may take several hours). Rinse.

If this does not work, cover stain with a cloth dampened with hydrogen peroxide. Cover with a dry cloth, and press with an iron as hot as is safe for fabric. Rinse well.

If the stain is still there, you will have to accept the fact that it cannot be removed because the fabric has been damaged too severely by the scorching.

Nonwashables. Follow hydrogen peroxide techniques, as with washables.

SHELLAC

Washables and nonwashables. Sponge stain with alcohol, or soak it in alcohol (see page 166 f.). If alcohol will damage the dye, try turpentine. Alternately sponge the stain with turpentine and with detergent as many times as necessary.

SHOE POLISH

Because no single cleaning method will work for every kind of shoe polish, it may be necessary to try more than one technique.

First try:

Washables. Apply a commercial spot remover, then rub a detergent directly into the stain and wash the fabric in warm, sudsy water. Rinse thoroughly.

Nonwashables. Apply a commercial spot remover, and allow to dry. If this doesn't work, then try:

All Fabrics. If safe for fabric dyes, sponge the stain with rubbing alcohol (see page 166 f. and chart on page 170). If a stain still remains and if it is safe for the fabric, use a chlorine or powdered peroxygen bleach (see charts on pages 168 f. and 170). If these bleaches aren't recommended, have the garment professionally dry cleaned.

Smoke. See **SOOT AND SMOKE,** below.

SOFT DRINKS

Washables. Sponge the fabric with cool water immediately, and then launder by machine or by hand. If the spot remains, use chlorine or peroxygen bleach (see charts on pages 168 f. and 170).

Nonwashables. Sponge stain promptly with cold water. If stain remains, sponge detergent into the spot. If it still persists, try commercial spot remover or chlorine of peroxygen bleach (see charts on pages 168 f. and 170).

SOOT AND SMOKE

Washables. Apply undiluted liquid detergent to stain, or dampen it and rub in soap or dry detergent until thick suds appear. Work in until outline of stain is gone, then rinse well. Repeat, if necessary. It may help to dry fabric between treatments.

Nonwashables. Use commercial spot remover. (See chart on page 170.)

Syrups. See **CHOCOLATE AND SYRUPS,** page 172 f.

TAR

(See also stains on **HANDS AND FEET,** page 189.)

Washables. Scrape off excess with a dull knife, and then wash by your regular method. If stain remains, dampen the spot. Rub in soap or detergent (dry or liquid), and then rinse with warm water. On some wash-and-wear or permanent press fabrics, if the stain is still visible, rub detergent or soap into the stain, and allow it to stand for several hours or overnight before rinsing.

It may be necessary to use a commercial spot remover; this is effective even after the article has been washed. Cover stain thoroughly with spot remover and allow to dry. Repeat, if necessary. If the stain remains, sponge with turpentine.

Nonwashables: Start with a commercial spot remover, then use hydrogen peroxide, if necessary. (See charts on pages 169 and 170.)

Tea. See **COFFEE AND TEA,** page 173.

TOBACCO

Washables and nonwashables. Dampen the spot. Work in soap or detergent, then rinse. If safe for the dye, sponge stain with alcohol (see page 166 f. and chart on page 170). If stain remains and if fabric permits, use a chlorine or powdered peroxygen bleach. If not, use hydrogen peroxide (see charts on pages 168 f. and 170).

TOMATO JUICE AND SAUCES

This kind of stain can be very stubborn, so remove it as quickly as possible.

Washables. Sponge stain with cool water, or soak in cool water for 30 minutes or longer. If stain remains after sponging and soaking, work in soap or detergent, then rinse. If stain remains after detergent treatment, use a chlorine or peroxygen bleach (see pages 168 f. and 170).

Nonwashables. Sponge the stain with cool water, or force cool water through the stain with a small syringe. Use a sponge under the stain to absorb the water. If the stain remains, rub on soap or detergent, and work it into the fabric. Rinse. A final sponging with alcohol helps to remove the soap or detergent and to dry the fabric more quickly (see page 166 f. and chart on page 170). If stain remains after rinsing, use a chlorine or peroxygen bleach (see charts on pages 168 f. and 170).

URINE

Washables. Soak in cold water, and then wash by regular laundry methods. If the color of the fabric has been changed, sponge stain with household ammonia. For wool or silk, dilute the ammonia with an equal amount of water. If this treatment does not restore the color, sponging with vinegar may help. If the stain remains, soak it in alcohol (if it will not harm the fabric), and rinse thoroughly. Then use chlorine or peroxygen bleach (see charts on pages 168 f. and 170).

Nonwashables. Instead of soaking, sponge stain with cold water, work in detergent, and rinse. Then follow procedures for washables.

Varnish. See **PAINT AND VARNISH,** page 178 f.

VOMIT AND MUCUS

Washables. Scrape off as much as possible with a knife. Then treat the area with a lukewarm solution of ¼ cup salt to 1 quart of water. Sponge stain with solution, or soak stain in it. Rinse well and launder.

Nonwashables. Treat as washables, but sponge the fabric instead of soaking it. If stain is not removed, send to the dry cleaner.

(See also stains on **CARPETS AND RUGS,** page 186.)

WAX

FLOOR, FURNITURE, OR CAR WAX

Washables. Regular washing, either by hand or machine, may remove wax stains. Some can be removed by rubbing soap or detergent into the dampened stain and then rinsing with warm water. On some wash-and-wear fabrics or permanent press, it may be necessary to rub soap or detergent thoroughly into the stain and to allow it to stand for several hours or overnight before rinsing.

You may have to try a commercial spot remover; this is effective even after the garment has been washed. Saturate the stain thoroughly with spot remover and allow to dry. Repeat, if necessary.

If stain has been set by age or heat, yellow stain may remain after the spot remover dries. To remove this, use a chlorine or peroxygen bleach, if safe for the fabric (see charts on pages 168 f. and 170). The strong sodium perborate treatment described on page 168 is very effective.

Nonwashables. Use commercial spot remover, and then if stain remains, rub in soap or detergent, and rinse spot with warm water. If stain still persists, use hydrogen peroxide (see charts on pages 169 and 170).

CANDLE WAX

Washables and nonwashables. Scrape off surface wax with a dull knife. Place the stained area between clean white blotters, paper towels, or several layers of facial tissue and press with a warm iron. To remove remaining stain, sponge with a commercial liquid spot remover.

If it is safe for the fabric, try pouring boiling water through the spot.

For really stubborn stains, sponge with a solution of 1 cup of rubbing alcohol to 2 cups of water. Check to be sure alcohol will not hurt the fabric (see chart on page 170).

WINE AND LIQUOR

Washables. Sponge immediately with soap or detergent and cold water. If the stain remains, and it is safe for fabric, pour boiling water through stain. Repeat until stain is removed.

An alternate method, if safe for the color of the fabric, is to sponge the stain with clear rubbing alcohol (see page 166 f. and chart on page 170). If stain remains, use a chlorine or peroxygen bleach (see charts on pages 168 f. and 170).

Nonwashables. Sponge stain with cool water, work in soap or detergent, and rinse. If stain remains, force water through stain, holding a sponge underneath to absorb the water. If safe for fabric, use alcohol (see page 166 f. and chart on page 170). If stain remains, use chlorine or peroxygen bleach (see charts on pages 168 f. and 170).

YELLOWED FABRICS

Washables. Use as many of the following treatments as necessary to clean the article, but be sure those you use are safe for the fabric (see chart on page 170).

Wash the piece, then mix 1 to 2 tablespoonfuls of powdered sodium perborate with 1 pint of lukewarm water for wool, silk, and modacrylic fibers such as Dynel ® or 1 pint of hot water for other fabrics. Prepare the mixture just before using. Apply to stain with medicine dropper if the stain is small. If the whole item is yellowed, dip it in the solution, wait a few minutes, and then rinse well. Rinse again with 1 cup of vinegar added to the rinse water. Then rinse with fresh water.

If this still does not work, sprinkle powdered sodium perborate on the fabric, and then dip it into the hottest water safe for the fabric. Do not use on wool, silk, or modacrylic fibers.

For white fabrics, you may have to resort to a color remover.

OTHER STAIN-REMOVAL PROBLEMS

The constant battle with dirt and stains is not limited to clothing. Stains on carpets, floors, furniture, wallpaper need special handling. After reading this section, you won't need to panic when a pan is scorched, the iron sticks, or your child gets chewing gum in her hair. Some hints on cleaning suede and leather are also included here.

Caution! Never mix household cleansers. In an effort to do a very thorough job, some housewives have mixed such products as toilet bowl cleansers and chlorine bleaches. When the acid in the bowl product is added to the bleach solution, a deadly chlorine gas is released. Its toxic effect can prove fatal.

CARPETS AND RUGS

STAIN REMOVERS

Plain soda water acts as an instant spot remover—providing the stain is fresh. Just pour some on the spot, sponge it up, and that may be all you have to do.

Foam is a good spot remover for both synthetic and wool carpets and for rugs. It can be made by beating liquid or powdered detergents and water in the electric mixer. If you have shaving cream on hand, however, it is an excellent substitute because it is drier and often more effective than the self-mixed foam.

For older or more stubborn stains, you may have to try other methods. One stain-removal solution you can mix yourself is 1 teaspoonful of a mild detergent, the kind used for washing delicate fabrics, and 1 teaspoonful of white vinegar mixed with 1 quart of warm water.

Commercial stain-remover solutions similar to spot removers used on fabrics can be purchased at supermarkets, hardware, or carpet stores. If you have none at hand, use the same spot remover you apply to fabrics.

STAINS

The first thing to do when confronted with a stain on the carpet is to dab up as much as you can. Scrape up any solids, and then blot gently with a clean white cloth or paper towel. Begin at the outer edge of the stain and blot toward the center. Do not rub. Try to classify the stain and treat it accordingly:

Beverages (alcoholic, soft drinks). Use soda water or foam. If necessary, apply detergent-vinegar solution (see above). Dry carpet, and repeat as necessary.

Blood. Use soda water or foam and if necessary, apply detergent-vinegar solution (see above). Allow carpet to dry and apply spot remover.

Candlewax drippings. Remove from carpet and rugs by placing a blotter, paper towels, or several layers of facial tissues over the wax spot. Place a warm iron over the absorbent material. In about two minutes, the wax will be absorbed into the blotter, cloth, or paper towel.

Candy and syrup (except chocolate). Use soda water or foam. If necessary, apply detergent-vinegar solution (see above). Allow carpet to dry, and repeat as necessary.

Chewing gum. Press ice cubes against the gum until it becomes brittle and breaks off. Then use spot remover to remove the last traces.

Cigarette burns. The first thing to do when you see a burn in the carpet or rug is to make sure there are no embers at work. If not, brush the burned spot and use sandpaper to clean the hole of any remaining charred threads. Put a small amount of rubber cement or plastic glue into the hole and spread it evenly with your fingers. While the adhesive is setting, take a single-edged razor blade and lightly scrape the top of the carpet in an area that most closely matches the burned section. When you have scraped enough lint, drop it loosely into the hole, and push it down gently with your finger. In a few days, after normal use, it will be hard to find the spot that was burned.

Crayon, heavy grease, lipstick, shoe polish, tar. Apply commercial spot remover, then detergent-vinegar solution (see above). Allow car-

185

pet to dry, and reapply spot remover. An alternate method for grease is to give the stain a liberal coating of baking soda, which should be rubbed well into the nap. Allow it to stand overnight, and then vacuum.

Food (all greasy foods, chocolate, coffee, milk). Use soda water or foam. If necessary, apply detergent-vinegar solution (see page 185). Allow carpet to dry, and apply spot remover.

Paint, varnish. Apply a few drops of turpentine to clean cloth, and dab carpet lightly. Apply nonflammable spot remover.

Pet stains. Use soda water or foam. If necessary, apply detergent-vinegar solution (see page 185). Allow carpet to dry, and apply spot remover.

Rust. Use a solution of ⅛ cup household detergent that contains ammonia to 1 gallon of hot water. Scrub area lightly with a soft brush and rinse.

Shellac. Apply a few drops of denatured alcohol to clean cloth, and dab carpet lightly. Apply nonflammable spot remover.

Vomit. Use soda water or foam. If necessary, apply detergent-vinegar solution (see page 185). Allow carpet to dry, and apply spot remover.

CHINA DISHES

Cigarette burns. There is always the possibility that someone will inadvertently rest a cigarette on the saucer of a coffee cup or on some other piece of your favorite china. If dishwashing doesn't remove the nicotine stain, rub the spot with a cork, or a soft rag, dipped in baking soda.

Coffee and tea stains. Even a little coffee or tea left in a cup for a short time can cause a brownish stain that doesn't yield to detergent or soap. You can remove these stains by rubbing them with a damp cloth dipped in baking soda.

COFFEEPOTS

To restore the gleam to the inside of the coffeepot, remove all the parts, then fill the pot with hot water just high enough to cover the stains. Add 1 teaspoonful of detergent. If the coffee maker is electric, turn it on until the water is very hot, then empty it and rinse. If the pot is not electric, do the same thing, but put the pot on the range until the water is hot.

To freshen a coffeepot, fill it with cold water and add 2 tablespoonfuls of baking soda, and let it stand for several hours. Then rinse with cold water. Stale smells and tastes will vanish.

Mineral deposits or scale can be removed with commercial products specifically made for this purpose. Or you can achieve the same result by adding 1 teaspoonful of cream of tartar to water in the pot, then bringing the water to a boil.

FIREPLACE

To clean a brick or stone fireplace blackened by soot, cover the stained area with a paste made of concentrated ammonia and powdered pumice

186

(available at hardware stores). Let the paste remain on for about two hours. Scrub off with hot water and soap. Rinse with clear water and dry.

FLOORS AND COUNTERS

STAINS ON VINYL, ASPHALT, RUBBER OR ASBESTOS TILE, LINOLEUM

Alkalis, including lye and drain cleaners. To neutralize these stains, apply a 1-to-1 mixture of white vinegar and water. Let stand for several minutes, then rinse and dry.

Beverage and fruit stains. For stains caused by coffee, fruit, juice, or alcoholic beverages, rub with fine (#00) steel wool. Then pour on hydrogen peroxide (see page 167). Wash, then wax.

Crayons and black heel marks. Crayon marks can be removed with silver polish even if the crayons have been mashed.

To remove black heel marks, take a pencil eraser and go to work. This removes the mark without scrubbing.

Ink, iodine, mercurochrome, or merthiolate. To remove ink, iodine, mercurochrome, or merthiolate stains from a tile floor or counter, rub the stain with fine (#00) steel wool dipped in a strong liquid detergent. Wet a white cloth with household ammonia, and place it over the stain for several minutes. Wash with clear water, dry, and apply wax. For linoleum, rub with fine steel wool dipped in detergent. Rinse and wax.

Fingernail polish remover, acids, and blood. Rub with fine (#00) steel wool, rinse, and let dry. Apply wax.

Paint, varnish, shoe polish, or fingernail polish. Clean up as much of the spilled material as you can with a paper towel or clean cloth, using a pick-up motion toward the center of the spill to avoid spreading it. Remove the excess or dried material with a spatula or dull kitchen knife. Ice cubes in a plastic bag held over the spot for a few minutes sometimes makes removal easier. Sprinkle abrasive cleaner onto the area and rub with fine steel wool. Take up the abrasive and rinse. Let dry and wax.

STAINS ON WOOD

Black heel marks. Use a pencil eraser to remove marks.

Burns. Scrape out the charred wood with a sharp knife or single-edged razor blade in a holder. Work with the grain. Sand smooth. If the hole is not too deep, fill it with plastic wood. Plastic wood (available at hardware stores) must be stained to match the area surrounding the burn. After the plastic hardens, sand smooth, and wax the floor.

STAINS ON FORMICA ®

Burns. Burn stains on Formica ® cannot be removed.

Common stains. Scrub with powdered household cleanser. Then apply appliance wax and polish the surface.

Rust. Apply ammonia or chlorine bleach and polish with appliance wax.

187

FURNITURE

STAINS ON OILED WOOD

Alcohol and water stains or rings. Dip a fine steel wool pad into one of the following:

Oil used in finishing
Lightweight mineral oil
Paraffin oil or lemon oil
Boiled linseed oil (if wood is badly scarred)

Rub carefully with the grain of the wood. Wipe the entire surface with a cloth slightly moistened with one of the above oils. Wipe dry.

Burns. Burns or heat marks on oiled wood cannot be removed.

STAINS AND SCRATCHES ON VARNISHED SURFACES

Alcohol spots or rings. Rub with rottenstone (available at paint stores) and a cloth dipped in salad oil.

Candle wax. Scrape off as much wax as possible with your fingers, and then remove the rest with a dull table knife.

Crayon or lipstick marks. Use a commercial cleaning wax.

Fingernail polish. You may be tempted to use fingernail polish remover or other lacquer thinner on the varnished surface, but don't do it. Scrape the polish off gently with the point of a knife. If the surface is scratched, use rottenstone and a cloth dipped in salad oil.

Paint spots. Scrape off gently with the point of a sharp knife. Then if the surface is scratched, rub it with rottenstone and a cloth dipped in salad oil.

Paper stuck to surface. If paper becomes stuck to a varnished table top, don't try to scrape it off with a knife. Pour olive oil, or any salad oil, a few drops at a time, on the paper, and rub with a soft cloth. Repeat the procedure until the paper is completely gone.

Scratches. Cover up minor scratches on red, finished mahogany, with iodine; for mahogany that has turned brown, use brown paste shoe polish. For maple, dilute iodine with denatured alcohol, using a 50–50 mixture.

Scratches can also be rubbed with the meat of a walnut, or a similarly oily nut, or with floor paste wax.

For larger scratches, fill by rubbing with a wax stick made for use on furniture. You can touch up with matching oil stain applied with a small artist's brush.

The alternative is to sprinkle rottenstone (available from a paint store) on the scratch, and then rub with a cloth dipped in salad or sewing machine oil. Work with the grain. This will take off quite a lot of the finish and you may have to refinish it with oil stain. But if you haven't cut through the varnish to the wood, several applications of paste wax will hide the scratch.

Water and heat marks. When the party's over and you find a water ring on your furniture, don't fret. It can be remedied with quick action.

If you wax or polish over a water ring on a table top before it has dried thoroughly, you will set it permanently. If the ring is new, place a clean white blotter over the spot and press with a warm, not hot, iron until the ring disappears.

If you are reluctant to try this method, or don't have a blotter, you can rub mayonnaise or petroleum jelly into the ring and leave it overnight. Then wipe clean with a flannel cloth. An alternate method consists of applying a little salad oil. Rub it in gently with a soft cloth.

The techniques mentioned above will also work with heat marks. If the spot turns out to be rough after treatment, rub ever so lightly with fine (#00) steel wool, and then go over the entire surface with a soft cloth dipped in salad oil.

HAIR

If chewing gum gets caught in your child's hair, rub a dab of peanut butter on the spot. Gently massage the gum, hair, and peanut butter between your fingers until the gum is loosened. Remove with a facial tissue and shampoo hair in the usual manner.

No peanut butter available? Freeze the gum with ice cubes, and then peel it off the hair.

HANDS AND FEET

Hands and feet often get stained during the day's work. Here are some hints on how to remove some of the more common stains:

Ball-point pen ink. Rub hands well with the moistened tip of a paper match, and then wash hands vigorously.

Fruit stain. Mix a little cornmeal or cornstarch with vinegar, and massage the spots.

Ink. Dip an old toothbrush or nailbrush into vinegar and then in salt, and scrub the stains until they disappear.

Tar. Rub with the outside of an orange or lemon peel and the tar will come off. Or, rub spots with kerosene.

PILLOWS

Young children or people who are ill often stain pillows. If you want to be able to use the pillow again, it is wise to wash it promptly.

First check for any open or weak seams. Then put the pillow in a pillowcase, and baste the open end. Wash two pillows at a time for a balanced load, or add towels for balance. Fill the automatic washer with warm water, and push pillows down to saturate them completely before turning on the regular wash cycle. Stop the washer and turn pillows over half way through the washing. To dry, put feather pillows (but not foam rubber pillows) in an automatic dryer set at low heat. It will take about one and a half hours to dry them completely. Foam rubber pillows may be gently squeezed to remove water and allowed to dry for several days in a warm, dry, place.

189

POTS AND PANS

SCORCHED AND BURNED

There are several things you can do about burned pans besides using elbow grease. For pans made of aluminum, stainless steel, porcelain, porcelanized cast iron, ceramic, and heat-proof glass, partly fill with water and a little detergent and simmer the mixture for 10 minutes. As it simmers, scrape the sides and loosen the burned particles with a wooden spoon. Or, instead of adding detergent to the water, put an onion in the water and boil. Chances are the burned food will come off without a tear.

Burn stains on glass pans and casseroles can also be removed by soaking the dishes in a mixture of baking soda and cold water—2 teaspoonfuls of baking soda to 1 quart of water. Be sure the solution completely fills the inside of the stained container. In an hour you'll be able to wash the dish clean. Burned enamel pans should be cleaned with household cleanser and a sponge.

Put a scorched pan aside overnight. Fill it with a solution of ¼ cup water to 1 cup household bleach. Wash it clean in the morning.

STAINED

Aluminum. If the insides of aluminum pans have darkened, mix 2 teaspoonfuls of cream of tartar mixed with 1 quart of water, and boil for 10 minutes. Then use steel wool.

Teflon ®. Stained Teflon ® pots and pans can be cleaned by boiling 2 tablespoonfuls of baking soda, ½ cup of liquid household bleach, and 1 cup of water in the container. Then wash in warm suds. Don't let the solution contact any surface other than the Teflon ®. Rub with 1 teaspoon of salad oil before using again.

Cast-iron. Cast-iron skillets or pans can be cleaned very easily with commercial oven cleaner. Be sure to take the same precautions you would when cleaning the oven. Place a lot of newspapers under the skillet so the cleaner won't touch the counter top or sink, and protect your hands with rubber gloves. Let stand two hours. After you rinse the pot, you may find an accumulation of black stains inside. These can easily be removed with vinegar and water.

SUEDE AND LEATHER

Suede leather and grain leather are both tanned animal skins that are treated at the tannery with fine oils and dressings to make them soft and durable. Leather loses its tannery oils as a result of wearing, soiling, and natural evaporation. The loss is increased by improper cleaning, so avoid using cleaning fluids, saddle soap, wire brushes, steel wool, or other harsh abrasives, which usually result in ugly rings, discoloration, or other damage. A gum eraser or fine sandpaper, however, can be quite effective on small stains. But do it gently. Lipstick, ball-point pen ink, and other such stains are best removed by a leather-cleaning specialist.

Garments or trim made of smooth leather can be surface-cleaned by using a sponge or soft cloth dampened in water containing a small amount of mild soapsuds. Wipe the surface clean, and then dry with a terry towel.

Blood, food, or milk. If any of these is spilled on suede or another type of leather, blot the stain immediately with a soft cloth dampened in cool water. Do not rub hard. Feather out the stained area with a terry towel. The garment should then be dried at room temperature. Brush it lightly with a soft bristle brush when it is dry.

Coffee, cola, fruit juices, perfume, or tea. Stains caused by one of these liquids will set and turn brown if not sponged up immediately. Once set, it may be impossible even for a leather-cleaning specialist to remove the stain.

Mildew. Allow a cloth to soak in a solution of 1 cup of denatured alcohol and 1 cup of water. Squeeze it out, and use it to wipe off the mildew stain. Repeat, if necessary.

Rain spots. Suede doesn't fare too well when splashed with water, so if a suede or leather garment gets wet, allow it to dry at room temperature. Sponge or brush to remove rain spots and raise the nap of the suede.

UPHOLSTERY

FABRIC UPHOLSTERY

There are a number of products designed for cleaning upholstery, but if you do not have one on hand, and do not think the stain requires a professional cleaner, try foam. Foam is one of the most useful upholstery cleaners for new stains and ordinary dirt. Shaving foam right from the container is excellent for this purpose. If you want to make your own foam, put 1 tablespoon of liquid detergent or soap and 1 cup of water in your electric mixing bowl. Beat slowly, increasing the speed as the foam forms. Keep whipping until the bowl is full, and then apply the foam to the upholstery with a clean sponge, brush, or cloth, depending on the delicacy of the fabric. Wipe off with a clean, damp sponge.

There are some upholstery stains, however, that need special handling, such as:

Grease, oil or blood. Sprinkle talcum, cornstarch, or chalk on a fresh grease, oil, or blood stain. Rub in well, and let stand until the stain is absorbed; then brush off. Repeat until the stain disappears. For older stains, rub on a paste of cornstarch and water. If possible, put the stained piece in the sun near an open window, or outdoors. The sun will help to draw the stain out into the cornstarch. Brush off the dry cornstarch, and if the spot is not completely gone, repeat the process.

Other types of stains. When foam does not work, treat upholstery stains as you would any fabric stain (see pages 170 to 184) if you know what caused the stain and the fiber content of the fabric (see chart on page 170).

LEATHER UPHOLSTERY

Most stains can be removed by rubbing gently with a damp cloth dipped in mild soap or detergent suds. Rinse the cloth in clear water, and wipe off the suds. Then finish the job by going over the surface with a cloth dipped in a well-beaten egg white. Allow to dry, and polish with a soft, dry cloth.

WALLPAPER

Washable. Stains can usually be removed from washable wallpaper with a sponge dipped in soapy water. After rubbing with the sponge, rinse with a clean sponge or soft cloth dipped in clear water. When the paper is dry, a soft gum eraser may be used for any stains that remain.

Nonwashable. Use a gum eraser. If the stain still remains, you still have ways to remove it.

For greasy stains. Make a thick paste of commercial spot remover and a powder such as cornstarch or cornmeal. Cover the stain with the paste and let it remain until it is thoroughly dry. Then brush it off with a soft cloth. Repeat several times, if necessary.

For nongreasy stains. Use a solvent such as turpentine or alcohol, but be sure to test an inconspicuous spot first to see if it removes color or affects texture.

WHITE WOODWORK

White shoe polish will cover up marked, scuffed, and stained white woodwork.

travel

If there's one thing worse than facing an emergency at home, it's facing an emergency away from home. However, if you know the answers to common travel problems, you will be prepared to handle them.

First of all, prior to starting out on any trip, whether for pleasure or necessity, plan ahead. Know just what you are going to do and where you will do it. Allow yourself ample time—trying to crowd too much into a single trip is unwise.

If immunizations are required, get them early so you don't suffer from the reactions on the trip.

Before you leave home, make sure any medical or dental problems are taken care of by your doctor or dentist. If you wear glasses, carry an extra pair or a written prescription for them. If you take medication regularly, be sure you have an adequate supply.

Ask your physician for an antidiarrhea medicine. Even if you are traveling in the United States, you may need one. Ask also if a broad-spectrum antibiotic should be taken along—just in case. In a strange town, at a strange hour, it is often difficult to find a physician or a drugstore.

Other health supplies to pack in your hand luggage include: a Fahrenheit-scale thermometer, aspirin, adhesive bandage strips, a motion-sickness remedy, hand-washing packets, and, if your doctor recommends them, an antihistamine and a nasal decongestant. You may also need an insecticide, depending upon the locale of your trip.

You have probably heard the expression: "Take half as many clothes as you think you need, and twice as much money (preferably in travelers' checks)." This is wise advice because unnecessary clothing is an extra burden. As for unnecessary money, you can always bring it back. In the meantime, by having enough, you avoid one of the most common emergencies—running out of funds.

Make a calendar of the days you will be away; then list all the outfits you think will be needed. Repeats, of course, are fine. Lay out all the garments plus shoes, belts, scarves, underwear, and jewelry. Be sure the clothes you select are appropriate for the climate and local custom. Don't forget to include at least one good pair of walking shoes.

Write a check list of all little extras you probably will need; spot remover; your own house keys, and a second set of luggage keys; sewing kit plus roll of cellophane tape for instant mending; clothesline; pocket flashlight; spoon; extra pen, safety pins; and any other item that you know from experience may be handy in a minor emergency.

No matter what your means of travel, carry a compass and, if possible, maps of the area you are visiting. The compass may just be a convenience in a city, but it is essential in a wilderness area.

Before departing, leave copies of your itinerary with a family member, a neighbor, and a friend. In case of any emergency at home, it will be possible to get in touch with you promptly.

When you leave home for a vacation, business trip, or even just for a local event that has been announced in the newspaper, create a "lived-in" look for your house. Keep two lights lit at all times, or install an automatic timing device that turns on your lights at dusk. A light in the bathroom and one in the hall discourages burglars. Leave shades or blinds in a normal position—not completely drawn or closed. A radio playing while your home is empty can be an inexpensive method of keeping burglars out.

If you are going to be away more than 24 hours, cancel all deliveries and services, including newspapers and mail. Ask a neighbor to remove circulars that may accumulate. Do not mention your planned absence to strangers.

Make arrangements to have your lawn mowed and watered, and snow shoveled or plowed in winter. Leave your keys with a neighbor and ask that he or she check your house periodically. Place valuables and important papers in the bank vault, if possible. If you live in a small community, notify the police of dates of departure and return.

Once on your way, it is nice to follow your inclinations and go off on unplanned tangents, but if you're going to do it in the height of the tourist season, or you are traveling with young children, you would be wise to have reservations. If you have none, try to arrive at lodgings before 3 P.M. to increase your chances of getting rooms.

If you are going to fly, make sure you have confirmed reservations.

Sightseeing can be very tiring, so try to schedule it for only half a day and rest and relax the other half.

Avoid extremes of hot or cold. Don't try to get a suntan all in one day.

Refrain from trying to crowd a year's exercise into two weeks; Forego playing golf or tennis under the broiling sun if you are unused to such activity. Do only what is best for you within your own physical limitations.

Some of the unexpected things that happen on a trip are fun. Some are not.

A travel emergency, as you will read in this chapter, can be as minor as arriving at a hotel and finding no rooms available, or it can be as major as a serious illness or a plane hijacking.

If you get caught in an emergency while traveling, there are well-tested, standard procedures, and there is almost always professional help available for travelers in trouble in the United States and in almost every nation with which the United States has diplomatic relations.

Airsickness. See **MOTION SICKNESS,** page 105.
Accidents, Automobile. See page 36 ff.

ARREST, ACCIDENT, OR DEATH OVERSEAS

If you or someone for whom you are responsible gets into difficulty in another country, the first thing to do is to contact the American embassy or consulate. The staff will try to help an American citizen.

Should you be unable to contact the embassy or consulate or, for some reason, your problem is not serious enough for official help, consider seeking aid from local members of your religious denomination or fraternal organization. Religious groups usually are equipped to offer social services, and fraternal groups such as Rotary Clubs or the Masons consider a member from another part of the world a brother. The same kind of helpfulness is available to members of international women's organizations.

BAGGAGE—LOST OR DAMAGED

What do you do when you arrive at your destination and find that your baggage has gone astray? Report the loss immediately to the airline personnel. The bags may still be on the plane and a prompt search may unearth them without delay. If they are not on the plane, report the loss to the airline before leaving the airport. A claim made later may not be honored by the carrier. You will probably be asked to identify the type of luggage from diagrams of various shapes and sizes. If you plan ahead, however, such identification can be made easier. Applying bright, self-sticking tape conspicuously on all your bags will make your luggage easy to spot. Use your initials or some distinctive design.

Before each trip, you should remove old destination tags and tape an identification card inside each bag, as well as your itinerary, with the dates and places where you will be stopping. Do not use address tags on the outside of your luggage if you and your spouse are traveling together. It tips off burglars that your home may be empty.

Any medicines that you must take should be carried with you in case your luggage does get lost. If you must carry valuables while traveling, they should always be kept with you rather than in a suitcase. Always carry your passport with you. Never leave it in luggage or in a hotel room.

Keep a list of the contents of your luggage at home and a copy with you so that if there is a loss, you have an accurate record.

If your luggage is lost and you have no change of clothes, contact a representative of the airline at the terminal, or the Travelers Aid Society for advice and help.

If the luggage is eventually recovered, the airline may deliver it to your home or hotel without expense to you.

Should your baggage be damaged by the airlines at any time, report it immediately to airline personnel at the airport or ticket office. The agent will complete a Baggage Damage Report form, and ask you to describe the damage. If it is due to your luggage being dropped, or if the handles have been torn off, or if there is any other damage which could have been prevented, the airlines will pay. However, they will not pay for damage caused by packing the luggage too full, or by packing breakables.

For lost or damaged baggage on domestic flights, the airlines' liability is usually up to $500 per fare-paying passenger. You should find the liability amount printed on your ticket.

BUMPED FROM A PLANE

Even if you purchased a ticket on a scheduled airline well in advance of your flight, you may be forced off the flight list because the airline has oversold, or flights have been canceled.

Bumpings occur most frequently during peak travel periods—holidays, summer weekends, and almost any Friday afternoon. Therefore, avoid departing during these periods, particularly on the eve of a major holiday. If you must fly then, try to depart early in the day.

The Civil Aeronautics Board has ruled that an airline must put you on another flight that will arrive at your final destination no more than two hours later than your original flight, or give you a refund as fixed by the CAB. In addition, you do not have to accept alternate transportation in a light plane or air taxi.

If your flight has been canceled, or you have missed a connecting flight because of delays, some airlines provide expenses such as hotel, meals, telephone, and transportation to and from the airport. They seldom publicize the fact, so ask an airline representative at the terminal about this service.

Car Sickness. See **MOTION SICKNESS,** page 105.

CHILDREN TRAVELING ALONE

Sometimes it is necessary for children to travel by themselves when going to and from relatives' homes or when going off to schools, camps, etc.

In some cases, an airline will take responsibility for a child, but be sure to call in advance to see if they provide this service. Most airlines won't be responsible for a child under 6 years of age (they suggest you pay to have someone escort the child), and they charge full fare for a child traveling alone. Special agents no longer escort the child to connecting flights or buses.

Similar problems are involved in rail transportation. Amtrak (the national railway system) will not assume responsibility for a child alone, so be sure to make arrangements accordingly.

Death, Overseas. See page 195.

FINDING A DOCTOR

Most hotels and motels in the United States have a physician on call so phone the front desk and request a doctor.

When someone becomes ill while traveling by car, you can stop at a service station, store, or phone booth, and call the police. Describe the situation, and the police will advise you what to do. Or you may ask directions to the nearest hospital emergency room.

Hotels and motels in Europe and other areas catering to Americans usually have an English-speaking physician on call. If not, contact the American embassy or consulate, the Red Cross, travel agencies, police, hospitals, clinics, American business or cultural institutions, religious groups, American armed forces installations, or the American Express.

To be prepared in advance, investigate the services of the organizations listed below:

The International Association for Medical Assistance to Travelers compiles a directory of hospitals and clinics abroad where doctors speak many languages (including English). A small fee entitles you to the directory and a membership card. Doctors' fees are lower for members. The directory and more information can be obtained by writing to: IAMAT, Membership Dept. 350 Fifth Avenue, New York, New York 10016.

The World Medical Association, 10 Columbus Circle, New York, New York 10019, publishes an *International Medical Directory* listing physicians abroad who are approved by the Medical Association of each country. You can obtain a copy for a small charge.

For a nominal fee, The Medical Passport Foundation offers a pocket-sized Medical Passport that contains a standardized medical record (a comprehensive questionnaire) to be filled out by you and your doctor. The passport and medical record will supply the physician abroad with a current condensed, detailed medical history. Write to: The Medical Passport Foundation, Inc., 704 N. Kansas Ave., DeLand, Florida 32720.

HANDICAPPED TRAVELERS

People with physical handicaps need not miss the pleasures of traveling. There are many places they can tour just like anyone else. The President's Committee on Employment of the Handicapped, Washington, D.C. 20210, has issued a list of guidebooks for handicapped travelers. The list includes the names and addresses of scores of tourist meccas that provide special facilities, not only in the United States, but overseas as well. Write to the committee for the list.

ILL PERSON NEEDS TRANSPORTATION

Transporting an ill person from a hospital, or from one hospital to another, or to an airport may be accomplished by contacting a local first-aid squad or commercial ambulance service. Often these volunteers or professionals will drive a person by ambulance from one town to another or even longer distances.

When a person on a stretcher is to be transported by plane, arrangements must be made in advance with the airline involved. Carriers prefer to have the passenger's physician make the arrangements and assure them that there will be no problems in flight. The airline will make arrangements with airport authorities to have an ambulance waiting at the landing field. Prices for transporting a stretcher case by plane vary but usually amount to at least the cost of two seats.

Should you or anyone you are traveling with become ill on board a plane, call a steward or stewardess. They have been trained in first aid and are there to help with oxygen and other first-aid supplies.

If the illness is a dire emergency, the plane will, if possible, land at the nearest airport and the pilot will radio ahead to have an ambulance and medical personnel waiting.

Most ships, on the other hand, carry fully equipped infirmaries, including an operating room, and at least one physician and one nurse. If an illness or emergency requires hospitalization on shore, the Coast Guard will be notified and, if feasible, arrangements will be made to pick up the passenger by helicopter.

NO ROOM AT THE INN

It's frustrating to arrive at a hotel or motel and find no rooms available, especially if you have made reservations. The best insurance against such a situation is to guarantee your reservation by paying at least one night's stay in advance.

If you find yourself without a room for the night and you have confirmed reservations, the manager should find suitable similar accommodations for you elsewhere. Most reputable hotels and motels will make every effort to do this.

All American Hotel and Motel Association members make available to guests, at their front desks, a copy of the *Hotel and Motel Red Book,* which enables visitors to select alternate accommodations in the same city or area if the hotel of their choice is overbooked.

If you arrive without an advance reservation and find the hotel or motel of your choice has no rooms available, look for a convention bureau or tourist information office. Many of the larger cities and resort areas maintain such facilities where tourists can find out about the availability of accommodations in the area.

The earlier you arrive at a hotel or motel, the better your chances of getting a room for the night.

For information on what to do if you are out of funds and have no place to stay, see **STRANDED WHILE TRAVELING,** page 200.

OUT OF FUNDS OVERSEAS

If you should find yourself without funds in a foreign country, the American embassy or consulate may offer advice but little else. As a rule, the maximum they may lend you is $10.

One of the fastest and safest methods of obtaining funds is to go to one of the 400 American Express offices, or one of the 5,000 banking correspondents they deal with, and explain your plight. An American Express representative will help you prepare and transmit a cable home to your family or bank. For a small fee the recipient of the cable can arrange to transmit the funds in either local or foreign currency through any of the local American Express offices. An average of three days is required for the transfer of funds, but the process can be speeded up by paying an additional cable fee. (See also **MONEY NEEDS TO BE SENT FAST,** page 143.)

PET TRAVELING WITH YOU

Before leaving on an extended trip with a pet, take it to the veterinarian for a checkup, rabies shots, and other necessary vaccinations.

On an automobile trip, carry a bottle of water and a water dish, so you won't have to hunt for a place to stop. Just fill your pet's dish when he gets thirsty. Stop off the road every hour or so, for elimination and a stretch. Keep your pet under control. If traveling overnight, pack a blanket or whatever the pet normally sleeps on at home. Check accommodations before booking to make sure pets are accepted. Don't feed the pet until it has had an hour's rest from traveling.

If you have to leave a pet in your car while you stop at a restaurant to eat, be sure there is enough ventilation for comfort, and that the car is sheltered from the hot sun.

Don't let your pet mingle with other animals if you stop at a picnic area or campsite. You can't be sure the other animals are disease-free. And don't let your pet wander off if there is a chance that it will tangle with wild animals. They could be carrying rabies.

Check to be sure that your pet's identification tag is firmly attached at all times. (See also **TRANSPORTATION FOR A PET,** page 158 f.)

PLANE IS HIJACKED

In the event of a hijacking, the Federal Aviation Administration recommends that passengers try to remain calm and do absolutely nothing. A threatening gesture or even a remark by a passenger could have catastrophic results. Passengers have no choice but to follow orders of the flight crew in this very delicate situation.

Seasickness. See **MOTION SICKNESS,** page 105.

STRANDED WHILE TRAVELING

What do you do when you are in a strange city and you have no money, no place to stay, and no transportation? You can contact the local police, the Salvation Army, or Travelers Aid.

Police usually are very cooperative and will advise you about local agencies that may help out in such circumstances. In some cities throughout the country, the Salvation Army has residences that may offer services to a traveler in trouble, although they are not specifically designed for transients. The Travelers Aid Society was founded for the specific purpose of helping travelers and their services are available in many bus, airport, and railroad stations. If you cannot find their offices, look up Travelers Aid in the phone book or ask the telephone information operator for the number of the nearest office. (See also **OUT OF FUNDS OVERSEAS,** page 199.)

TRAILER OR CAMPGROUNDS FILLED

If you are traveling by trailer or camper, reservations in camps or national parks are a necessity at the height of the tourist season. If you find such sites are fully booked and local laws will not allow you to stop in the open, head for a gas station or diner and ask for permission to spend the night. Notify the local police of the arrangement.

TRAVELING WITH CHILDREN

Children can make family travel a wonderful and memorable experience. Nevertheless, there are pitfalls to be avoided.

When traveling with very young children, pin identification tags to their clothes each day. Include such information as the child's name, place of temporary residence (hotel or motel), home town, and auto license number and make if traveling by car.

Give each child a whistle to blow if he or she gets lost. This works in crowded cities and shops as well as in open country.

In strange hotels or motels, children who cannot read will be able to find the door to their rooms if you paste a sticker on the outside or if you tie a ribbon to the door handle.

Sightseeing with young children should be limited to no more than two or three hours. They usually do not take well to long bus tours. (It is often cheaper to rent a car and guide when a family is involved.) Schedule rest stops every hour, and if you are traveling any distance by car with young children, carry snacks, bottled water, and toys or games for diversion. A blanket and pillow will add to their comfort. A few paper or plastic bags might prove useful if a child is subject to car sickness.

A damp washrag in a plastic bag is good for quick cleanups, and don't forget an extra change of clothing for "accidents" that may occur.

When traveling with children by automobile, here are some precautions to take to avoid serious problems:

Children under four or weighing less than 40 pounds should not be strapped in by the standard safety seat belts. They should, instead, have car beds or car seats of their own. The car seat or bed should be of sturdy construction and strapped to the seat by the seat belt. There are no Federal safety standards for car beds, at this writing, but there are for car seats and harnesses. The car seat should have a head restraint to prevent whiplash injuries and a full harness to protect against collision forces. Parents should look for the label "Federal Motor Vehicle Safety Standard No. 213" for car seats and "Federal Motor Vehicle Safety Standard No. 209" for safety harnesses.

Although a child may prefer it, never hold a youngster on your lap or in your arms when the car is moving. In an accident, the child may be crushed by your weight, or thrown through the windshield, window, or door. Strapping the child with your lap belt will only make matters worse in an accident. The belt will be pressed by your weight into the child's abdomen, with serious consequences.

Children should sit in the back seat, if possible, because it is safer. Never allow children to have their heads, arms, or legs out of the window.

When traveling with children, discipline may be a matter of life or death. Do not allow them to distract you. If a fight occurs in the back seat, pull over to the the side of the road. Do not attempt to discipline them while the car is moving.

In addition to the usual pillows and blankets, airlines carry infant beds (if ordered ahead) and often provide toys and coloring books. Just ask the stewardess. Often a mother with young children can get seats in the front of the tourist section where the additional space makes handling children, especially infants, easier. Special meals including such child favorites as hamburgers and hot dogs will sometimes be provided if you give the airline advance notice.

The key to safe and happy travel with children is not allowing them to get too tired or too hungry, so plan your schedule accordingly.

weather emergencies

Although people can heat their houses in winter, and cool them in summer, they still can do little more than talk about the weather. There is no way to control the whirl of a tornado, level the snow, halt the floods, or cool the sun-heated atmosphere.

There are, however, certain actions that can be taken in anticipation of weather disasters.

1. Every house should have a "storm box" containing:

   > Bottled water
   > First-aid supplies
   > A flashlight painted with luminous paint so it is visible
   >   in the dark
   > Fresh batteries
   > Matches (do not, of course, use matches if there is the
   >   slightest danger of leaking gas)
   > Fuses
   > Candles

2. Keep a working battery-powered radio or television set and extra batteries on hand. These appliances may be your only contact with the outside world during a weather emergency.

3. Check your supply of both heating and automobile fuel. In a severe storm, it may be several days before you can get more. If time does not allow for replenishing household fuel, obtain an alternate such as wood for the fireplace, or portable heaters.

4. An emergency supply of food is a "must" for residents of storm-prone areas:

   > Food that doesn't require cooking or refrigeration in case
   >   of power failure (see **FREEZER,** page 20). Include
   >   any of your family's favorite foods.
   > Canned or powdered milk for young children
   > Soda or canned fruit drinks
   > Cans of soup that can be eaten hot or cold and do not
   >   require dilution with water
   > Tins of crackers, cookies, and unsalted nuts (if you do
   >   not have tins, wrap and seal the boxes in plastic
   >   bags)
   > Jelly or jam
   > A nonelectric can opener
   > A bottle opener
   > A chafing dish with Sterno or a camp stove with appropriate
   >   fuel, or a fondue pot with an alcohol burner. Such
   >   appliances can be used for heating meals and water
   >   for hot beverages.

5. A working fire extinguisher (see page 75 ff.) should be kept within easy reach for fires caused by storms.

6. It is also a good idea to have games, toys, and books on hand to calm children and keep them busy.

7. If severe storm warnings are broadcast by the weather bureau (officially the National Weather Service), sterilize the bathtubs, jugs, bottles, and cooking utensils with household chlorine bleach or disinfectant and then fill them with drinking water, since city water service may be interrupted.

8. Store or secure everything that may blow away or be torn loose. Garbage

cans, garden tools, toys, signs, porch furniture, awnings, and other objects become missiles in high winds.

9. In any weather emergency, stay off the telephone except to report an emergency and don't go sightseeing. You may keep vital help from getting to those who really need it.

BASEMENT FLOODED

Basements are always the first areas to be flooded when waters rise. Should you be lucky enough to have sufficient warning, move everything to higher ground. Shut off all electricity at the fuse box and disconnect all wire cords in the basement *before* flooding occurs. Never enter flooded basements under any circumstances until the utility company representative has given his permission. In flooded basements, it is not necessary to touch electrical equipment to be electrocuted—currents in the water can do it. Naturally, too, no appliances should be touched if the floor is wet, unless the electricity is turned off or you are wearing rubber-soled shoes.

If you have a portable basement telephone, remove it and seal its outlet with plastic kitchen wrap or other waterproof material and water-proof tape. Again, do this only *before* flooding occurs. Make sure the covering is watertight. Should you have a persistent problem with flooding, it may be worthwhile to install waterproof telephone outlets (sold in electric supply stores) for outdoor use. (See also **FLOOD,** page 206.)

DISASTER SERVICES

During and immediately after a disaster, you may obtain emergency help from a number of sources. If you must leave your home, radio broadcasts will tell you where to go, usually to a public building such as a school or church. If phone lines are not down, you may obtain information about available aid from your local or state civil defense departments, the police, churches, synagogues, the Salvation Army, Red Cross, or other community service agencies. Such agencies generally set up facilities to provide shelter, food, clothing, and emergency medical care.

As soon as possible, notify your insurance company because your agent can advise you about steps to take in reporting damage and finding other shelter. Hotel costs may be covered by your policy.

If you are in a declared disaster area, government funds may be made available for your needs. Families and individuals can now receive grants from the Department of Housing and Urban Development of up to $5,000 —which need not be repaid—after natural disasters. The grants are awarded by the state in which the disaster occurred to persons whose homes or business properties have been damaged by floods, tornadoes, or hurricanes. Check with your local government for referral to the proper agency.

Keep an exact account of your losses not only for the insurance company but for the Federal government. The value of personal property, including your home and its furnishings, lost or damaged during an act of nature, may be deducted from your income tax if the loss exceeds $100. Your deductible loss, of course, cannot be greater than the cost of your property before the disaster, and you may not deduct losses for which you were reimbursed by insurance.

Losses to your business property which were not covered by insurance are deductible up to the amount of your depreciated cost, and you need not subtract the first $100.

EARTHQUAKE

When an earthquake occurs, you feel as though you are standing on the deck of a rolling ship. The tremor lasts only a short time, but when you feel it, your immediate reactions may mean the difference between life and death. At present, earthquakes are not predictable, but there may be a few seconds in which to take emergency measures.

Falling debris presents the greatest danger, so if you are indoors, keep away from windows and shelves. Take shelter under a table, bench, or desk, preferably one against an inside wall or in a hallway. Douse all fires and do not light a match, a candle, stove, or fireplace either during or after a tremor. A gas leak could cause a bigger blast than the one you experienced from the earthquake.

If you are caught outdoors, avoid the temptation to run inside a building. Stay out in the open, away from utility wires, trees, and buildings (if possible).

If you are in an automobile, stop as quickly as possible, and stay inside. The springs in the car deflect the tremors, and the body of the car protects you from debris. If a wire falls on the car, do not attempt to get out. Wait until help arrives.

After the shaking stops, do not try to turn utilities on. The quake may have damaged water, gas, and electrical lines. Wait for official instructions, or until your house can be checked by the proper authorities.

If you smell gas, open the windows, and shut off the main valve. Don't take the time to look for it if you aren't sure where it is. Evacuate the house immediately, and don't return until your utility service tells you it is safe.

If water pipes are damaged, shut off the supply at the main valve. Do not drink any water from the tap until water officials say that it is potable; water pipes and reservoirs may be damaged in your area.

If electrical wiring is shorting out, shut off current at the main meter box. If there is no problem with the electricity (or you use battery-operated appliances), turn on a radio or television set to get the latest emergency bulletins.

Do not use the telephone unnecessarily. Make a call only to report damage or to seek help.

Do not go sightseeing. Do not enter damaged buildings until all danger of aftershocks is past and building authorities tell you it is safe.

If you live near the seashore, an earthquake may be the forerunner of a tidal wave. As soon as the tremor stops, head for high ground and stay there until officials advise you to return.

FLOOD

You can do little in a flash flood except try to get out of its path by escaping to high ground or going to the highest place in your house.

Before the flood. If you are forewarned of the possibility of a flood, you will have time to make preparations:

Keep the radio or television on to listen for late reports.

Move household goods to high ground or to the highest floor.

Sterilize the bathtubs with chlorine bleach or with alcohol, or cleanse with soap and water. Fill the tubs with water, and store extra water in various clean containers in case service is interrupted.

If dishes, bedding, and furniture are to be moved, pack them well, and write your name and address on the carton and on the back of each piece of furniture with a crayon or indelible marker. Put portable telephones in plastic bags and seal.

Plug electric outlets to keep out silt by taping layers of plastic wrap around outlets with waterproof tape.

Turn off the water heater and board up the windows, if possible. All electric appliances that can be moved should be taken to an upper floor or high ground.

All outdoor furniture and other such items should be brought inside.

Turn off the main electrical switch to your house before departing, or before the water rises. (See **BASEMENT FLOODED,** page 204.)

Escaping a flood. If possible, eat a light meal before leaving home.

Take along prescription drugs, infant formula, and special diet requirements. Don't forget eyeglasses, false teeth, and other necessaries.

Be sure the car's gas tank is filled. Electric pumps in gas stations may be short-circuited by the flood water.

Avoid areas like valleys subject to sudden flooding. If walking, do not attempt to cross a flowing stream when the water is above your knees. If driving, do not attempt to travel over a flooded road—you could be stranded and trapped. Head for high ground.

Food, shelter, clothing, and first aid are made available as quickly as possible at community shelters, usually a school or other public buildings. Listen for announcements on the radio.

Should sickness or injury occur, seek the necessary medical care at the nearest hospital or community shelter.

After the flood. Do not use fresh food that has come in contact with floodwaters, and do not drink any water from the tap unless it has been tested first or okayed by health authorities.

If the house is flooded or seriously damaged, it must be inspected by public health officials and building inspectors before you may reoccupy it.

Refrain from visiting the disaster area. You may place yourself in further danger or hamper rescue operations.

Do not handle live electric equipment in wet areas. Electrical equipment should be dried and checked by an electrician before using. Proceed with extreme caution. Flashlights, not torches or lanterns, should be employed to examine buildings, as there may be flammables inside.

Report any broken utility lines as soon as possible to appropriate authorities.

HEAT

Living in a modern, air-conditioned environment, people forget that heat can cause sickness and even kill. The human body takes about a week to acclimatize itself to very hot weather and even after acclimatization, it requires special care when performing hard work.

Physicians caution that temperature and humidity, and not sun, are the critical factors in heat exhaustion and heat stroke (see page 103 f.). These hot weather ills can occur in the shade as well as in the sun.

During hot, humid weather, if you are not working in an air-conditioned environment, schedule your hardest work for the cooler, early morning and evening hours. Avoid wet jobs around the house, like mopping and washing clothes, during the heat of the day. These chores only increase the humidity. Rest from 15 to 30 minutes after every hour of strenuous activity, and wear white or light-colored clothing to reflect heat. (Lightweight clothing permits heat and perspiration loss.) Do not wear plastic-coated or rubberized garments during hot weather. They increase dehydration.

Body fluid and salt loss will be high especially during the period of acclimatization, but extra salting of food within the limits of taste will often be sufficient to replace lost salt. Taking salt tablets, especially on an empty stomach, can be irritating, and the salt is poorly absorbed. Water should be restored on an hourly basis.

One method of providing both liquids and salt is to add from ⅛ to ¼ teaspoonful of salt to 1 quart of noncarbonated soft drink. Plain salted water (¼ teaspoon of salt per 8 ounces), with a bit of lemon if you wish, is also recommended.

To keep your home cool, draw shades, blinds, and draperies on windows directly hit by the sun. Turn on the kitchen exhaust fan before starting the oven or dryer to keep hot air from escaping into the rest of the house.

If you have air conditioning, close windows and doors when you turn it on to keep out heat, dust, and humidity. For most efficient operation and economy, keep the machine at one temperature day and night, but set as low as possible.

Another hot weather consideration is conservation of electric power to avoid blackouts. Follow these guidelines:

> Heavy appliances such as washers and dryers should be used before 9 A.M. or after 5 P.M. to cut down the drain on electrical power during peak hours.

All appliances should be shut off during voltage reductions (brownouts), not only to conserve energy, but also to protect the appliances against damage from fluctuations in voltage. This would include washers, dryers, electric water heaters, television sets, radios, etc. If possible, try to limit the use of your air conditioner.

During a complete blackout, all appliances should be disconnected except refrigerators or freezers, which are insulated against voltage changes. Food perishables should last from 4 to 24 hours without power. (See page 21 for information on freezer care in case of power failure.) Do not turn appliances on again until 10 minutes after power returns.

Keep candles, battery-powered radios, and flashlights stocked in a dry, easy-to-find spot. Keep transistor radios on during power problems.

How do you know there is a power problem? You will hear loud humming from the motors of heavy equipment, or see a dimming of electric lights and a shrinkage in the television picture.

HURRICANE

A hurricane is an intense tropical storm with roaring winds above 74 miles an hour that spin counterclockwise around the center or eye. A hurricane moves slowly at about 5 to 18 miles per hour, usually on a west-northwest course toward the United States.

Winds of 90 to 100 miles per hour are common in a hurricane, but speeds up to 200 miles per hour have been recorded. Accompanied by torrential downpours that can dump 5 to 10 inches of rain, hurricanes can stir up to 10- to 30-foot tides that may whip the shoreline.

When the National Weather Service issues a "hurricane watch" it means that there is no immediate danger but that everyone in the area should take precautionary action. Garbage cans, garden tools, toys, porch furniture, awnings, signs, and other unattached objects should be stored or secured. They can become deadly missiles if carried by the wind. Storm shutters should be fastened. If windows are not equipped with storm shutters, they should be boarded up, covered with tarpaulins, or taped with crosses of adhesive or masking tape to prevent shattering.

Boats should be hauled out of the water or moored securely. Fill gas tanks in cars before the storm, if possible, since electric failure would prevent gas pumps from working. If feasible, the car should be stored in a garage or moved to high ground away from trees and wires.

When the weather service issues a "hurricane warning," the storm is approaching, and immediate precautions must be taken.

If you are a resident of a coastal area and ordered to evacuate, turn off all gas and electric applianes and leave immediately. Keep a transistor or car radio turned on for further instructions.

If not ordered to evacuate, stay indoors and be sure that a window or door is opened on the lee side of the house—the side opposite the one facing the wind. Bathtubs should be sterilized with chlorine household bleach and hot water and then filled with water. Jugs, bottles, and cooking pots should also be filled because city water service may be interrupted.

Emergency food supplies that do not require cooking or electrical refrigeration or freezing (see page 203) should be stored in the safest part of the house.

If the eye of the storm passes directly over your area, there will be a period of calm lasting up to half an hour, but the wind will return suddenly from the opposite direction, frequently with even greater violence.

Once you are sure the hurricane is over, check for damage. Do not touch any loose or dangling wires. If you see downed wires, report the damage to the police or the utility company.

Unless you are qualified to render expert aid, stay away from affected areas. If you must drive, drive cautiously, watching for debris and avoiding streets that are under water. If a live wire falls on your car, do not touch any metal parts of the car. Just stay inside and await help.

If your insured property has been badly damaged, causing a real hardship, report the loss to your insurance agent promptly, after the storm is over. If the damage is less serious, wait a day or two so that those with more severe damage can be taken care of first.

LIGHTNING

Lightning carries quite a jolt—from 12,000 to 200,000 amperes—compared with a 100-watt light bulb that contains less than 1 ampere.

Lightning storms usually occur in hot, humid weather, but there are sometimes "bolts out of the blue." To determine whether a lightning storm is approaching, turn on a transistor radio. Heavy static indicates that there is a storm in the area and precautions should be taken.

If you are indoors, stay there. Avoid open doors and windows, fireplaces, radiators, stoves, metal pipes, sinks, and all plug-in electrical appliances such as radios, hair dryers, and electric razors. Don't use the telephone during the storm—lightning may strike telephone lines outside. If you have laundry on the line, leave it there. Don't handle flammable material in open containers.

If you are outdoors, keep away from metal objects such as fishing rods, wire fences, garden tools, clotheslines, golf clubs, and golf carts. Golfers should remove cleated shoes. Stop any tractor work, especially when the tractor is pulling metal equipment, and don't work on fences. Avoid hilltops, open spaces, and exposed sheds.

If you are in your car, stay there (automobiles offer excellent lightning protection). Never stay in the water if you are swimming or boating. Head into shore immediately.

Always seek shelter as soon as possible. If there are no buildings in the area, your best protection is a ditch or cave. When there is absolutely no shelter, crouch or lie down in the open, taking care to avoid the highest object. If there are isolated trees nearby, stay away from them (note their height, and keep at least twice that distance away).

If your hair stands on end or your skin tingles, lightning may be about to strike you, so drop to the ground immediately.

ROOF LEAK

A telltale drip during a rainstorm or water staining on the rafters or roof sheathing are sure signs of a roof leak.

If water drips in, the first thing to do is put a bucket or basin under the leak. Then find the place in the ceiling where the drip originates. If it is near an electric fixture, unscrew the fuse to avoid a short circuit. Hammer a long nail into the ceiling at the point from which the drip starts. The nail should be long enough to go through the ceiling up into the attic floor or crawl space. Search the roof above the nail for the origin of the drip. If you can, hammer a long nail through that spot in the roof. Then call a roofer, who will repair the roof from the outside. If you don't mark the spot and the drip stops before he comes, he will have a hard time finding the area that needs repair.

If you find only water stains, and you cannot determine the source of the leak, check or have someone check the flashing at the valleys and around the chimney. Defective flashing is often the cause of leaky roofs, but it can be repaired with heavy applications of roofing cement under and around all edges. If necessary, it can be tacked down with aluminum or galvanized nails.

Other common causes of leaks are exposed nails that rust away or work out, split shingles, and unfilled nail holes. Slow seepage usually indicates a loose or missing nail. Leaks that appear only during driving rainstorms are caused by water being driven upward under broken shingles, through a crack or into areas where not enough shingle over-lap was allowed.

If you can locate any of these as the source of trouble, have the nails or shingles replaced.

TORNADO

Although few people have even seen a tornado, these violent, twisting windstorms cause millions of dollars worth of damage each year, and take scores of lives. Texas has more than any other area of the United States—about 109 a year, but they can occur anywhere in the world. Whirling at a speed of 300 miles an hour or more, tornadoes are usually 300 yards wide around the top and funnel down toward earth. The funnel often yo-yos up and down from a mass of black clouds. From "birth to death," tornadoes frequently last less than 30 seconds in any one spot, and cover about 16 miles. Caused by a clash of cold and warm air, they occur most often on hot, sticky afternoons.

The National Weather Service issues "alerts" about possible tornadoes, and when a tornado funnel has actually been sighted, or has been detected by radar, the weather service issues a "warning." When you hear an "alert," keep an eye on the weather and listen for bulletins on the radio. If you hear a "warning," seek shelter immediately. The basement is usually the safest place, but if there is no basement, get under a heavy table or workbench in the center of the house. If time permits, douse all fires, shut off fuel and electric lines, and partially open some windows. Then keep away from them.

Other places that can protect you from a tornado are caves, vaults, underground parking facilities, hallways, steel-reinforced office buildings, and tunnels. Avoid parked vehicles, flat open land, and structures with large but poorly supported roofs, such as auditoriums or gymnasiums. Because mobile homes are particularly vulnerable to overturning during strong winds, their occupants should leave them and seek shelter in a safe place.

If you are caught in the open and do not have time to seek shelter, lie flat in a ditch or other low ground and protect your head with your arms. (See also **HURRICANE,** page 208 f.).

WATER NEEDS PURIFYING

When a natural disaster occurs or the water supply protection system fails, you must purify the water yourself. Boil it from 5 to 10 minutes, and to improve the taste, pour from one container to another several times after boiling.

If you cannot or do not wish to boil the water, you may add 1 drop of household bleach to each quart of clear water or 3 drops to each quart of cloudy water, and let it stand for 30 minutes before using. Another method is to add 2 to 3 drops of household iodine to each quart of clear water and 8 to 10 drops to a quart of cloudy water, and let stand for 30 minutes.

WINTER STORM

Local weather bureaus usually give ample warning of approaching winter storms, but if you are in the path of a storm, there are certain tried and true precautions you should take:

Indoors. Check your battery-powered equipment before the storm arrives. A portable radio or television set may be your only contact with the outside world. Also check emergency food supplies, cooking facilities, and flashlights.

Check your supply of heating fuel to be sure you have enough to last through an emergency. Fuel carriers may not be able to move if a winter storm buries your area in snow. Make sure there is plenty of wood for the fireplace if your house has one and be sure camp stoves and lanterns are filled.

Outdoors. If you are caught in the open without a car and you cannot find any shelter—car, cave, house, or barn—it is possible to survive a storm by digging a hole in the snow, preferably next to a tree. Trees give off heat and afford solid protection from the wind. Climb into the hole, covering the top with newspapers, branches, or anything else available that will afford some protection from the cold. Shake snow from the covering periodically, so that air can come in and there is not too heavy a buildup of snow when you want to get out. Be sure to clap your hands and move your arms as much as possible from time to time to avoid freezing. (See also **DRIVING THROUGH WINTER STORMS,** page 42 f.).

INDEX